TALK'S CHEAP, ACTION'S EXPENSIVE

THE FILMS OF ROBERT L. LIPPERT

By

Mark Thomas McGee

Published in the USA by:
BearManor Media
P O Box 71426
Albany, Georgia 31708
www.bearmanormedia.com

ISBN: 978-1-59393-558-0
Printed in the United States of America
Book design by Robbie Adkins

For Wendy Wright,
my love, my life

Contents

INTRODUCTION

In the summer of 1960, the untimely passing of 20th Century-Fox's production chief, Charles "Buddy" Adler, left a lot of people in the Hollywood community wondering who the devil was going to fill his shoes. Who had his background? Who had his experience? Who had an Oscar for Best Picture, a Lifetime Achievement award, and an Irving Thalberg Award on his mantel? Believe you me, it took a lot of soul-searching and butt-scratching before studio president Spyros Skouras came to the inescapable conclusion that there was only one man capable of making the kind of important decisions that Adler had made and that man was Spyros Skouras. A few years later the stockholders forced him to resign over his mismanagement of *Cleopatra* (1963), the movie that brought the studio to its knees. Darryl F. Zanuck was persuaded to come back and take over the studio. He fired just about everyone on the lot, everyone that is, but Skouras' cigar smoking, golfing buddy, Bob Lippert.

Robert Leonard Lippert was a stocky, round-faced guy with brown hair, brown eyes, and a little cropped mustache. He spoke frankly, often bluntly, in a rapid and crisp tenor voice. He wore black and gray custom-made suits, with custom-made white shirts and narrow, plain ties. He loved movies, had no use for alcohol and was in the habit of borrowing money that he never paid back. He'd been making low budget movies since 1945, and since 1956 he'd been making them for Fox. He was more qualified to run the place than Zanuck. Lippert knew every facet of the motion picture business—exhibition, production, *and* distribution.

"It all started when I was 8 years old," Lippert said in a 1956 interview. "I gave out programs at the Strand Theater in Alameda. I just kept going from there."

Lippert managed several theaters before he built his own theater in 1942, The Grand. He was told that an independent theater was not a good risk, but he cleverly built the theater near a shipyard and a military base. By keeping it open around the clock he did a good business.

He built the first drive-in theater in Northern California and by the end of the decade he owned more than fifty theaters in California and Nevada and was making money hand over fist. He became a movie producer because he got fed up with the prices he had to pay the major studios for their movies.

The same year that Lippert opened his first theater, the Society of Independent Motion Picture Producers let it be known how unhappy they were with the studios and their "block-booking" system, whereby the exhibitor was forced to buy three or four mediocre films to get one good one. As one exhibitor put it, "Even an exhibitor can smell a stinker." The government stepped in and abolished block-booking and forced the studios to give up their theaters in 1948. By that time, Lippert's movie-making machine was up and running.

The critics were often unhappy with Lippert's movies. He couldn't have cared less. "I don't worry about what the critics say," he said. "I make pictures people what to see." His target audience was the small town, rural audience; people who went to the movies each and every week. These were people who didn't come for enlightenment or lofty soul-searching. They came for entertainment.

"I'll take a chance on production," Lippert told the buyers, "but you fellows have to help by proper booking."[1] But they didn't help. For all of their talk about the need for product, the buyers often booked Lippert movies as a last resort. Lippert never expected to get the primo playdates in the major markets, but he thought he'd get a break from the small-town theaters, which he did, but not as often as he should have.

"The exhibitor has never seen fit to bail the producer out," Lippert complained.[2] It was ironic that the same exhibitors who would not play, or rarely played his movies cried foul when, in an effort to recoup some of his losses, Lippert sold a package of films to television in the early 1950s.

Exhibitors! As far as Lippert was concerned they were the world's worst retailers; a bunch of lazy jackasses. They'd book a picture and hope the damn thing would sell itself. "In recent years only a handful of exhibs, as far as I can observe, really take a film and do something with it," Lippert noted. "The average theater operator just keeps aimlessly decrying the product shortage. He keeps saying he needs more pictures; he hasn't even the imagination to say he needs more 'box office' pictures."[3]

When Producers Releasing Corporation, one of the major suppliers of B-movies, went belly-up, Lippert warned the exhibitors that unless they supported the B-movie-makers, they would find themselves without low cost second features. He reminded them that people felt cheated if they did not get two pictures, which was true. Then, while keeping a straight face, he added that in some of the small southern, western, and Midwestern towns, "audiences would rather sit and watch one of our little B's rather than most A's."[4] Some audiences in some towns. Almost sounds vague enough to be true! Lippert continued to drive home the need to keep B-movies alive by attacking the exhibitors where it hurt most—the snack bar.

"Confection sales represent 50% of gross receipts for most drive-ins," Lippert reminded them. "On a single bill, concession sales would be less than 20% of the gross. Without those sales, 90% of the drive-ins would go out of business."[5]

Some of the exhibitors liked having Lippert around and let it be known. "Hats off to Lippert for making movies that move!" raved small town theater owner David S. Kline. "What other company can compare with this one when it comes to features released that are playable at a small town theater?" Ralph Raspa asked his fellow exhibitors. Kansas theater owner Bill Leonard said: "If you are in a small town with rural patronage, just line up with these Lippert pictures, and you and your patrons will be happy."

Some agents, fearing an appearance in anything but an A-movie might damage the value of their clients, kept them out of Lippert's movies. In an unprecedented move, Lippert sent out a questionnaire to the exhibitors, asking them what they thought about it. Most of their replies, often bitter, expressed the belief that the picture made the star rather than the other way around. Good pictures with no names often did better than the poor ones loaded with star power. The prevailing sentiment was that the agents and the producers needed to come down from their ivory towers if they wanted to know what was going on. The plain, simple truth was the exhibitors were hungry for good pictures, regardless of who made them or how much they cost.

It wasn't until Lippert had a few hit movies under his belt that people started to take him seriously. Suddenly, "the Quickie King" (as Time magazine called him) was praised for putting shoestring movies on a big business basis. Variety reported that Lippert could expect around a $15,000 profit on every picture he made. "That gives him a nice return, considering that he makes 10 or more a year, plus

Lippert line-up for 1951. The Steel Helmet grossed over two million bucks, setting the benchmark for all low budget movies that followed.

the fact that his own distributing company also makes a good fee for handling them."[6]

Profit with Lippert. That was the slogan on his press books. It should have been on his tombstone. Above everything else, making money was Lippert's passion. This is not to say he didn't love his theaters, and he most certainly loved movies, but he didn't love *making* movies. He rarely came to the set, he did not watch rushes, and he

Barbara Britton and John Ireland from the critically acclaimed I Shot Jesse James, *Sam Fuller's debut feature.*

never read scripts, many of which were written around his titles. Making deals was what Lippert liked. Making deals and making money.

A lot of filmmakers got started with Lippert because he knew first-timers were willing to work cheap. "He broke in more directors than anyone in Hollywood because he paid them no money," Lippert, Jr. told Keith Gleason from *Alameda Magazine.* Charles Marquis Warren, James Clavell, Andrew McLaglen, and Samuel Fuller got started with Lippert.

"When I made *I Shot Jesse James* in 1949 for producer Robert Lippert, we closed the deal on a handshake because he liked my yarn," said Sam Fuller. "It was a business, damn straight, though big profits were not the only motivation. My contract did not even show up until six months later. When the movie unexpectedly made some dough for Lippert, I was happy for the guy. He shared the profits with me exactly as we'd agreed."[7] (Insofar as profit sharing was concerned, Fuller was one of the few people who claimed to have gotten a square deal from the tight-fisted Lippert.) Fuller called Lippert "a dynamic guy with a pioneering spirit and, most important, integrity."[8]

Writer Robert M. Fresco was once approached by *Collier's* to do a piece on Lippert. Fresco thought Lippert was a sleazy, but fascinating character and someone well worth writing about. He was quite certain that when all was said and done, Lippert would not emerge as a villain. It is too bad that *Collier's* folded before Fresco could finish his article. It would have been most informative, I am sure, and badly needed, as so little has been written about the movie mogul from Alameda, California. Of course, one would not expect to find the sort of articles and books that have been devoted to producers like Sam Goldwyn or David Selznick, but one would expect to find a guy who produced over 200 movies to be in the pages of Ephraim Katz's *The Film Encyclopedia*. I will go further than that— Lippert should have a star on the Hollywood Walk of Fame. Alas, I am afraid he will have to settle instead for this book.

Before we get started I would like to thank all of the people who made this book possible. First and foremost there is Kit Parker. Kit and I were strangers when I asked his permission to use the information on his website and the interviews contained on the Lippert DVDs he released through VCI Entertainment. Kit told me where to go for this and that, arranged interviews, corrected my errors, and did everything but actually write the text, and he even did some of that. Without Kit this book wouldn't exist and I am forever in his debt.

Tom Weaver was also there for me above and beyond the call of duty with suggestions and phone numbers. Film historians owe a debt of gratitude to Tom for his treasure-trove of interviews with all of the actors and filmmakers from years gone by.

Maury Dexter wrote a book about his experience in the film business, and when I phoned him to ask his permission to quote from his book at length, he told me he was glad that I called. There were a couple of stories about Lippert that he'd forgotten to include.

Margia Dean and her husband, Felipe Alvarez, were kind enough to invite me into their home (with a little prodding from Kit) to talk about old times, after which I was treated to dinner and a concert. It was a lovely afternoon and evening.

Thanks also to John Agar, Edward Bernds, Whit Bissell, Robert Clarke, Gene Corman, Roger Corman, Kevin Fernan, Beverly Garland, Brett Halsey, Jerry Harrah, Marty Kearns, Steve Latshaw, Bob Lippert III, Ace Mask, Wyott Ordung, Nick Seldon, Gary Smith and Bob Villard.

And a special thanks to BigScreenGoodies for most of the hard-to-find photographs in this book. Check out their website.

Notes:

1. *Variety* December 4, 1950, page 5.

2. *Variety*, March 20, 1952, page 5.

3. *Variety*, August 3, 1960, page 17.

4. *Motion Picture Herald*, February 11, 1950, "Lippert Sees TV as Real Threat," page 42.

5. *Variety*, January 6, 1955, page 3.

6. "Medium Budgeters B.O. Dimout—Hit-or-Miss Biz Stymies Indies," *Variety*, March 20, 1950, page 7.

7. Fuller, Samuel, *A Third Face, My Tale of Writing, Fighting, and Filmmaking*, Alfred. A. Knopf, New York, 2002, page 8.

8. Ibid, page 245.

Prologue
Movies — One Cent

"As long as I gave a cup or a saucer away each week, I got them for a year to complete their set."
                              Robert L. Lippert

It was a typical Saturday afternoon in northern California. The children were forming a line in front of the Alameda Theater. Every week, rain or shine, they came for the children's matinee. It didn't matter what was on the program. They came looking for excitement. They came hoping for thrills. But mostly they came because it was free. Bob Lippert could see them through the glass doors, a sea of anxious little faces, only minutes away from Tom and Jerry and John Wayne. Lippert had been the manager of the Alameda when it opened back in 1932. He was 23-years old then and still had his hair. Now he was 65-years old and his hair was history but now he owned the place, lock, stock and barrel. He owned a lot of theaters but the Alameda was something special. He'd spent over $85,000 to fix it up and would have spent three times that amount of money if he'd had to. You can't put a price on the dream of a lifetime. And he'd always dreamed of owning the Alameda.

Robert L. Lippert had done okay for a nameless little ragamuffin, left like a sack of laundry on the doorstep of the Catholic Charities Orphanage in San Francisco back in March of 1909. He was adopted after 22 months by a hardware store owner with a roving eye named Leonard Lippert and his wealthy, Jewish-German socialite wife, Esther. Lippert did not know they were not his real parents until his mother died. His grandmother found the papers while she was cleaning out the house.

Leonard and Esther raised the boy in the Jewish faith, but Lippert never put much stock in religion. His place of worship was the local movie theater, which he always pronounced *the-a-ter*. His whole life had revolved around movie theaters in one way or another. He saw just about every movie made. Once he had a place of his own, he turned his living room into a theater.

"Every week he ran first run movies for his friends," said his grandson, Bob Lippert III. "He'd give me the newspaper and tell me to pick out a movie. After everyone had gone home, he'd sit with me and watch whatever piece of junk I'd picked out."

Lippert had been running movies since he was eight years old. It all started in the basement of his parents' home at the corner of High and Madison streets in Alameda, California. Every Saturday afternoon he showed scraps of 35mm nitrate film on a toy projector for the neighborhood children. He put a sign on the door that read, "Movies 1 cent." A few years later he ran movies at school.

Instead of working in his father's hardware store, he ran errands for the manager of the Bay Theater. There was not much money in it, but he saw all of the movies for free. Eventually, he ran the projector. During the day he supplemented his income with a job at the Strom Electric Company as their radio expert. He also edited a couple of school newspapers and had as many as four paper routes.

The boy wonder!

He was 14-years old when the *San Francisco Bulletin* called him that in a piece they ran about him the year his father died. The Lipperts were living at 1726 Lincoln Avenue then, a few blocks from the Bay Theater. Years later, when asked about his father, the only thing Lippert had to say was that he did not remember much about him, which is not surprising. They had never been close. The same could be said of Lippert's relationship with his own son. He had been too busy earning a living to spend much time with him when he was young. In later years the two would be at each other's throat. Some people thought it was because they were so much alike, a suggestion that made Bob Lippert Jr. bristle. He didn't think he was anything like his dad, but he was competitive like his dad, and he was a womanizer like his dad. A bet made during a game of golf that involved a young lady resulted in the two Lipperts not speaking to each other for two years. And they were both vindictive. Senior saw Junior's car parked in front of the house of a young actress Senior was dating. He got so angry he sent Junior to Mexico, which was on the brink of a revolution at the time, to make movies.

During his years at Washington High Bob Lippert was put in charge of showing 16mm movies on Friday afternoons. He would pick up the movie from the exchange on Thursday, return it the following Thursday and exchange it for a new one. It wasn't long before it dawned on the enterprising young Lippert that he would be a fool not to take advantage of the situation. He put out some feelers and before long he was running movies all week, at the Elks Lodge one night, the American Legion the next and maybe a church or some civic group.

One Friday afternoon, while he was threading the projector, Lippert noticed a young lady he'd never seen before. She'd come to Alameda from Milton, Massachusetts and was the Irish daughter of Charles M. Robinson and Alva Margaret Hamilton. Her name was Ruth Elizabeth and was 16 years old, one year younger than he. It was love at first sight. Three months later they ran off to San Jose to get married. Her parents were furious. Her father dragged them into court.

"Mr. Robinson," the judge asked, "why do you think this marriage should be annulled?"

"They're too young," Mr. Robinson replied. "I want someone who can support my daughter!"

And that's when Lippert pulled out a wad of bills and defiantly waved it in his father-in-law's face. "Well, here's two thousand dollars!" he said. "How much have *you* got?"

It had been a short-lived moment of triumph. With a wife to support, Lippert dropped out of high school and took a job at Dettner's Printing Shop, which was as boring as the hardware business. After two long years of this soul-crushing tedium, opportunity came knocking once again. Talking pictures were becoming all the rage, but a lot of towns were too small for a theater. So, Lippert rented some sound equipment, bid farewell to Dettner's, and travelled up and down the eleven western states running sound movies in school auditoriums. He made good money while it lasted.

Money was already tight when Ruth gave birth to a boy on February 28, 1928. They christened him Robert Leonard Lippert, Jr. ("They must have gotten stupid when they got to me," said Bob Lippert III. "My middle name is Leonard too only they spelled it L-E-N-A-R-D.")

Lippert was making $25 a week running three theaters in Oakland when Junior arrived on the scene. Ruth was making $7 as a cashier. Always looking for new ways to make money, Lippert moved his family to Detroit and went into the dish business. He convinced the exhibitors that they could boost their ticket sales if they participated in what he called "Dish Night." Once a week, anyone who bought a ticket was entitled to a free dish. There were fifty-two dishes in a set. If the customers wanted a complete set they had to come back every week. Later he switched to "Book Night." Ticket-buyers were given a volume of a *Wonder Book* each week, which was a bargain basement version of the *Encyclopedia Britannica*. There were thirty-six volumes in a set.

From Detroit the Lipperts moved to Chicago, then to Los Angeles, selling dishes and books. Lippert developed relationships with the exhibitors that served him well in the years that followed. He managed to keep out of the draft by eating until his weight exceeded the allowable standards for induction.

Lippert glanced at the clock on the wall. Only a few minutes more and it would be time to open the doors and let the kids in. As he fished for the keys in his pocket he recalled the time that one of the trade magazines had asked him to write a piece about his most memorable moment in show business. A lot of moments had come to mind. There was the time he bought his first theater with $800 he borrowed from Arthur Richard. And there was the time that he and Bill Foreman tossed a coin over territories to build their drive-in theaters. And what about the day the word came down that The Steel Helmet *had grossed over $2 million bucks? The whole industry was buzzing about it.*

Gene Evans in Sam Fuller's gritty The Steel Helmet *(1951).*

As he inserted the key into the lock the children cheered. He opened the door and the kids scurried in.

Let the show begin.

CHAPTER ONE
SCREEN GUILD

"I'm not in this for personal glory. I'm giving the public and the exhibitors the films they want for purely commercial reasons."

Robert L. Lippert

In 1945 Harry S. Truman became the President of the United States, U.S. troops dropped atomic bombs on Hiroshima, the Empire State Building was struck by a B-25 bomber, the Independent Republic of Vietnam was formed with Ho Chi Minh as its president, Charles De Gaulle was elected president of France, and theater owners Robert L. Lippert and John J. Jones decided to make movies. They moved into an office in San Francisco and formed two companies—Action Pictures and Screen Guild Productions. Action Pictures produced the movies that Screen Guild released. Jones was the president (he would later resign on June 30, 1948), and Lippert was the vice-president and general manager. Like any other organization, it took some time to assemble a team. F. A. Bateman became the general sales manager (Madison Schwer was his assistant), John L. Franconi was the secretary, M. S. Schulter was the treasurer (Sam K. Decker was his assistant), Jack Cartwright was in charge of public relations, and I. H. Prinzmetal was the company attorney. He continued to be Lippert's attorney until the day Lippert died.

In 1947, at the company's first annual sales convention, a new public relations job was filled by the company's former publicity and advertising director, Jack Cartwright. Warner Bros. publicity man Jack Leewood also joined the company. Action Pictures had evolved into Golden Gate Pictures with Joseph Blumenfeld, of the Blumenfeld Theaters, in charge. He handled the international distribution. His vice-president and production chief was William B. David, the general manager of the Redwood Theater chain in San Francisco.

Before coming to Hollywood, William B. David claimed that he could make better pictures than the ones he booked. Although he had no illusions about revolutionizing the industry, he expected an easier time of it than he got when he was given a chance to put his money where his mouth was. He quickly discovered that low budget filmmaking was guerilla filmmaking. While a major studio was happy to get two or three camera set-ups a day, Screen Guild logged in anywhere from fifty to seventy set-ups a day. B-movie directors have a lot in common with traffic cops. They are not hired for their artistic abilities. They are hired because they have a history of bringing films in on time.

David produced Screen Guild's first release, *Wildfire, the Story of a Horse* (1945), a Cinecolor western that cost $36,000.

It is no surprise that Screen Guild's first release was a western. There was an old saying in Hollywood: "If you wanna make money make a western." And Lippert loved westerns. He owned property near Rogue River in Oregon that was ideal for shooting westerns.

Wildfire was directed by Robert Emmett Tansey. Tansey, a veteran of short schedule westerns, approached each project in the same way: twenty minutes of riding, ten minutes of shooting, ten minutes of fighting, and twenty minutes of plot. If he ran behind schedule, he cut the plot.

Wildfire (1945) was Screen Guild's first release. It cost $36,000 to make and grossed $350,000.

Bela Lugosi was one of the screen's most famous bogeymen. Here he's seen with Angelo Rossitto in Scared to Death *(1948), one of the most boring and confusing movies ever made.*

After two years of fast schedules, egos, and testy temperaments, William B. David called it quits and retreated to the safety of theater management. His last Screen Guild production, *Scared to Death* (1947), is noteworthy because it is the only color movie to star Bela Lugosi, the actor who became famous for his portrayal of Count Dracula on stage and screen.

Lippert tried his hand at directing once. The picture was called *The Last of the Wild Horses* (1948). To his horror, after only three days, he fell hopelessly behind schedule. True to form, he did what he would have done to any director who fell behind schedule, he fired himself. The film's editor, Paul Landres, took over and finished the film without credit. Landres also directed *Grand Canyon* (1949), the only film to feature Lippert in the cast. The poster claimed the movie was "funny 'nuff to make a mule laugh." The mule friendly comedy concerned the trials and tribulations of a film crew shooting a motion picture at the Grand Canyon and Lippert played (what else?) the producer.

Like Paul Landres, Lee Sholem was another editor-turned-director. When he was just starting out in the business, he worked a hundred and eighteen hours the first week. The second week he worked a hundred and twenty-six hours. He had completed one hundred and thirty-hours the third week when he passed out. He earned the nickname, "Roll 'em" Sholem because nothing could stop him from bringing a movie in on time. He directed one of Lippert's most famous movies, *Superman and the Mole Men* (1951) and never worked for Lippert again.

"[By] knowing exactly what I was going to do," Sholem said, "I could walk on the set in the morning and say to the crew, 'Eleven shots from now I'm going to make a dolly shot, from *here* to *there*.' By knowing and telling them that, it gives them a chance, whenever they have a few minutes' break, to go ahead and lay the track, put the dolly on there, and set a camera and tripod on it. So by the time we got to that eleventh shot, everything was ready! *This* is where you save time."[1]

John T. Bambury, Tony Boris, Billy Curtis, Jerry Maren and George Reeves from Superman and the Mole Men *(1951). Maren had the distinction of being two commercial icons. The first was Buster Brown in the Buster Brown Shoe commercials. He also played Little Oscar whenever the Oscar Mayer Wienermobile came to town.*

Every camera movement and every angle was mapped out on the back of each page of the script; Sholem wasn't taking any chances.

"Talk's cheap. Action's expensive," Lippert would often say, and who could argue with him? Obviously, it took a lot more time to stage a fist fight or a chase sequence than it did to shoot a scene of two people sitting at a table, talking each other to death. This is why low budget movies are often long on conversation and short on action.

All of the writers who worked for Lippert had to be able to fashion stories around three or four locations with as few characters and as little action as possible. Maurice Tombragel and Orville Harris Hampton were two of the writers that Lippert came to depend on.

Tombragel had written several mysteries for Universal and Columbia before writing *Thunder in the Pines* (1948) for Screen Guild. His comedy-drama about two lumberjacks fighting over a gold-digging dame was the first of what was supposed to be twelve features that producer William Stephens signed on to make for Screen Guild. He made six.

All in all, Tombragel wrote twelve features for Lippert before moving into television, where he was more active than ever as a writer for some of the most successful shows of the era: *Stories of the Century*, *The Life and Legend of Wyatt Earp*, and *Walt Disney's Wonderful World of Color*, to name just a few.

Orville H. Hampton was a former news journalist and radio announcer stationed in the Hawaiian Islands during World War II. After his discharge in 1946, he moved to Hollywood and sold his first script to Lippert in 1950. It was a western titled *Bandit Queen*. He and Ron Ormond, another prominent figure in Lippert's history, had a brief working relationship that came to a rather abrupt and unexpected end. Ormond owned an airplane and gave Hampton a couple of flying lessons. One afternoon Hampton lost control and crashed the plane. The experience rattled him so that he was unable to move at first. Then he crawled out of the plane, walked off the field, and Ormond never saw him again. During his prolific career, Hampton wrote over 500 television shows and 100 features.

Ron Ormond's background was in vaudeville. He was performing his magic act at the Capitol Theater in Portland, Oregon when he met June Carr, a singer-dancer who was also on the program. Three weeks later they were married. When they started making movies, June did the make-up, the costumes, kept track of the continuity, and did just about anything else her husband needed. She also organized the personal appearance tours with actress Peggy Stewart and cowboy star Lash La Rue. As for Ron, he wrote the scripts and made the deals. If he made a bad deal, June posed as his business manager and got him out of it. She was one tough cookie.

Lippert had seen the Ormonds perform on stage many times and was one of their biggest fans. One afternoon he went back stage and suggested they make a vaudeville movie. *Square Dance Jubilee* (1949) proved to be a profitable venture for both the Ormonds and for Lippert. The star of their film was a hillbilly fiddle player named Donnell Clyde Cooley, better known as Spade Cooley[2] the "King of Western Swing." He became the host of a local KTLA-TV variety show in Los Angeles, California, that ran from 1949 to 1959.

Co-starring with Cooley was the film's executive producer, Donald M. Barry. To his fans he was known as Don "Red" Barry, a nickname he was given after appearing in Republic's twelve-chapter serial, *Adventures of Red Ryder* (1940). Barry hated his nickname with a passion, but there was nothing he could do to shake it. He makes fun of himself in *Square Dance Jubilee*. He and Wally Vernon play a couple of New York talent scouts who've been sent out west to find some authentic western singing acts. In their search, they encounter cattle rustlers, murderers, and a pretty rancher played by the charming Mary Beth Hughes. "We were looking for the old west. We found it," Barry tells Vernon. "An old town, a beautiful blonde, changing brands, rustlers, dry gulching...reminds me of a Don 'Red' Barry western." Vernon enthusiastically replies: "Don 'Red' Barry? He's my favorite actor. Did you see the picture where..?" Barry cuts him off. "I never liked him!"

Barry was winding down his career as a leading man when he signed on with Lippert, but he continued to have an active career as a supporting player, often as villains.[3] He made eight more pictures for Lippert—*The Dalton Gang, Red Desert, Tough Assignment, Ringside* (all 1949), *Border Rangers, Gunfire, I Shot Billy the Kid* and *Train to Tombstone* (all 1950). Ron Ormond produced three of them.

Ormond brought the Lash LaRue series to Screen Guild. The series started at PRC with director Robert Tansey. Tansey had been looking for someone to play a supporting role in an Eddie Dean western called *Song of Old Wyoming* (1945) when LaRue walked into his office looking for a job. "He told me he could handle a bullwhip

Screen Guild's line-up for 1949.

when I hired him," Tansey remarked. "But he also told me he could act—and I believed that too!"[*] LaRue lied about knowing how to use a whip, but he assumed that he could learn quickly enough. He rented a couple of whips to practice with.

Looking at the first day's rushes on *Song of Old Wyoming*, it was obvious to Tansey that La Rue was stealing the film from Eddie Dean, which was not all that hard to do. Dean could sing well enough, but

Lash La Rue and his sidekick Al "Fuzzy" St. John on tour.

he was one of the least dynamic cowboys to hit the saddle. Tansey asked La Rue if he would be interested in doing three more pictures at a slightly higher salary. That was when LaRue felt obliged to confess that he did *not* know how to handle a whip. He'd been practicing but it had not gone as well as he thought. To prove it, he gingerly peeled away his shirt to show Tansey the damage he had inflicted on his body. At the sight of the red and blue streaks Tansey burst out laughing. He hired someone to give La Rue lessons. It wasn't long before the amount of fan mail La Rue received prompted PRC to give him a series of his own.

The novelty of a having a sinister looking, whip-wielding cowboy hero gave La Rue an edge over his competition. His sidekick, Al "Fuzzy" St. John, was one of the original Keystone Kops, a former sidekick to Bob Steele and Buster Crabbe. Fuzzy was as popular as La Rue. In some foreign territories the movies were advertised as Fuzzy St. John movies. La Rue thought he was the greatest ad lib artist in the world. "He could stumble over a matchstick and spend fifteen exciting minutes looking for what he stumbled over," La Rue observed.[5] L. D. Montgomery, a theater owner in Texas, said: "Fuzzy St. John has a drawing power in these smaller towns that usually exceeds that of the so-called stars he plays with."

The two made eight pictures before PRC was absorbed by Eagle-Lion, leaving La Rue without a distributor. That's when Ron Ormond took over the series. He and director Ray Taylor made six more features that were released by Screen Guild: *Dead Man's Gold, Frontier Revenge, Mark of the Lash, Son of Billy the Kid* (all 1948), *Outlaw Country,* and *Son of a Badman* (both 1949).

Sometimes you will find an actor on the way up or on the way down in low budget movies, but mostly you will find people who aren't going anywhere at all. They are never going to be stars, and they're never going to make the big money, but some of these people are the best actors in the business.

"They don't get the acclaim but when you think about it, the actors in these little pictures have to be good," said actress Margia Dean, a veteran of many Lippert movies. "They don't have rehearsal time. They don't get any help from the director. If they hit the mark and don't flub the lines they move on to the next scene. They do not get to do the scene over and over until it is perfect."

"There was a stigma to B-pictures," said Beverly Garland, the star of Lippert's *Badlands of Montana* (1957) and *The Alligator People* (1959). "You were nothing if you were in B- pictures. The only way you can be any good is to get out of B-pictures."

Lippert had a stable of actors that he used time and again. The smooth and charming dancer-turned-actor Cesar Romero was a Lippert favorite. He'd been the star of The Cisco Kid series at Fox but was usually cast in supporting roles during the fifteen years he was under contract to the studio, holding his own against the studio's biggest stars. Because he loved to attend movie premiers, art shows, and other public events it was said of him that he would attend the

Cesar Romero and George Brent are FBI agents in Lippert's FBI Girl *(1951)*

opening of a napkin. His career got a second wind in the mid-60s when he appeared as The Joker on the *Batman* television series. His Lippert credits include, *FBI Girl, The Jungle, Lost Continent, Scotland Yard Inspector, The Shadow Man,* and *Villa!*

Robert Lowery was equally comfortable playing heroes or villains at Lippert. He'd been the star of a couple of cliffhangers and was a supporting player at Universal and Fox during the 1940s. In the 1950s and 60s, he was extremely active in television, the star of his own series, *Circus Boy,* and later one of the nighttime soaps. His Lippert credits include: *Arson, Inc., Border Rangers, The Dalton Gang, Gunfire, Highway 13, I Shot Billy the Kid, Queen of the Amazons, Shep Comes Home* and *Western Pacific Agent.*

Richard Travis starred or co-starred in eight Lipperts. "I had been doing fairly well in pictures—making $15,000 to $18,000 a year," he told *The Miami News* in 1958 (the year he made his last movie, *Missile to the Moon*). "But the caliber of pictures I was offered was pretty crummy." So he quit acting, changed his name to William Justice, and became a successful real estate salesman. His Lippert credits include: *Danger Zone, Fingerprints Don't Lie, Mask of the Dragon, Motor Patrol, Operation Haylift, Pier 23, Roaring City* and *Sky Liner.*

Reed Hadley had one of the best voices in the business, so it's no surprise to learn that his acting career started in radio. He narrated dozens of feature films and government documentaries, often without credit, and was the star of his own TV series, *Racket Squad*. His Lippert credits include: *The Return of Wildfire*, *Jungle Goddess* (voice only), *I Shot Jesse James*, *Rimfire*, *Grand Canyon*, *Red Desert* (voice only), *The Baron of Arizona*, *Motor Patrol*, *The Return of Jesse James*, *Little Big Horn* and *Moro Witch Doctor*.

Sid Melton was in more Lippert movies than any other actor, mostly as a supporting player. He was working in a nightclub revue at Ciro's on the Sunset Strip when Murray Lerner gave him a part in *Tough Assignment* (1949). Lippert put him under contract after that at $140 a week.

"And he did a terribly sneaky thing, Lippert, may he rest in peace," Melton told Tom Weaver. "I was on a loan-out from him, because Bob Hope wanted me for a part in *The Lemon Drop Kid* [1951] at Paramount."

The studio paid Lippert six or seven hundred dollars a week for Melton's services. Lippert paid Melton his usual salary and kept the balance, which was standard operating procedure. Every studio did

Sid Melton is intimidated by psychopathic Mickey Knox in this scene from Western Pacific Agent (1950.)

it. Then, when tax time rolled around, Lippert wanted Melton to pay the tax on the full amount. The actor went to an attorney who put a stop to that nonsense.

"Robert Lippert liked me very much," Melton remarked. "Why shouldn't he? If I may be immodest, aside from working cheap, I think there are very few that can do what I do." Melton can be seen in *Everybody's Dancin, Fingerprints Don't Lie, Hi-Jacked, Holiday Rhythm, Lost Continent, Leave It to the Marines, Mask of the Dragon, Motor Patrol, Radar Secret Service, The Return of Jesse James, Savage Drums, Sky High, The Steel Helmet, Stop That Cab, Three Desperate Men, Thundering Jets, Treasure of Monte Cristo,* and *Western Pacific Agent.*

The angelic Mary Beth Hughes was signed by Lippert to a multi-picture deal in 1948. She had been under contract to MGM when Fox borrowed her to replace the wonderful Jean Rogers in *Free, Blonde and 21* (1940). Fox signed her to a contract. Other than her brief appearance in *The Ox-Bow Incident* (1943) most of the movies she made for that studio were programmers. She was not given much to do at Lippert other than to look pretty. Her credits include: *Grand Canyon, Holiday Rhythm, Last of the Wild Horses, The Return of Wildfire, Rimfire* and *Square Dance Jubilee.*

Spunky Pamela Blake once starred opposite Cesar Romero in one of the Cisco Kid movies. She spent most of her career as a freelance actress, in westerns and thrillers, trapped in the B-movie jungle. Her Lippert credits include: *Border Rangers, The Case of the Baby Sitter, Gunfire, The Hat Box Mystery, Highway 13, Rolling Home,* and *Sky Liner.*

Then there's Margia (pronounced Mar-juh) Dean, the Queen of Lippert, born Marguerite Louise Skliris in Chicago on April 7, 1922. She was Miss San Francisco, Miss California, and a runner-up in the 1939 Miss America contest. Her first screen role was in Republic's *Casanova in Burlesque* (1944) and on television she was a regular on *Dick Tracy* (1951). Her career was in a slump when she was introduced to Lippert by a mutual producer friend and he gave her the lead role in *Shep Comes Home* (1948). Four or five movies later she and Lippert were lovers.

"I'm not proud of it," Margia said. "I knew what I was doing was wrong. I was running around with a married man. I don't think I ever really loved him, but he was crazy about me. He gave me all this work and he was pleasant to be with. He made it easy for me."

Charles Robinson had been right when he'd said his daughter was too young to get married. It didn't take long for the romance between Ruth Robinson and Robert Lippert to fade, leaving a vacuum soon filled by contempt. Ruth turned to alcohol (and an occasional lover) for comfort. Robert turned to Margia, though not exclusively. Sometimes he would brag about some of the women he had slept with.

"He told me he slept with Marilyn Monroe," Margia recalled. "He would stop by my place after work because he didn't want to go home. He liked to smoke his cigar and talk about how miserable he was at home. We talked about him mostly; about the things he

Margia Dean, "the Queen of Lippert," from The Baron of Arizona *(1950)*

wanted to do. We never talked about his business or anything like that. Sometimes he would ask my opinion about something but I never had any influence over anything."

"I like Margie," Lippert Jr. remarked. "I think she's a hell of a person, and my father, frankly, should have divorced my mother and married Margie Dean."

Lippert would say time and again that he was going to leave Ruth, but she would have taken him to the cleaners and he knew it. And since money trumped every other consideration, including peace of mind, Lippert never made good on his promise. After sixteen years of this bumpy romance Margia had had enough. She said goodbye to show business and her backdoor romance with Lippert and married Felipe Alvarez, an architect, writer and singer. Lippert was furious. He offered her money to break with Alvarez and sent her some expensive gifts which she returned. Lippert used his considerable influence to have Alvarez deported and when that didn't work he tried to ruin the couple financially. He hired a couple of extras that looked like thugs to drive away the customers at her coffee shop in Beverly Hills. It was Jack Leewood who told Margia that Lippert was going to hire a hit man to murder Alvarez. She went to the police and the FBI and told Lippert that if anything happened to her or Felipe, they'd know who was responsible. And that brought an end to Lippert's reign of terror. After all was said and done, Margia and Felipe had the last laugh. It seemed that once Margia gave up acting she discovered there were other things that she enjoyed doing just as well. Besides the already mentioned coffee shop, she opened a dress shop in Brentwood and went into real estate as Buckeye Realty and Management, also in Beverly Hills. She is now retired and is still happily married to Felipe. Her credits include: *Ambush at Cimarron Pass, Badlands of Montana, The Bandit Queen, The Baron of Arizona, The Big Show, The Creeping Unknown, Fangs of the Wild, FBI Girl, Fingerprints Don't Lie, Frontier Gambler, Grand Canyon, Kentucky Jubilee, The Last of the Desperados, Leave It to the Marines, Loan Shark, Lonesome Trail, Mask of the Dragon, Mr. Walkie Talkie, Pier 23, Red Desert, The Return of Jesse James, Rimfire, Ringside, Savage Drums, The Secret of the Purple Reef, Seven Women from Hell, Sins of Jezebel, Sky High, Stagecoach to Fury, Superman and the Mole Men, Tales of Robin Hood, Treasure of Monte Cristo,* and *Villa!* She was also seen in Screen Guild's most famous and successful film, *I Shot Jesse James* (1949), which marked the directorial debut Sam Fuller.

An ex-crime reporter and pulp novelist, Samuel Fuller had written a couple of screenplays before coming to Lippert. "I was anxious to direct," he told the *Daily News*. "The last few pictures I'd written, the directors didn't direct them the way I wrote them. It used to get me a little burned up once in a while. I guess there has to be a difference of opinion as to how a script should be directed. If you give 30 directors the line: 'Joe looks furtively' to direct, they will probably have 30 different interpretations of the word 'furtively.'"

After Lippert read Fuller's novel, *The Dark Page*, he tracked the writer down through a secretary in the New York office of Duell, Sloan and Pearce. He knew that Fuller wanted to direct, and he was willing to give him the chance, provided that he could make a film fast and cheap. Fuller told Lippert that he wanted to do a film about Cassius and his plot to kill Caesar. Lippert did not want to make a movie about a lot of guys "running around in bed sheets" so Fuller suggested a film about another assassin, Bob Ford, the man who shot Jesse James. "Now," Lippert said, chomping on his cigar, "we've got a movie!"

Barbara Britton and John Ireland from Sam Fuller's debut motion picture I Shot Jesse James *(1949).*

Fuller was paid $5,000 plus a percentage of the profits for his services as a writer and director. He had ten days and $110,000 to make the picture. In his autobiography, *A Third Face*, Fuller praised Lippert for encouraging the kind of subversive movie that he wanted to make, going so far as to say that the major studios would have squashed him the second they saw the rushes from the first day. Lippert frankly admitted that he would have been more cautious if the picture had cost him a lot of dough, but since it did not, he was willing to take a risk. He left Fuller alone to make the movie his way. The only concession that Lippert asked of him was to open the film with a horse chase, which Fuller later admitted probably helped the picture.

The manager of New York's Palace Theater couldn't help but notice the phenomenal business that Fuller's picture was doing in the Bible belt. Though he'd never played a Screen Guild movie before, he decided to give *I Shot Jesse James* a chance, and he wasn't sorry. It was an absolute smash, opening the door for other independent pictures to play the major movie houses across the country.

Still, Lippert thought business should be better, and he blamed the exhibitors who were, in his opinion, a bunch of lazy old men. They didn't bother to look at the pictures they bought and made no effort to sell them. Even worse, they insisted on set change dates. A picture could be making money hand over fist and the fools would dump it to play some other picture that they had already booked. In his own theaters, Lippert promoted each and every picture to the tastes of the community, and each attraction was allowed to run until it stopped making money. As a result, in comparable situations, he was able to double the box office returns. If things were ever going to change, the exhibitors needed to exercise some selectivity, flexibility and, most of all, showmanship. It was as if producers and exhibitors lived on two different planets! Producers did not know what was going on in exhibition and the exhibitors did not pay a lick of attention to what was going on in production. In no other industry were the two ends so far apart. Lippert had even heard some exhibitors gloat when a film company went broke. What did the idiots think they'd do if *all* of the companies went broke?

Interference from the banks was not helping matters either. Bankers knew nothing about show business and yet they thought they should have a say in casting, story treatment, and other things that were none of their damn business. It wasn't as if they were lending money to just anyone. They were giving it to people who'd proven that they knew what they were doing so let them do it! After all, producers didn't tell bankers how to run *their* shop.

In the midst of all of the hassle with bankers and exhibitors, Lippert continued to build his theater empire. The February 1, 1947 edition of *Boxoffice* magazine announced that Earl Henning, the construction supervisor for the Robert L. Lippert Theaters, was ready to break ground on a new drive-in theater, located on the outskirts of Medford, Oregon. Lippert had acquired the property when he purchased the nine-theater circuit of Leverette Interstate Theaters. At this point in time, Lippert had drive-ins in Fresno, Visalia, Modesto, Sacramento, and Concord. Bob Lippert III remembered driving with his Grandpa to look for new places to build theaters: "He'd have the game on the radio. He loved baseball. And he loved driving. He just liked driving around."

Lippert created the Motion Picture Financial Corporation whose sole purpose was to supply financing for Screen Guild movies. He had twenty-two features scheduled for release in 1949 and he wanted to be sure the money would be there to make them. In a meeting with Franconi, Schulter, Sam Decker and Prinzmetal, he explained how the thing would work. The MPPC would loan seventy-five percent of the $60,000 budget on any given film to Screen Guild. This would prevent one or two features from drying up the available financial pool. Stock purchases would be limited to $3,000 per individual. A stock issue of $270,000 would be matched by bank loans to create a $500,000 revolving fund. Eventually the stock would split into one share of preferred stock and one share of common stock at a price of $100 each. The preferred stock would carry a five percent interest rate with the intention of retiring half of the issue within the first two years. Cash advances would be guaranteed by various Screen Guild franchise holders. De Luxe Laboratories was willing to participate with cash and deferred credits.

"I have considered the financial plan for some time as it basically concerns the small, independent exhibitor who exists on 'bread and butter' product," Lippert told his associates. "In the past eleven months I have invested more than a million in cash in nineteen pictures, the financing of which was made possible by my personal signature and the cooperation of banks in northern California. However, there is a limit to such credit and I now find it impossible to continue single-handed as sole owner of Lippert Productions. Rather than resort to paying large bonuses to 'loan sharks,' I decided to form this financial corporation. Besides fulfilling an exhibitor demand for product, he has the opportunity to invest in his future and share additional profits."[6]

One year later the MPFC had netted a ten percent profit before taxes and declared its first dividend.

As the decade drew to an end, Lippert decided that his franchise holders were far more trouble than they were worth. They'd blocked his efforts to make bigger pictures and, for a time, had considered relinquishing control of the company to a joker named Carl Leserman, who offered them a million dollars for the privilege. The positive reaction to, and the unprecedented bookings for I Shot Jesse James made the franchise holders change their minds, but it was too close for comfort to Lippert's way of thinking.

Using Fuller's film as leverage, Lippert persuaded the 28 franchise holders to merge Screen Guild with Robert L. Lippert Productions, an action that put Lippert in charge of the distributing-producing combination. His first order of business was to liquidate Screen Guild's assets for a 5% overhead charge, after which he bought out the franchise holders and set up his own string of exchanges. Later he would sell his exchanges and, once again, operate on a franchise basis.

As the newly formed Lippert Pictures, Inc., Robert L. Lippert was about to have his most successful year.

Notes:

1. Weaver, Tom Interviews with B Science Fiction and Horror Movie Makers, McFarland & Co., North Carolina, 1988, page 228.
2. Spade Cooley's popularity took a nosedive in 1961 when he murdered his wife, Ella Mae. He thought she was having an affair with Roy Rogers so he smashed her head against the floor and stomped on her belly until she stopped breathing. Then he burned her flesh several times with a cigarette to make sure she was dead. He told the jury she'd fallen while taking a shower, which would have hardly accounted for her condition. His 14-year old daughter's eyewitness account of the crime was all the jury needed to send him to jail for first degree murder.
3. Donald M. Barry's off screen exploits were far more interesting than anything he ever did on screen. Even though he had been relegated to supporting roles by the mid-Fifties, apparently he was still a leading man in the bedroom. As one actress put it, "I don't exactly know what he's got but whatever it is he should bottle it." He was having an affair with Susan Hayward when the actress found him in bed with Jil Jarmyn. Miss Hayward punched Miss Jarmyn in the kisser and threw her out of the house. The public had all but forgotten this little bedroom drama when Barry's name was plastered all over the newspapers again, this time for pulling a gun on a painting contractor who was trying to collect the money that Barry owed him. Barry's reckless and violent behavior made headlines again when

he cornered one of the four thieves who had stolen the purses of three women in three different shopping centers. Barry's wife saw one of them running down the street, and while the police went after the other three, Barry (still in his pajamas and slippers) grabbed his gun and chased after the boy. A few years later, when his wife (Peggy Stewart) divorced him, she told the judge, "He had quite a bad temper—a little impossible." In 1980, the police were called to Barry's North Hollywood home to quiet a family dispute. Thinking everything was under control, the policemen were on their way back to their car when Barry walked out of the house, put a .38 caliber revolver to his head, and blew his brains out.

4. Lewis, C. Jack White Horse, Black Hat: A Quarter Century on Hollywood's Poverty Row, Scarecrow Press, Inc., Maryland, 2002, page 20.

5. Dellinger, Paul, Lash La Rue, The Old Corralb-westerns.com

6. Boxoffice magazine, July 9, 1949, page 8.

Chapter Two
Lippert Pictures, Inc.

"People are a sight smarter than they used to be. You can't get away with the old stuff that used to go. All the names in the business won't carry a picture unless the story is there."
                    Robert L. Lippert

Everyone may have thought that Robert L. Lippert was talking through his hat when he announced his intentions to produce four features with budgets of two million dollars. Producers routinely say outrageous things to keep their names in print, but Lippert was quite serious. Low budget movies were losing ground for the simple reason that they weren't much better than what the public was getting for free on television. If he wanted to stay in business he had to make bigger-budgeted pictures. Two of the movies at the top of his list were adaptations of Jules Verne's 20,000 *Leagues Under the Sea* and *Isle of Zorda*. The big question was: where would he get the money?

He had a few meetings with Steve Broidy, the president of Monogram. Walter Mirisch, the studio's vice president, had convinced Broidy that the company needed to upgrade its image to stay in business. Since Monogram and Lippert had a full line of exchanges (some owned, some franchised), it stood to reason that if the two companies combined their exchanges and dumped the ones they didn't need, they'd save a lot of money, money that could be used to make bigger pictures. Broidy assured the press that the arrangement would in no sense be a merger of the two companies as the trade magazines had reported. For reasons never stated, Broidy walked away from the deal, a deal which would have affected only Lippert's distribution setup but not his production unit.

A few years later Lippert discussed a similar arrangement with Jack Broder at Realart Pictures, but nothing came of that either, possibly because Lippert was in hot water with the Screen Actors Guild at that time. We will get into that a little later.

Lippert was also working on a deal with Metro-Goldwyn-Mayer's Louis B. Mayer. Mayer was going to make four movies a year for Lippert; each one budgeted at $1 million dollars or more, to be

Vincent Price as con-man James Addison Reavis in one of the actor's
personal favorites, The Baron of Arizona *(1950).*

released through Lippert's low cost exchange system. But that deal
fell through as well.

With no immediate source of revenue in sight, Lippert hocked his
chain of Northern California movie theaters to finance Sam Fuller's
next feature, *The Baron of Arizona* (1950), based on the life of con-
man James Addison Reavis.¹ Once an employee of the Federal Land
Office in Santa Fe, Reavis had forged a Spanish land grant and stole
66,000 square miles of land in the Southwest in 1872. Sam Fuller
had written an article about Reavis for the *American Weekly* and
thought the story would make an interesting movie. It sounded like

Ellen Drew, Reed Hadley and Vincent Price from The Baron of Arizona *(1950)*.

a good idea to Murray Lerner, Lippert's vice-president, so Lippert told Fuller and producer Carl K. Hittleman to get busy. Fuller chose Vincent Price to play Reavis.

The critical reception to the picture was less than enthusiastic. Perhaps *Variety* put it best: "Fuller misses in scripting and direction. He tries to be too erudite, losing the fast action needed to put this one over with the general ticket buyer."

Still, of all of the films in Vincent Price's canon, *The Baron of Arizona* was one of his favorites. It was also one of a handful of films that Lippert was proud of, even though it was not the money-maker that he had hoped it would be. Two months later, however, he had a hit on his hands.

Kurt Neumann walked into Lippert's office with a science fiction script he'd written. Neumann had been writing, producing, and directing movies at a B-level for almost twenty years, jumping from genre to genre, from studio to studio, wherever he could find work. Now, he'd written this script called *Journey into the Unknown* about some astronauts who discover prehistoric animals on Mars. To avoid expensive special effects, cost-conscious Neumann intended to use the dinosaur footage from *One Million B.C.* (1940). Those scenes were marked with a triple "x" in his script.

Lippert liked the idea of combining rocket ships and dinosaurs, but he believed that the days when characters like Flash Gordon and Buck

Rogers explored the solar system were long gone. Nobody was making outer space movies anymore. Lippert sent Neumann on his way.

A few weeks later Jack Rabin approached Lippert with a story about a trip to the moon. Rabin had a special effects company on the Eagle Lion lot, and he was looking for a way to drum up a little business. Lippert sent him on his way, too. Then he saw a nice spread in *Life* magazine about *Destination Moon* (1950), an outer space movie that a guy named George Pal was making at Eagle Lion. All of a sudden, everybody was talking about this picture. *Popular Science*, *Popular Mechanics*, and a dozen other publications ran articles about it.

The wheels began spinning in Lippert's head. He could take advantage of all of this publicity by beating Pal into the theaters with a rocket ship movie of his own. He got Neumann on the phone and told him to come back to his office. "Kid," he said, "we're going to the moon."

At first Lippert couldn't settle on a title. *Rocket to the Moon* sounded good for a while. Then, *None Came Back* seemed more appropriate since all of the astronauts die at the end of the film. He felt like a fool when he realized that in order to hitch a ride on Pal's publicity wagon, the title had to have the word "moon" in it. So he changed it to *Rocket Trip to the Moon*. It went into production as *Rocketship Expedition Moon*.

George Pal got wind of what Lippert was up to and threatened to sue him. Lippert didn't' want any trouble. He told Neumann they were going to do what Neumann had wanted to do in the first place—they'd go to Mars. The title was changed for the last time to *Rocketship X-M* (1950).

Now that he was committed to the project, Lippert was determined to make a quality picture. He gave Neumann's script to Dalton Trumbo to see what he could do with it. A few years earlier a writer of Trumbo's stature would have been way out of Lippert's price range. Trumbo was one of the highest paid screenwriters in the business, earning as much as $4,000 a week; however, his refusal to testify before the House's Un-American Activities Committee had earned him a little jail time and a place on the Hollywood blacklist.

This communist witch-hunt was one of the darkest times in America's history. Communists, socialists and liberals were under attack because they'd been instrumental in the formation of labor unions. The ruling class wanted them put into the same category with traitors and terrorists. People like Trumbo suddenly found that the only way they could work was if they were paid under the table, at a cut rate, and without credit.[2]

The focus of Trumbo's rewrite was on the second half of Neumann's scenario. He threw out the business with the dinosaurs.

Poster for Rocketship X-M (1950).

Instead, the astronauts find that Mars is a nuclear ravaged planet. The few survivors of the holocaust have reverted to stone-age savagery. This was the first time a film had warned the public about the danger of nuclear war, a warning that echoed throughout the decade. Trumbo had turned Neumann's silly story into something dramatically more satisfying and relevant.

Lippert's space opera was playing in theaters while Pal's film was still being edited. It cost $94,000 to make and grossed over $600,000. *The Hollywood Reporter* called it "first rate." It is ironic that for all of the effort and energy that went into making *Destination Moon*, Lippert's cheaper rip-off was more entertaining. Both films are credited with kicking off the cycle of science fiction films that were so popular during the decade.

After the success of *Rocketship X-M*, Kurt Neumann seemed like a good choice for *20,000 Leagues*. Contracts were signed. Neumann would get $9,000 to direct the picture, and Carroll Young would get $2,500 to write it. The budget was set at $500,000, but the movie never happened. Lippert finally sold the property to Walt Disney.

One of the more interesting projects that fell through the cracks was a movie about Herbert Emerson Wilson, a minister who became a thief. He made off with more than $15 million before the law caught up with him. *Collier's* magazine ran a five-part article about Wilson called, "King of the Safecrackers" and Lippert took an option on it. One reporter glibly remarked: "By utilizing the best tricks of both trades, the 'king' might even be qualified to pry an occasional kopek out of Lippert's tight-fisted production impresario, Murray Lerner."

Ron Ormond and Maurice Tombragel came to Lippert with an outrageous proposition. They told him they could make six westerns in twenty-one days by using the same cast, crew, sets and locations. Costumes and horses would be chosen based on how closely they matched the costumes and horses ridden by the actors in the action footage they planned to crib from some old westerns. Lippert estimated that each feature would cost about $7,000. At that price, he couldn't lose.

The stars of these harried horse operas were James "Shamrock" Ellison and Russell "Lucky" Hayden, once sidekicks to William Boyd in the Hopalong Cassidy series. Their leading lady was newcomer Betty Adams. In her autobiography, *The Lucky Southern Star*, the actress wrote: "When the movies began filming I did my own hair

THE FILMS OF ROBERT L. LIPPERT

and makeup, and for each new scene tried very hard to remember which 'girl' I was playing."

The six features—*Hostile Country, Marshal of Heldorado, Crooked River, Colorado Ranger, West of the Brazos,* and *Fast on the Draw*—were released in 1950 and went over well with the exhibitors and their audiences.

Russell Hayden's and Jimmy Ellison's acting careers were winding down when they signed on for these movies. Hayden had been a film cutter and a production manager with no aspirations toward being an actor until producer Harry Sherman told him he'd pay him $1,000 a week to play Hopalong Cassidy's sidekick. During the war Hayden purchased a chunk of agricultural acreage in the San Fernando Valley. These days they call it Studio City. He also invested in Pioneertown, a frequent location for Gene Autry, the Cisco Kid, and countless other cowboys during the early days of television when westerns filled the airwaves. He produced a few TV shows of his own—*Cowboy G-Men* (1952-53), *Judge Roy Bean* (1955-56) and *26 Men* (1957-59). When Hayden retired, he and his wife (Lillian Porter) lived in Pioneertown in the house they'd built for the *Judge Roy Bean* TV series.

Jimmy Ellison also made a buck in real estate. He bought a chunk of land in Beverly Hills where he built some high-priced homes on what came to be known as Ellison Drive.

As for Betty Adams, she changed her name to Julie Adams after signing with Universal-International and became the studio's most active actress. She played opposite all of U-I's heavy-weights—James Stewart, Charlton Heston, Glenn Ford, Rock Hudson, Van Heflin, Tony Curtis, George Nader, Francis the talking mule, and the Creature from the Black Lagoon.

1951 turned out to be a landmark year for Lippert. He would experiment with what he called dual purpose features, produce the first Superman movie, begin a relationship with the writer and director of one of television's longest running series, enter a successful co-production deal with Hammer Films in England and have his biggest hit movie ever!

After completing *The Baron of Arizona,* Sam Fuller had gone to Warner Bros. to write a script for a Gary Cooper movie. Lippert wanted him back and knew how to get him. He promised Fuller complete autonomy—he could write, direct, produce and edit any picture he wanted to make and he wanted to make a movie about the war in Korea.

After World War II the Korean Peninsula had been divided into two separate states. The northern half was occupied by the Russians, the southern half by the United States. The 38th parallel was the political border between the two. Cross-border skirmishes and raids eventually escalated into war. On June 25, 1950, North Korean forces invaded South Korea. A security resolution was quickly passed authorizing military intervention, and the U.S. sent over 300,000 soldiers to aid the South Korean forces in what U.S. President Harry Truman called "a police action."

The movie that Fuller had in mind was not going to be full of typical John Wayne type of phony baloney heroics and patriotic flag waving. It was going to focus on the confusion, brutality, and futility of war. It would not say "THE END" at the close of his film. It would say instead: "THERE IS NO END TO THIS STORY."

Fuller delivered his script to the Pentagon a few days before the film went into production. The motion picture section of the Defense Department's public information division made suggestions that would have meant a complete rewrite. Since no changes were made, the film went into release without the Defense Department's approval.

In his article for *The Citizen News*, Victor Riesel quoted a high ranking, anonymous military officer who said Fuller's script was technically inaccurate and seemed to be a vicious attempt to put the military in a bad light. Among the many scenes the officer objected

James Edwards, Steve Brodie, Robert Hutton, Richard Loo and Gene Evans . *from* The Steel Helmet *(1951)*

Advertisement for The Steel Helmet.

to was one in which a communist prisoner of war argues with a GI sergeant over the reasons they're at war. General Anonymous said: "[The] communist is firm and decisive and has the answers while the GI is weak, and fumbling, and doesn't know what to answer. The impression is clearly left that he (the American) either has no idea why he's fighting or doesn't really believe he should be fighting." Imagine that.

Fuller returned to the Defense Department in November with the unfinished film in hand and a request for some footage from the Signal Corps. They gave him 1,000 feet of unedited and unclassified footage, out of which he used about 150 feet. The Motion Picture Association assumed that this act meant the Army approved of Fuller's film. It was given the production code seal without a second's thought.

The Steel Helmet (1951) had its Los Angeles premier in mid-February. Victor Riesel claimed that someone from Lippert's office had asked the Army for a band and parade to publicize his film. Riesel was glad they did not get it because he was outraged that the filmmakers had the audacity to brag that "for the first time an American Motion Picture shows the murder of a Prisoner of War by American Soldiers." What gall! "There's already enough stuff in Chinese union halls in and around Peking today showing the American G.I. as one who wantonly smashed the skulls of his wounded buddies for fifty cents and as men who shoot down Chinese workers just for sport without the U.S. Army helping to publicize a movie portraying a murderous G.I.," Riesel bristled.

Fuller took issue with Riesel's account and let the law firm of Kaplan, Livingston, Goodwin and Berkowitz take care of the matter.

The Fox West Coast Theater chain played The Steel Helmet in their first run houses. It was held over for a second week at the United Artists Theater in downtown Los Angeles to the best business the place had seen for two years. It was also the first Lippert movie to play New York City's Loew's State Theatre. In the first week it took in $26,000. By February, it was playing in first-run theaters in five major markets, and (probably to Victor Riesel's surprise) was booked into the entire Army and Air Force circuit, even though it had been denied the War Department's seal of approval.

"There is a difference," a spokesman for the Army and Air Force Motion Picture Service told Variety, "between the Army giving its seal of approval to a film, and merely not objecting to a picture. The Army does not censor any pictures."

Dick Williams, the entertainment editor for *The Mirror*, was pleasantly surprised. Even though Fuller's movie was produced on a low budget and a fast-schedule, it was not the "shoddy, quickie makeshift" he expected. It was, he said, "a first-class job." He thought Ernest W. Miller's photography was as good as anything turned out by the major studios.

Whatever its shortcomings, *The Steel Helmet* is not a film that can be easily dismissed. It is about as subtle as a hand grenade going off in your face and does about as much damage to the psyche. It has one of the best openings ever seen on film, and Gene Evans is perfect in the lead role. It is doubtful that anyone could have been more convincing.

Four months after the picture went into release, Lippert was in the hospital for gall bladder surgery. When the reporters asked Marty Weiser how he was, Weiser (never one to miss a promotion opportunity) replied: "They found 21 gall stones and four frames from *The Steel Helmet*."[3]

By July the film had garnered over a million dollars and was expected to play at least another 7500 domestic dates. Lippert was forced to double his usual print order from 300 to 600 prints. Once the figures were in on the foreign market, which brought in about 40 percent of the total revenue, the film earned over two million in profits, setting the bar for high grossing low budget features.

The Steel Helmet and *Rocketship X-M* boosted Lippert into a higher bracket. He was finally able to command a percentage of the box office, giving him some leverage to make bigger pictures. He moved the home office of his distribution company from San Francisco to 145 N. Robertson Boulevard in Los Angeles. His production unit was moved from KTTV studios in Hollywood to Beverly Hills. Yet, in spite of the success he was enjoying, Lippert told *Variety* that the market for B-movies was drying up.

Lippert took a lot of heat from the exhibitors when he sold a package of Screen Guild movies to television in the early 1950s. It was one way to recoup the negative costs on the films that had not made money. He was accused of aiding the enemy and there were those who wanted to boycott his movies. Lippert wondered if they'd noticed there were fewer B-movies being made. He told them:

"Unless you are willing to pay higher rentals for program pictures, to make them profitable, they will continue to disappear."[4]

For a short time, Lippert experimented with what he called "dual purpose movies." These were 57 minute movies with two separate stories. As soon as they'd finished their theatrical run they were split in half and sold as half hour TV programs.

It began with the three Dennis O'Brien movies—*Danger Zone, Roaring City*, and *Pier 23*—released in 1951. Soft-spoken William Berke directed the series. The star was Hugh Beaumont, a dependable B-actor who would later become famous as Ward Cleaver on the popular *Leave It to Beaver* television series. Beaumont played Dennis O'Brien, a bitter, wise-cracking loser who earned his living by renting his boat and taking whatever odd jobs came his way. The odd jobs always led to murder and O'Brien was always the prime suspect. Richard Travers played the hard-boiled, not-so-bright cop who was always certain O'Brien was guilty. O'Brien eventually turned to his drunken ex-doctor friend (Edward Brophy) for help, and between the two of them they flushed out the killer.

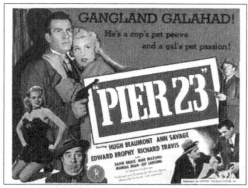

This formula should sound familiar to anyone who listened to the syndicated *Pat Novak for Hire* radio show. The O'Brien scripts were adapted from six of the half hour radio scripts written by Richard L. Breen, Herbert Margolis,

Above: Poster for Pier 23. *Below: Hugh Beaumont, (unidentified actor), Edward Brophy, Richard Travis, and Raymond Greenleaf from* Pier 23 *(1951).*

Tom Neal, Pamela Blake, Virginia Dale, and Hugh Beaumont from Danger Zone *(1951).*

and Louis Morheim. There was another radio program starring Jack Webb called *Johnny Modero* that is often listed as the source for these screenplays. With Webb involved in both programs, it is quite possible that one borrowed from the other.

Lippert went into partnership with Hal Roach Jr. to make twelve more dual purpose movies. Roach had a lot of standing sets from *One Million B.C.*, *The Bohemian Girl* (1936), *Captain Fury* (1939), *Joan of Arc* (1948), and *Jack and the Beanstalk* (1952). These sets made it possible for Roach to deliver his and Lippert's first effort, *Tales of Robin Hood*, for a mere $30,000. Roach hoped he would be able to turn *Robin Hood* into another hit TV series like *The Stu Erwin Show* (1950-55), *Racket Squad* (1951-53), or *My Little Margie* (1952-55).

"We've got our operation down to the point now where there isn't any waste," Roach told a reporter from the *New York Herald Tribune*. "We put up the sets close to each other so there are no expensive camera hauls. When we finish a scene we don't strip the stage, as they do in the major studios, but leave all the scaffolding standing. Chances are most of it can be used as it is again."

However, the exhibitors were not happy with these television-ready movies and showed their disapproval by not booking them. Then, the unions came knocking at Lippert's door wanting their cut of the action. Lippert decided it was not worth it. After two service comedies, *As You Were* and *Mr. Walkie Talkie* (both 1951), Lippert severed his deal with Roach.

"If you were an exhibitor, you never really knew where you stood with Lippert," said Robert Clarke, the star of *Tales of Robin Hood*. "You might book one of his pictures, thinking it was first run only to find out after it was too late that it had already played on television. I don't know if that happened with our film but I know it happened."

Superman and the Mole Men was the last of the dual purpose movies, modestly bankrolled by National Periodicals Publications (DC Comics), to promote the Superman television series which went into production a month after the feature was completed. In a way, the movie was a pilot, though pilots traditionally introduce all of the principal characters of a series. George Reeves and Phyllis Coates were the only two actors in the feature who would be part of the series. Reeves played the dual role of Clark Kent and Superman.

Advertisement for Superman and the Mole Men.

Phyllis Coates was Lois Lane and, for my money, is still the best Lois Lane of them all.

"George and I laughed through the whole thing!" Miss Coates told Tom Weaver. "Somebody recently sent me a still of George and the mole-men, and one of the midgets is holding an Electrolux vacuum cleaner, which was their weapon! It really was funny."

Superman was shot on the RKO-Pathe lot in Culver City, a few hundred yards from the oil derricks that play such an important part of the story. The budget was probably around $125,000 with a 12-day shooting schedule. According to the *Hollywood Reporter*, Robert Maxwell and Bernard Luber produced the movie, but their names do not appear on the film. Instead, the producer's credit goes to Barney A. Sarecky. All three of these gentlemen were involved in the TV series. Both Sarecky and Luber had made other films for Lippert, which may explain how Lippert became involved in the project.

Lippert never held the copyright on this movie. Once it finished its theatrical run, it was no longer part of his library and was not seen for two years. That's how long it took for the series to find a sponsor. *Superman and the Mole Men* was edited, split into two parts, and shown as the last two episodes of the first season under the title, "The Unknown People."[5]

Lippert made an insidious arrangement with Rudolph Flothow, the producer of the syndicated TV series *Ramar of the Jungle* (1952-54). The show was produced in four sets; each set contained thirteen episodes. Flothow made sure that each set had three episodes with a related story line so they could be edited together into feature length. For the record, the titles of these features were: *White Goddess, Eyes of the Jungle* (both 1953), *Thunder Over Sangoland,* and *Phantom of the Jungle* (both 1955).

Rather than admit his dual-purpose films had been met with hostility from the exhibitors and the unions, Lippert told the press: "Production technique for motion pictures made for theaters and television is radically different; it's impossible to combine the two methods."[6] He claimed that he was through with television unless conditions for sales dramatically improved.

"Exhibitors who fear that B pictures might be offered to television in competition with theater bookings are working up unnecessary ulcers," Lippert wrote in a piece for *Boxoffice*. "The television industry can't afford them...and doesn't need them." He added that the movies

Above: Phyllis Coates, George Reeves, Walter Reed, and Jeff Corey. Below: Jack Bambury and Tony Boris as they appear in Superman and the Mole Men *(1951).*

currently running on television were so old the box office potential had been completely drained and, therefore, could hardly be considered as competition. He was talking through his hat; of course, they were competition. The movies may have lost the power to lure people to the box office but as free entertainment they could keep people home.

Around this time, Lippert hooked up with a writer named Charles Marquis Warren, whose fascination with frontier lore would ultimately lead to the production of some of television's most popular western series: *Gunsmoke* (1955-75), *Rawhide* (1959-66), and *The Virginian* (1962-71). It was Lippert who gave him the chance to direct *Little Big Horn* (1951).

In January of 1950 Lippert had purchased a script called *Little Big Horn* from a writer named Sydney Byrd. Since Byrd's name does not appear on the film, we can assume Warren tossed his script and started from scratch. Warren gets the screenplay credit and Harold Shumate gets the story credit, a story based on a real incident in which a Seventh Cavalry patrol raced against time to warn General Custer that Sitting Bull was setting

Poster for White Goddess *(1953).*

a trap for him at the Little Big Horn. Manny Farber called Warren's picture "tough-minded" and "unconventional."

F. Scott Fitzgerald was the one who discovered Warren. In his letter of recommendation to Metro-Goldwyn-Mayer, Fitzgerald called him, "...amazingly varied. He writes, composes, and draws...I haven't believed in any body so strongly since Ernest Hemingway."[7] Fitzgerald sent Warren to Hollywood to work on a screen treatment of *Tender Is the Night*. In spite of the author's endorsement, Warren had little success as a screenwriter. But he did find a home in magazines. He sold more than 250 pulp fiction stories and eventually became a regular contributor to the *Saturday Evening Post*. Three of his serials—*Only the Valiant, Bugles Are for Soldiers* and *Valley of the Shadow*—became best-selling novels.

When World War II broke out Warren joined the Navy and served in the Photo Science Laboratory, filming amphibious landings. He was wounded by a Japanese grenade in the South Pacific and received a Purple Heart, a Bronze Star, and five battle stars. He was recuperating in a Guadalcanal hospital when he learned that Warner Bros. had purchased the rights to *Only the Valiant*. Before hooking up with Lippert, Warren wrote a number of successful screenplays, including *Beyond Glory* (1948) and *Streets of Laredo* (1949). Directing changed his viewpoint about movie writing. Whenever directors had changed his scripts, Warren had suffered the usual agonies that all writers do. Now, *he* was the director and he was cutting his script to the bone. "I've been cutting it as I go along," he told a reporter from the *Daily News*. "I've been tightening scenes, eliminating dialog, and condensing action." He cut 10 lines of dialog down to one, and trashed the first 14 pages of introductions to the characters. "You stand or fall on this sort of thing," he remarked. "It's a challenge. If the picture turns out lousy, you can't blame anybody."

Warren's picture had a strong cast of Lippert regulars including Lloyd Bridges, John Ireland, Reed Hadley, Jim Davis, and Hugh O'Brien. Joanne Dru, the star of Howard Hawks' *Red River* (1948), was married to John Ireland at the time, and she tested for the role that ultimately went to Marie Windsor, another Lippert regular. She's only in the first few minutes of the movie.

For the most part, the critical reaction to the film was positive. It did good business and was another film that Lippert was proud of.

Lippert decided to follow the lead of the major studios and take advantage of the British government's Eady Plan. The exhibitors in England collected a tax at the box office which was, in turn, given as a subsidy to the producers of locally made films. The computation of the bonus paid to individual producers was based on the proportion of the film's gross to the overall annual national theater gross,

Poster for Little Big Horn *(1951).*

and the payments were made to a central fund out of the gross receipts. Sir Wilfrid Eady, second Secretary to the Treasury, let it be known that despite an avalanche of protests from every section of the industry, the trade could expect no remission in the volume of

John Ireland and Marie Windsor from Little Big Horn *(1951).*

entertainment tax in the foreseeable future. In an address before the Theatre Owners Association of America (TOA) a few years later, producer Walter Mirisch told the group it was high time for an American version of the Eady plan. "The Eady Plan saved a dying British film industry and assured a steady flow of product to the theater operators," he told the crowd. "Three percent of the $1,300,000,000 per year average national gross of the American motion picture business during the last ten years would roughly be $40,000,000 per year, an amount sufficient to produce ten more blockbusters per year or twenty more major motion pictures, a welfare fund that would assure the health and continued growth of the industry."

Producer Alex Gordon was responsible for bringing Lippert together with Michael Carreras of Hammer Films in England. "I was in New York and had dealing with Bill Pizor, who handled Lippert's foreign sales," Gordon recalled.[8]

Carreras and Lippert hit it off right away as they had a lot in common. Both men operated on the fringe of the motion picture business and, like Lippert, Carreras' father was a former exhibitor. Enrique Carreras formed a partnership with Will Hinds, an ex-vaudevillian known as Will

Hammer. They founded Hammer Films, created to supply more features for Exclusive Films, a company that Hammer and Carreras owned. It was a set-up remarkably similar to Lippert's operation.

To make their co-productions more acceptable to U.S. audiences, Lippert supplied Carreras with an American actor (or actors), sometimes a writer (usually Richard Landau), and sometimes a director. In return, Exclusive Films distributed Lippert's product in the U.K. Hammer got the revenue from England, Scotland, Wales, Northern Ireland, the Channel Islands, Malta and Gibraltar and Lippert usually got the rest of the world. It was a great arrangement for both parties. It allowed Lippert to lower the cost of his productions and enabled Hammer to develop its North American market.

Lippert was there when the cameras rolled on their first co-production, *The Last Page* (1952), starring George Brent and Diana Dors. It was an unbelievable tale of blackmail and murder, lethargically directed by Terence Fisher, who would become Hammer's most famous director. Lippert trimmed six minutes from the film and changed the title to the more provocative *Man Bait* for the U.S. release.

Satisfied that things were running smoothly at Hammer, Lippert returned to the U.S. and struck a deal with Famous Artists Corporation, a talent agency that represented a number of writers, directors, producers, and actors. Lippert promised their clients the freedom to make the kind of pictures they wanted to make. He encouraged writers or actors who wanted to be directors to pick a project. It was a clever way of getting these people to work for a fraction of their normal price. To make the deal more attractive, Lippert offered to stretch their profit participations over a period of years to ease the tax burden and supply long-term revenue from theatrical, video, and other future markets. For his trouble, Lippert got a 30% distribution fee.

Loan Shark (1952) was the first of what Lippert called these "story-to-can" packages. The budget for this crime drama was $250,000, unusually high for a Lippert picture. $25,000 went to the film's star, George Raft. In the film he is coerced into infiltrating a gang of loan sharks that have been preying on factory workers. It is not on the level of the type of movie Raft made at Warner Bros. but taken on its own terms, it is very entertaining with a fine supporting cast that included John Hoyt and Paul Stewart.

George Brent finds Diana Dors to be more stimulating than a few swigs of Geritol in this scene from Man Bait *(1951).*

As *Loan Shark* went into production, Lippert cut deals with Irving Reis and Stephen Longstreet to direct a couple of features. Charles Marquis Warren was signed to deliver three pictures, beginning with *Hell Gate Prison* and *Galveston*. The most surprising of the lot was the production deal he negotiated with Carl Foreman.

Carl Foreman was the screenwriter who was responsible for such hard-hitting films as *Champion, Home of the Brave* (both 1949) and *The Men* (1950). He had recently completed *High Noon* (1952) for producer Stanley Kramer and was getting offers from just about everyone in town. It was a bit of a shock when this "hot property" told the press: "I have chosen to associate myself with Robert L. Lippert because I consider him one of the most dynamic and forward-thinking men in the industry today."⁹Foreman was set to write, produce and direct three features for Lippert at a cost of $306,000 a piece.

Back in 1950, Lippert and actor Gary Cooper had formed Mayflower Productions to make a western called *Three Desperate Men* (1950). Cooper was one of the shareholders in this new deal with Foreman, along with attorneys I. H. Prinzmetal, Sidney Cohn and publicist Henry C. Rogers. It all came to a sorry end when HUAC reared its ugly head and accused Foreman of being a Communist. He told the committee he was not a Communist when he signed the Screen

Writers Guild loyalty oath, but evoked his Constitutional right not to answer questions concerning his past political affiliations. Pressure was put on the Coop to withdraw from the deal, which he did, but he made it clear to the committee and anyone else who cared to listen that he believed Foreman was a loyal American.

The deals with Irving Reis and Stephen Longstreet also fell by the wayside. Only Charles Marquis Warren's *Hell Gate Prison* (retitled *Hellgate*) came to pass. It was one of Lippert's best pictures.

Lippert did not trust Hammer's writers to keep their idioms out of their screenplays, so for *Stolen Face* and *Scotland Yard Inspector* (both 1952) he supplied the scripts, and for the latter film, he supplied the director—Sam Newfield.

"Doubt as to how the British technicians might adapt themselves to American methods was dispelled on the first day of shooting when, with twenty-five camera setups, no fewer than nine minutes of quality screen time was put in the can," reported *The Kinematograph Weekly* in their September 11th account of the making of *Scotland Yard Inspector*. Hammer was so impressed with Newfield's speed they made an official request to the Ministry of Labor for the right to have an American director on their payroll on a permanent basis.

To qualify for Eady money, filmmakers had to adhere to the quota system which put a limit on the number of foreign artists permitted on British films during any given year. This is the reason why Sam Newfield's name does not appear on the British prints of *The Gambler and the Lady* (1953) even though he directed and wrote it. Pat Jenkins is given the director's credit; there is no screenplay credit.

Hammer made fourteen more pictures with Lippert. 1953: *Bad Blonde* with Barbara Payton and *Spaceways* with Howard Duff. 1954: *Terror Street* with Dan Duryea, *Black Glove* with Alex Nicol, *Heat Wave* with Alex Nicol and Hillary Brooke, *Blackout* and *Paid to Kill* with Dane Clark, and *The Unholy Four* with Paulette Goddard. 1955: *Deadly Game* with Lloyd Bridges, *A Race for Life* with Richard Conte, *The Glass Tomb* with John Ireland, and *Break in the Circle* with Forest Tucker. 1956: *The Creeping Unknown* with Brian Donlevy and Margia Dean, and *Blonde Bait* with Beverly Michaels and Jim Davis. With one exception, these movies played the United States before they were shown in England.

In 1951, the January 3rd edition of the *Hollywood Reporter* mentioned that Lippert's production manager, Murray Lerner, was

Paul Henreid and Lizabeth Scott in Stolen Face *(1952), a psychological melodrama that bears some resemblance to Aflred Hitchcock's* Vertigo.

negotiating with actress Veronica Lake to star in a movie he was about to produce called *Lost Continent* (1951). Lake had been one of Paramount's hottest stars, having appeared in several of the studio's critical and financial successes, including *Sullivan's Travels* (1941) and *This Gun for Hire* (1942). But by 1948 the studio decided not to renew her contract because she had been hitting the bottle pretty hard, and people didn't want to work with her anymore. Out of work and out of options, she was the perfect candidate for Lippert. Nevertheless, she declined Lerner's offer for a day's work, and the part went to Hillary Brooke.

"It's my biggest venture to date," Lippert told the press, claiming the budget for *Lost Continent* was $500,000. It was more like $220,000, which was still high for one of his films. "We're even having a full-scale earthquake in the picture. We've built giant lava beds which will crack open and swallow up the actors. I guess if Metro has a call for an earthquake they do it this way. But it's unusual for a little outfit like us."[10]

Lippert flew to England with a print of the film to coordinate a U.K. premier with the one scheduled in the U.S. It opened in three theaters in Los Angeles—The Los Angeles on Broadway, the Vogue in Hollywood, and the Uptown on Western and Olympic. The co-feature was another Lippert release, *Highly Dangerous* (1950), a British spy drama with Dane Clark.

In her review of *Lost Continent*, Margaret Harford relates her experience watching the film. She told the young boy sitting next to her that she did not understand how the top of a mountain two or three times bigger than Mt. Everest could have a climate as warm as a Caribbean evening. "You can't be too literal about such things when it came to science fiction," he told her. Later, when Romero gets his first glimpse of one of the prehistoric animals, the young man blandly told Harford: "It's only a two-bit lizard photographed through a magnifying glass."[11]

Lippert made one more prehistoric movie, *The Jungle* (1952), the first American motion picture made in India with American actors. In the screenplay by Carroll Young, prehistoric wooly mammoths cause

Ex-Universal contract player Acquanetta and ex-20th Century-Fox contract player Cesar Romero in Lippert's mix of the past and the future, Lost Continent *(1951).*

Poster for The Jungle *(1952), the first American motion picture made in India with American actors.*

the elephants in Sunadur province to go mad. It is up to great white hunter Rod Cameron, Princess Marie Windsor and her protector Cesar Romero to resolve the problem.

Rod Cameron and Marie Windsor on a treacherous trek in William Berke's
The Jungle *(1952.*

On two occasions during the production of this movie, the State Department ordered director William Berke and his crew to stop filming so that the actors could represent the United States at the International Film Festival in India. It seemed that Gene Tierney had not shown up, leaving only director Frank Capra to steal the publicity away from the Russians. The Russians had been told they could bring 35 people. They brought 350. The State Department feared the U.S. propaganda would be trumped by Russian propaganda. Sundaram generously shouldered the costs of the shutdowns.

"When a company goes clear to India to film a feature," wrote Colorado exhibitor Bob Walker, "and they don't try to hold you up on the terms, every theater should give them a booking for their trouble."

Berke's $125,000 movie made $160,742 during its theatrical run and picked up another $32,170 from its sale to television.

Lippert began selling his twenty-eight exchanges to raise enough capital to finance two movies a year with million dollar budgets. L. Frank Baum's *Dorothy and the Land of Oz* was at the top of his list. Negotiations for the property had begun back in 1949, but it wasn't until March of 1951 that Lippert finally reached an agreement with

Director William Berke is attacked by a gorilla.

the owner of the copyright, Maud G. Baum. Lippert hoped to make the movie in England but, alas, it never happened.

At the stockholders meeting in 1953, with twenty-four low-budget features ready for release, Lippert told his audience that higher prices and the competition of television had gotten the public out of the habit of going to the movies every week, causing the gradual disappearance of small-budget pictures everywhere. Lippert believed the public would turn out for pictures they wanted to see, but they would probably continue to stay away from what he called "lesser films." Lippert stressed that he was determined to make nothing *but* big pictures. He chose to prove his point by naming two of his upcoming color features.

This was the year that Hollywood took a page from Cecil B. DeMille's playbook and started making big budget, heavy-handed religious epics. In 1951 20ᵗʰ Century-Fox made a lot of money with *David and Bathsheba*. Two years later, to introduce its new wide screen CinemaScope process, Fox chose *The Robe* (1953), based on a best-selling novel by Lloyd C. Douglas. Before *The Robe* went into release, the studio was already in production on a sequel. Not to be outdone, Harry Cohn put his favorite star, Rita Hayworth, in the most costly movie Columbia had made since Frank Capra's *Lost Horizon* (1937). The film, *Salome* (1953), featured a pillar-hugging, scene-chewing performance by Charles Laughton, as well as Miss Hayworth's provocative Dance of the Seven Veils, photographed in gorgeous Technicolor.

Sex and saintliness seemed to go hand in hand in these pious and humorless melodramas, so it should come as no surprise that two studios were poised to make movies about Jezebel, one of *The Bible's* most infamous sex sirens. Fox announced *The Story of Jezebel* in color and CinemaScope. Monogram jumped into the race with *The Siren of Jezebel*. Lippert beat them both to the punch with *Sins of Jezebel* (1953), one of those "big" movies that Lippert told the stockholders about.

Paulette Goddard was paid $20,000 to play the fiery hot Jezebel. Once the star of major motion pictures, she must have felt the swirl of her career circling the toilet when she signed on to this disaster. Although the film has the distinction of being the first movie to be photographed for projection in both conventional 4:3 and 16:9 widescreen, it also has the dubious honor of being the most impoverished "epic" ever made. It looks like one of those 16mm Bible films. Lippert spent more money to make *Lost Continent*.

Richard Landau's screenplay is absent of wit and low on drama. Reginald LeBorg's direction is pedestrian and listless. The cast is lethargic, save for John Hoyt, equally hammy and ridiculous as both the doomsayer prophet, Elijah, and the modern day preacher who introduces the story. Hoyt returns just before the climax to *tell* the audience how it all ended. That's right. There is no climax! If Lippert had had his wits about him the very last words Hoyt said to

Poster for Sins of Jezebel *(1954).*

the audience would have been: "Boy, you should have seen it. It was really exciting."

The other "big" picture that Lippert mentioned at the stockholders meeting was *The Great Jesse James Raid* (1954). Lippert loved movies with Jesse James in the title, but this one was made to capitalize on the headline-making, volatile relationship between Tom Neal and his girlfriend, Barbara Payton. Unlike Neal, who was always at the bottom of the B-movie bucket, Payton had been under contract to Warner Bros. For a short while it looked as if she might have been headed for a successful career. Ultimately, her well-publicized, reckless lifestyle and the near fatal brawl between her boyfriends Neal and Franchot Tone derailed her career. Lippert got the couple as a package deal and gave the job of producing the movie to his son.

During the Great Depression, when his father was selling and promoting "Dish Night" and "Book Night" across the United States, Robert Leonard Lippert Jr. attended six different grammar schools and spent the better part of his summer vacations with his Grandmother in San Francisco. There, he met a lot of seamen and aircraft pioneers, and their tales of travel and adventure made him all the more impatient with school. At fifteen he ran away to join the Canadian Navy. For that little escapade, he was given a four year sentence at the San Rafael Military Academy. Graduating as a Cadet Colonel Battalion Commander, he was forced to attend St. Mary's College in Moranga, California. After that, he went to San Francisco City College, but after a year he dropped out and went to work at one of his father's theaters, the one conveniently located near the airport where he took flying lessons. He continued to work for his dad, first as a theater manager, then as a film cutter, and a director. *The Great Jesse James Raid* was the first film he produced.

"The film was well-received by theater exhibitors," Junior said. "4,500 bookings in 1953 were exceptional for a 'B' or second feature.

Paulette Goddard and George Nader from the cheesiest of all of the Biblical epics, Sins of Jezebel *(1954).*

Considering that it had a budget of well under $100,000, *Jesse* made a nice profit."[11]

While his fellow exhibitors were scratching their heads, wondering which new process to invest in—CinemaScope or 3-D—Robert Lippert announced that he was going to install *both* formats in *all* of his theaters. He was ready to build the first 3-D drive-in theater until he realized the loss of light made that idea impractical. He did, however, buy 30,000 extra Polaroid glasses to keep on hand just in case the supplier could not keep up with the demand. He never produced a 3-D movie, but he did make a couple of 3-D shorts in 1953—*Bandit Island* and *College Capers.*

Lippert Jr. shot *Bandit Island* in various spots around Los Angeles, without permits, for $30,000. It had a small cast that included Glenn Langan as the policeman in pursuit of bank robbers Jay Lawrence, Jim Davis, and Lon Chaney.

"Lon instigated a lot of the stunts and he did some of 'em himself," Lippert Jr. recalled. "I was surprised. We had car chases, a helicopter and everything. Twenty-seven minutes of action...and no fuckin' story. The bandits pulled a robbery and took off so they would not get caught. Senior wanted all these 3-D gimmicks thrown at you, so we had to go action, everything coming at you, you duck in the

Barbara Payton, Tom Neal and Willard Parker from The Great Jesse James Raid *(1954). This was Neal's final film.*

audience. We shot the thing in four days, with all these gimmicks. We had these two cameras. They were very bulky, huge; two Mitchell cameras facing one another. You could hardly move 'em. It took four gaffers to move these damn things."[12]

College Capers featured Ed Wood star Dolores Fuller in a comedy about panty raids, which was shown recently for the first time in sixty years at a 3-D festival at the Egyptian Theater in Hollywood. Lippert also picked up a couple of 3-D shorts—*The Return of Gilbert and Sullivan* (1952) and *A Day in the Country* (1953), originally produced in 1941 under the title *Stereo Laffs*.

Lippert announced that he would be distributing six one-reel "Western Kid Komedies in Kolor." The titles of these shorts were as follows: *The White Phantom, Showdown at Sun-Up, Hal's Half-Acre, Last of the Good Guys, Hurry-Along Harrigan* and *Bar-Bar-Black Sheep*. Although some (or all) of these shorts were produced, there is no indication that they were ever released.

Lippert Jr. and Ollalo Rubio Gandara co-produced two movies— *The Black Pirates* (1954) and *Massacre* (1956). Gandara got the revenue from the Spanish speaking territories and Lippert Inc. got the rest of the world. Looking back on the two pictures, Junior said:

Posters for Bandit Island and College Capers (both 1953).

"The Black Pirates was shit and Massacre was no good either." He laughed when he recalled that they did not have enough money for a pirate ship: "[At] the beginning we showed a rowboat coming in from the ocean and the pirates getting' out! No ship! They were fun days, I'm tellin' ya, because you could get by with things like that. We made that whole goddamn thing for $108,000 in color."[13]

The star of The Black Pirates was Anthony Dexter, well-known in Latin America because of his portrayal of Rudolph Valentino in Edward Small's 1951 movie, Valentino. In Lippert's picture he was looking for gold in a Latin American town. Lon Chaney played the village priest who'd already found the gold and used it for charity. Chaney is shot by one of the pirates played by Eddie Dutko. Some of the uneducated locals who were watching from the sidelines thought Dutko had actually killed a priest and chased after him with their machetes.

Massacre, an Intercontinental Pictures production, was a tale about gunrunners stirring up trouble in Yaqui territory, selling bad weapons, and bad medicine to the locals. According to the New York Times, it had the distinction of closing in New York after a nine-hour run. Junior quit the business after that.

"My father was a son of a bitch to work for," he said candidly. "I couldn't make any money working for him. I had to quit."

Massacre sat on the shelf for over a year when Lippert's battle with the Screen Actors Guild forced him out of business.

It all began with the sale of his film library to television. The major studios were initially reluctant to license their movies to TV for fear of alienating the exhibitors, but Lippert was not worried about the exhibitors since they had never been worried about him. He traveled to all of the cities where television had taken hold and was ready to sell all of his 1946-47 features on the spot for $20,000 a piece. He sold 26 features to WGN-TV in Chicago for less than half of that. The widely reported demand for movies, save for New York and Los Angeles, simply was not there. Not then anyway.

Lippert was the first producer to sign an American Federation of Musicians contract, enabling him to sell his pictures to television at any time. The AFM had come to Lippert demanding five per cent of the gross of his television sale. Not wanting to pay, Lippert threw out the original scores and replaced them with tuneless organ music. No soap; the TV stations would not take the pictures. To make the sale, he was forced to restore (most of) the original scores and pay the AFM.

Lippert formed Tele-Pictures for the express purpose of selling more films to television. He put Junior in charge of it. The first sale of 33 more movies made $716,000. It was not long before the Screen Actors Guild (SAG) and the Writers Guild of America (WGA) wanted their cut of the action. Lippert told them to go fly a kite. SAG retaliated with the threat of a boycott. Lippert dug in his heels and reminded the guild that he had never signed a residuals agreement. SAG agreed to a 90-day truce while they worked out the terms.

"In approving the postponement," SAG stated, "SAG is not deviating from its firm policy of cancelling its contract with any producer who releases to television any theatrical pictures made after Aug. 1, 1948, without first negotiating an arrangement with the Guild for additional payment to the actors for such dual use. The Guild has this legal right of contract cancellation under its basic agreement with all the motion picture producers. Effect of such contract cancellation would be that no actor would work for such a producer."[14]

This truce was made on the condition that Lippert would not sell anymore of his post 1948 movies to TV, but he did, and SAG was furious. They put Lippert on their "unfair" list.

Lippert had been working on a deal with agent Bill White to finance a movie based on a Broadway play. White was going to act as the producer, and one of his clients, Sylvia Sidney, was to play the lead. Lippert accused SAG of squashing the deal: "The whole thing's up in the air, because I've been advised by SAG counsel that if I'm financing I'm in production."[15] SAG President John Dales Jr. denied the accusation. He said that they had not come to a decision regarding the matter. "It would depend on the circumstances of each particular case," Dales explained. "If Lippert only financed, and we had a contract with the producer or owner of the picture granting assurance the picture would not go to television, I can see no objection. On the other hand, however, if Lippert would be an owner or stockholder in the production, that would be another matter."[16]

When all of the shouting and finger-pointing was over, one thing was clear—somebody at SAG needed to put something in writing. Nobody knew who exactly was supposed to get what. SAG wanted a cut; the WGA wanted a cut; the AGM wanted a cut; but, nobody knew how much or on what basis.

"Certainly the smallest operator in the industry shouldn't set the pattern," Lippert told them. "When the pattern is set I then will be ready to sit down with the SAG."[17] He felt that the bigger companies, which had a far greater stake in the future, should be the ones to work out the details. He reminded everyone that producers should be entitled to recoup their production costs before a percentage of the gross was tossed into the union kitty, and not just for one union but for all of them. Lippert was willing to negotiate, but only after he knew where he stood.

SAG continued their boycott and Lippert became persona non grata in Hollywood. He tried to settle with them for $60,000, but they refused. According to SAG, an actor was supposed to receive 12 per cent of his original salary if the picture was sold for less than $20,000. If it sold for more, it was 15 per cent. SAG wanted to see a list of Lippert's films.

In the midst of his battle with SAG, Lippert had defectors in his own ranks. Two people in his New York exchange, David M. Sohmer and Robert Greenblatt, filed a suit against him in the New York Supreme Court. Assured by management that the exchange would not be sold, they read in the newspapers that the branch had, in fact, been sold to Favorite Films. Sohmer wanted $2,677 from Lippert, and Greenblatt wanted $892. In the five years that they'd worked for him they'd never had a vacation. The money they were asking for was for two weeks of vacation for every year they'd worked. Lippert probably thought their demands were outrageous. After all, he gave everyone an extra week's pay at the end of every year as a bonus? What was the matter with these people?

Finally, Lippert announced that his company was abandoning production. He would, instead, devote his time to the distribution of independently made films. Lippert's stated reason for this switch in gears was to enable him to devote most of his time to the financing bigger budgeted features.

Out of the blue, Lippert's executive assistant, Edmund J. Baumgarten, a former chief loan officer for the motion picture division at the downtown branch of Bank of America, became the president of Lippert Pictures, Inc. Of course, Lippert was still running the show. It was simply a bit of parlor magic to confuse SAG, a trick he would later employ when he went to work for 20th Century-Fox.

To further distance himself from the company, he was ready to change the company name to Screen Art. There were still a dozen or so pictures that would be going out with the old Lippert signature, but that could not be helped. The titles had already been shot and the campaign material had already been printed.

Attempting an end run around SAG, Lippert thought he could sell what was left of his library to a third party, and if that party happened to sell those movies to TV, SAG could not possibly hold him accountable. Or, so he thought. He cut a deal with producer William F. Broidy. In exchange for assuming the responsibility of the TV sale, Lippert would give him the money to make twelve features. Official Films agreed to represent Broidy in the matter. They sold the following package to KTLA, Channel 5 in Los Angeles: *There is No Escape, Mozart Story* (both 1948), *I Shot Jesse James, Tough Assignment, Treasure of Monte Cristo, Deputy Marshal, The Dalton Gang, Call of the Forest* (all 1949), *Baron of Arizona, Operation Haylift, Radar Secret Service, Holiday Rhythm, Gunfire, Motor Patrol, Train to Tombstone, Apache Chief, Hi-Jacked, Border Rangers,* and *Western Pacific Agent* (all 1950),

SAG was not fooled; they forced Lippert to shut his doors.

Notes:

1. In 1939, Warner Bros. announced that it was going to make a movie called *Prince of Imposters* with Edward G. Robinson playing James Addison Reavis. Brenda Marshall was to be his co-star and Anatole Litvak was slated to direct. Nothing came of it.

2. While Dalton Trumbo was on the blacklist he won two Academy Awards, one for *Roman Holiday* (1953), credited to writer McLellan Hunter, and one for *The Brave One* (1956), written under Trumbo's pseudonym, Robert Rich.

3. *Variety*, June 15, 1951, page 1.

4. *Variety*, January 6, 1955.

5. Some sources incorrectly state that SAG rules prevented *The Unknown People* from being shown until after 1960. Not so. I saw the movie at a children's matinee in 1952 and again on TV in 1953.

6. *Variety*, October 23, 1951, page 6.

7. Folkart, Burt A. "Charles Marquis Warren; Western Writer," *Los Angeles Times*, August 13, 1990.

8. Johnson, Tom and Deborah Del Vecchio, *Hammer Films, an Exhaustive Filmography*, McFarland & Co., North Carolina, 1996, pages 9-10.

9. *Variety*, April 24, 1951.

10. *Hollywood Citizen News*, September 8, 1951.

11. O'Dowd, John, *Kiss Tomorrow Goodbye: The Barbara Payton Story*, BearManor Media, Albany, GA., page 240.

12. Weaver, Tom *Earth Vs. the Sci-Fi Filmmakers*, McFarland & Co., Charlotte, NC. page 266.

13. Ibid: page 261.

14. *Variety* January 18, 1952, page 3.

15. Ibid.

16. *Variety* July 14, 1952 page 7.

17. Ibid.

CHAPTER THREE
REGAL FILMS, INC.

*"I'm running a school of opportunity. Lee Cobb is looking
for a story he can direct as well as star in. James Wong Howe
...came to me with a story he wrote, "The Umbrella God," and
we're going to let him make it."*

Robert L. Lippert

Lippert was sitting in his new office on the top floor of a two-story building, a building he owned. He was directly across the street from MGM studios on West Washington Boulevard in Culver City, in the larger of the two penthouse suites. His huge, mahogany desk was covered, as usual, with neat little stacks of papers. Behind it was a matching table full of curios: a knight in armor, a miniature torpedo, a bronze-covered wagon, a Grecian vase, and, of course, pictures of his family. He saw the pictures more often than he did his family. Being a workaholic, he all but lived in his office, and he loved it.

He was making movies again, just like before, only now he didn't have to worry about financing. 20th Century-Fox was bankrolling the operation.

After three years of concentrating most of their efforts on multi-million dollar blockbusters, 20th Century-Fox realized they needed to make bread and butter pictures again. For the first nine months of 1957-58, Hollywood cranked out 304 features compared to 238 in the same period in 1956-57. The newly-formed American International Pictures had taught the big boys a lesson. Exhibitors had made a bundle on AIP's low budget combo packages of science fiction and teenage pictures with no name actors. These packages were offered to the exhibitor for a fraction of what it cost for a single attraction from the major studios. Allied Artists, Columbia, and Republic quickly followed suit with low-budget combo packs of their own. Universal had never stopped making combo packs.

Spyros Skouras, the head of 20th Century-Fox, hired Lippert to make ten low cost, black and white CinemaScope features a year. In addition to his salary, Lippert would ultimately own the pictures. If Lippert had any problems he went directly to Skouras and vice versa. It was a very personal arrangement.

Sol M. Wurtzel had been Fox's go-to guy for bread and butter pictures in the 1940s. In the early 1950s, it was Leonard Goldstein's Panoramic Pictures. Now, Fox had a problem. Skouras promised the exhibitors that if they sprung for the cost of installing CinemaScope screens in their theaters, Fox would only make color—CinemaScope features. Rather than admit that Skouras had gone back on his word, Lippert's movies were treated as if they were independently made; Fox posed as a distributor only.

Regal Films was the name of Lippert's company. Ed Baumgarten was the President. He signed the checks, but Lippert ran the company. This piece of deception was designed to keep the Screen Actors Guild at bay. Everyone in town, including SAG, knew that Lippert was running Regal Films, but so long as his name did not appear on any of the movies, there was nothing they could do about it since their deal was with Fox.

A lot of the people who worked with Lippert during this period thought the reason he didn't put his name on the pictures was because it didn't matter to him. They believed him when he said Hollywood was nothing but a bunch of "pretty boys" and "pretty girls," and nobody should take it too seriously. It was what Lippert wanted people to believe, but come on, folks, the name of his previous company was Lippert Pictures, Inc. He cared.

Lippert was making the same kinds of movies he'd always made—westerns, thrillers and science fiction movies—three or four at a time. They were shot on independent sound stages rather than on the Fox lot, which was yet another way of separating Regal from Fox. Lippert wanted to stay clear of the lot anyway. He couldn't afford the overhead. Shooting on rental stages was cheaper.

Lippert's office building housed a projection room, cutting rooms, and a modest staff of 19 people. Jack Leewood, who left Lippert back in 1951 to run the Allied Artists publicity department, returned as a line producer and trouble-shooter. Jodie Copeland was Lippert's film editor, and John Mansbridge was his art director.

"Lippert kept me pretty busy," Mansbridge told Tom Weaver. Lippert had a motel and a house in Palm Springs that Mansbridge redesigned. "On top of that, in Indio he had purchased some houses, so I got involved with decorating and coloring some of *those* things. So he kept me busy when I wasn't busy!" When asked how he felt about Lippert, Mansbridge replied: "I like the man very much. I thought he was a very neat guy."

Former film booker and buyer Harry Spalding became Regal's production head and, more significantly, Lippert's right hand man. He was Lippert's voice, the guy who read all of the scripts and dealt with the talent. He also ran some of Lippert's theaters in his spare time, and William J. Magginetti more or less ran the company. Spalding, Magginetti and Magginetti's protégé, Maury Dexter, were the key players on Lippert's team at Regal. He relied on them to keep everything in running order because he did not have the inclination or the time to micromanage Regal. He still had his theaters to buy and sell. Lippert felt he could trust these guys because they were not "yes" men, which isn't to say that he didn't get sore when they disagreed with him. Sometimes he'd shout and bluster, but once he'd blown off steam, the storm was over, and it was back to business as if nothing had happened.

"He was an easy man to get along with, but he was totally concentrated," Harry Spalding remarked. "He and I had a pretty good relationship, 'cause we were both from San Francisco, we both knew the theater business, all that kind of thing. As a matter of fact, Lippert's employees were kind of his family a good deal of the time. He really took that attitude."[1] This might explain why Lippert still had his first banker, his first landlord, and his first projectionist on the payroll.

Maury Dexter had worked at Regal for about a year when he asked Lippert for the money his brother needed to start a cabinet business. Dexter and Lippert had never been what you would call close. Now and then Dexter would be a dinner guest in Lippert's home, but other than that they never saw each other socially.

"How much money are we talking about?" Lippert asked.

"Ten thousand."

Lippert sat for a moment, chewing on his cigar, got up, grabbed his coat and said, "Follow me, kid." They headed straight for the corner bank where Lippert had the teller make out a cashier's check in the amount Dexter had asked for. "Pay me back when and *if* you can, kid," Lippert told him. Six months later Dexter returned the money, but when he tried to give Lippert some interest, Lippert threw him out of his office.

Lovely and talented Mara Corday starred in Lippert's The Naked Gun *(1956).*

"I'm surprised to hear that story," Margia Dean remarked. "I never knew Bob to be that generous. You know he used to tell people that he bought my house which wasn't true."

During Regal's first year in operation the company made nothing but westerns—*Stagecoach to Fury, The Desperados are in Town, The Black Whip, The Naked Gun, The Quiet Gun, Frontier Gambler,* and *The Storm Rider.*

The Storm Rider was produced by Bernard Glasser who, like Lippert, had fallen in love with motion pictures at an early age. He quit his job as a teacher at Beverly Hills High School in the 1940s to become a production assistant. In 1950, he bought an old movie studio on the corner of Santa Monica and Van Ness in Hollywood and produced a comedy-western called *Gold Raiders* (1951) with Edward Ludwig Bernds.

Edward Bernds started in the business as a sound man, first at United Artists then at Columbia where he worked with Frank Capra.[2] His first credit as a director was *Micro-Phones* (1945) with the Three Stooges. Bernds and Glasser crossed paths with Lippert while they were looking for someone to distribute *Gold Raiders*. Lippert invited them to his home to screen it for some of his associates.

"Lippert was pleasant, but the deal he offered for distribution was not," Glasser recalled. He and Bernds got a better deal from United Artists. A few years later Glasser bought a western novel called *Long Rider Jones* which he hoped to produce. He had a meeting with David Brown, a story editor at Fox, who was interested in the property but not with Glasser as the producer. A few weeks later Glasser got a call from Brown. "He said that Bob Lippert had signed a multiple picture contract with the studio for the production of second features, and that if I was interested in making a budget Western, he would recommend my project to Lippert. I accepted his offer. *Long Rider Jones* was retitled *The Storm Rider* [1957] and was one of the first productions made under Lippert's Regal banner for 20th Century-Fox distribution."[3] Glasser wanted Bernds to direct it. "We made a pretty good team," Bernds remembered fondly. All in all, they made four more pictures for Lippert—*Escape from Red Rock* (1957), *Space-Master X-7* (1958), *Return of the Fly*, and *Alaska Passage* (both 1959).

Earle Lyon was another producer who made westerns for Lippert. He'd made an independent war movie in 1954 called *The Silent Raiders* which Lippert distributed. Lyon was in Montana working on *Stagecoach to Fury* (1956) when he got an urgent call from Lippert, who told him to drop everything and come to Las Vegas for a meeting. Lyon assumed that something had gone wrong. Maybe the boss was going to pull the plug on his picture, or cut the budget, or who knew what? Whatever it was, it probably wasn't going to be good. His stomach was in a knot when he walked into the meeting.

"Don't go one cent over the budget," Lippert said sternly. "Not one cent. Understood? Now get back to work."

Anyone who ever worked for Lippert knew that going over budget was punishable by death. Lyon wondered why Lippert felt the need to tell him again, and why he could not simply have done it over the phone. Harry Spalding could have told him why; he may have understood Lippert better than anyone.

"[Lippert] had no interest in the world at large; what he was interested in was what he was going to do tomorrow," Spalding said. "This is not to disparage him; it's just that he concentrated on the bottom line at all times. Like others of that kind, he was a little 'innocent,' in a way, because he was so concentrated in the one area he was successful in. As a result, some people didn't understand him. They'd come out of meetings with Lippert scratching their heads!"[4]

From time to time, Lippert would take off his producer's hat and speak out as an exhibitor, usually when he was upset about something or other. He certainly let his temper show when a reporter from *Variety* dropped by in early September of 1957 to see how things were going and found Lippert still upset over what he referred to as seasonal release pattern of the studios.

"When it came to the July 4 holiday, when they all suddenly started to release their top product, we made it a point of giving playing time to those companies that helped us out when we were starving for pictures," Lippert fumed. "I know some companies that had prints of pictures in their exchanges and wouldn't release them to us. When it came to booking them, finally, we deliberately gave our playing time to those distributors who [understood] our problems."[5]

Lippert was happy to take a swing at the exhibitors as well. When they referred to their drive-in theaters as strictly "warm-weather attractions," Lippert told them his drive-ins did good business all year round. Aggressive merchandizing was the answer. "Theater owners who book pictures and exhibit them with a laissez-faire attitude should be in some other business," he said. "A here-it-is, come-and-buy-it philosophy never made a profit in any business."[6]

Lippert kept a close eye on his own theaters; ever mindful that no one could possibly care as much as he did about how they were run. One evening, as Maury Dexter was leaving the office, he ran into Lippert in the hall. "Listen, kid," Lippert said, "I've gotta couple of things to do. How about having dinner with me?" Dexter had never been out with his boss on a one-on-one basis and though it was a little unusual, he said, "Sure," because everyone knows you do not say "no" to the boss.

Once they were in the car, Lippert told him he had something to drop off at one of his theaters, which was just around the corner, and it would take only a couple of minutes. However, as they walked into the theater, Dexter noticed that Lippert was not carrying anything. They stood at the back of the auditorium for a few seconds in silence. "Follow me, kid," Lippert whispered. They went upstairs to the projection booth where they found the projectionist idly leaning back in his chair with his foot on the desk.

"Get your foot off that desk!" Lippert snapped.

The projectionist nervously sprang to attention.

Lippert pointed at the window. "Look!" he ordered.

The projectionist obediently looked through the glass.

"Does it look good to you?" Lippert asked dully. "It looks fuzzy to me! Do your damn job!"

The projectionist uttered a subservient "Yes, Sir," and quickly adjusted the focus, certain that he was about to lose his job. Dexter thought so, too. On his way out Lippert told the guy to shape up, and that was the end of it.

When the unions complained about "runaway productions," Lippert took them on in much the same way as he did the projectionist. Lippert reminded the union big-wigs that twenty foreign governments gave their producers some sort of subsidy, and the crew and cast accepted lower salaries. "I have yet to hear of an American labor organization making concessions or constructive moves to bring Hollywood productions costs within a practical budget. The handwriting on the wall spells the inevitable end of 'B' productions in this country. Even 50-minute television films are costing over $100,000. 'Runaway production' isn't running away; it's being driven away."[7]

Kurt Neumann was the one who told Lippert about the science fiction story in *Playboy* magazine that would ultimately become Lippert's most famous film. Lippert quickly secured an option on the story, but he was not anxious to close the deal until he had a chance to talk with Skouras first.

The previous year Skouras had insisted that Lippert make a science fiction movie called *Kronos* (1957). It was a project that Jack

Rabin had brought to Lippert, and Skouras had been excited about it— excited enough to sign off on a budget that was more than triple what Regal was used to because the story required a lot of special effects. Then, just before the film went into production, Skouras got cold feet and slashed the budget. Nobody knows why. (Maybe somebody reminded him that Fox had not made a science fiction film since *The Day the Earth Stood Still* in 1951), which had not done the business Fox thought it would.) The script had to be quickly rewritten to fill in the huge gaps left by the absence of the special effects sequences that were cut. It was still a good movie, and it did good business, but it was not the movie it should have been. Lippert did not want that to happen with this new science fiction project. Lippert did not want it to happen with *The Fly* (1958).

Skouras read the story and liked it. Surprisingly, so did Buddy Adler. They liked it so much they agreed to an 18 day shooting schedule and a budget of $350,000, which was small potatoes for Fox. Since they'd be making it in color and scope, it could go out as a Fox film.

Kurt Neumann hired James Clavell to script it, a writer no one had ever heard of. He did such a good job that Neumann shot his script pretty much as it was written.

Two Fox contract players, Al Hedison and Patricia Owens, were cast in the leads. Vincent Price and Herbert Marshall were in supporting roles to give the picture a little class and Karl Struss was behind the camera.

As Lippert watched the project coming together, he was certain that he had a hit on his hands, and this time he wanted his name on it. The trade magazines announced that he was going to produce the picture. Before the month was out, the same magazines reported that Lippert had stepped away from the project and that Kurt Neumann was taking over. No one from the studio or the Screen Actors Guild would confirm or deny that Lippert's long standing feud with SAG was the reason for his withdrawal, but everyone knew that was exactly what had happened.

Apparently, Lippert's attempt to step back into the limelight so angered the folks at the WGA that they sued Lippert for breach of contract the following week. They wanted to see a list of the post-1948 features he'd released to television. They also wanted the names of the writers, the monies paid, and the monies received. Lippert decided it was a good time for him to get out of town. He went on an "inspirational and promotional tour," stopping at every U.S. and Canadian exchange across the country. He hoped to get them off of their behinds and engage in some old fashioned bally-hoo. At the close of his little pep talk, he ran some of the Fox movies that the exhibitors were told deserved their support.

The Fly opened in Los Angeles and pulled in $34,000 on the first day. By the end of the week, it had grossed over a million. In the end it made as much as Fox's bigger-budgeted *Peyton Place* (1958).The picture made Lippert a minor celebrity on the Fox lot and for the first time he had some

The Fly *(1958) was Lippert's most famous movie.*

real clout. From this point on, he would alternate between making low budget movies for Regal and bigger budgeted movies for Fox.

Lippert's art director, John Mansbridge, said the studio began using Lippert's unit as a training ground:

> "Fox would make deals with these actors, or so-called directors, and they'd say, 'Hey, we'll sign you up for two or three shows.' And if they did not have anything really ready for 'em, they would call Lippert and say, 'Okay, take this guy or this gal, and put her in a show.' Or, 'This cutter wants to be a director. Make him a director.' We got kind of the leftovers to finish out the contractual commitment Fox might have made, so this is how we got a lot of strange people. It was interesting, due to the fact that we did shows left and right. Matter of fact, we went down to Mexico and did two of 'em

back to back—that was with Brian Keith and Margie Dean, who I'm told was Lippert's girlfriend. Yes, we were kind of like the second cousin and, we just did our shows."

Patricia Owens and David Hedison are the doomed lovers in The Fly *(1958).*

David Hedison as The Fly *(1958).*

Poster for Villa! *(1958).*

Lippert's unit was also a training ground for all of the relatives of the studio big shots who wanted to get into the business. These people were jokingly referred to by Lippert's staff as "The Sons of the Pioneers." Lippert knew better than to let these people run amok without some supervision. First-time directors were given savvy cinematographers who would quietly steer them in the right direction. First-time producers had an experienced crew to work with.

Skouras sent his son, Plato, and his nephew, Charles, to learn the producing end of the business. One picture was all that Charles could take, but Plato stuck with it, aligning himself with director James B. Clark to make Regal's *Under Fire* (1957), *Villa!*, and *Sierra Baron* (1958).

On November 3, 1958, Judge Thurmond Clarke threw out WGA's suit against Lippert Pictures, Inc. on the grounds that Lippert was not bound by the 1951 pact between the Screenwriter's Guild and the Independent Motion Picture Producers' Association for the simple reason that he'd never been a member of the IMPPA. Lippert knew it was only a temporary victory; they'd be back, like bulldogs nipping at his heels.

Notes:

1. Weaver, Tom *Attack of the Monster Movie Makers*, McFarland and Co. Jefferson, N.C. 1994, pages 324-325.
2. Edward Bernds was the sound man on several of Frank Capra's movies at Columbia. The two men were on the train, headed back to Hollywood. "I couldn't understand why [Capra] looked depressed. We'd just had a couple of very successful screenings of *Mr. Smith Goes to Washington* [1939]. The audience was crazy about the picture. So I asked him what was wrong. He said, 'I wished they'd liked it in Washington.' I said, 'What do you care? They liked it everywhere else.' 'What do I care what those nitwits in the sticks think about my picture!' he said. What a phony he was; all that baloney about how he loved the people."
3. Weaver, Tom *Science Fiction Stars and Horror Heroes*, McFarland & Co., Jefferson, N.C. 2006, page 110.
4. Weaver, Tom *Attack of the Monster Movie Makers*, page 325.
5. *Variety*, September 4, 1957, page 6.
6. *Boxoffice*, Nov 21, 1960, page 15.
7. *Boxoffice*, November 6, 1961, page W-2.

CHAPTER FOUR
ASSOCIATED PRODUCERS, INC.

"There's still money to be made in the sticks."
                                        Robert L. Lippert

When Lippert's contract with Fox came to an end, he closed Regal Films and signed a new contract with the studio as Associated Producers, Inc. His new assignment was to make a slate of pictures that were even cheaper than the ones he'd made as Regal.

The exhibitors had already made it quite clear that they did not want any more cheap pictures. And they did not give a hoot about CinemaScope. As one exhibitor put it, a black and white CinemaScope movie looked like a jackass dressed up in a silk coat. The exhibitors wanted color! Well, they weren't going to get it. Not for $100,000! If they didn't like the pictures they didn't have to book them. Skouras didn't care one way or the other.

Fox sold their movies to television in packages. Each package contained thirteen titles. There'd be one or two premium titles, a lot of mediocre titles, and as an added bonus, they could toss in a couple of cheapjack Lippert's, like Styrofoam balls, to pad the package. If any of these stinkers made a couple of bucks from the sticks so much the better.

Although Lippert agreed to make the Styrofoam balls, he continued to make medium budget features that performed well at the box office. *Five Gates to Hell* (1959), written and directed by James Clavell, had taken in more than a million and a half bucks. Skouras and his buddies were beginning to think Lippert might know what he was doing. Maybe that's why Lippert was able to convince them that 1959 was the right year for a new comedy team. Since Dean Martin and Jerry Lewis split up three years before, nobody had stepped in to fill the void. And Lippert had just the boys to replace them—Tommy Noonan and Peter Marshall.

Peter Marshall was a stage and television actor whose most famous gig would be to host TV's *Hollywood Squares*. He had been in three Lippert movies—*Holiday Rhythm*, *The Return of Jesse James* and *F.B.I. Girl*. In the latter film, he and Noonan are shown on television performing what appears to be a Santa Mira variation of an

Abbott and Costello routine. Noonan was also in a couple of Lippert pictures. He and Marshall were a comedy team when they landed parts in *Gentlemen Prefer Blondes* (1953). Marshall was replaced by someone Darryl Zanuck liked better. Noonan was a big hit in the film, so Fox signed him to a contract, and he and Marshall parted company. Neither one of their careers were exactly on fire when they agreed to make *The Rookie* (1959).

Spyros Skouras was not convinced the world was waiting for a new comedy team, and even if they were, he wasn't sure they were waiting for Noonan and Marshall. Nevertheless, he reluctantly went along with Lippert's plan to promote the comedians and the movie. If things worked out, and the studio ended up with a hit, maybe they would have a money-making franchise on their hands.

Years later, when asked about *The Rookie*, Peter Marshall bragged that Buddy Adler told him it had saved the studio. From what? Big profits? The picture was a dud. It barely broke even. Lippert blamed the studio for not putting enough money into it. He told Lowell E. Redelings at *Hollywood Citizen News*: "Certain types of films require more money. There are some places where you cannot cut costs without it showing. Take *The Rookie*. This film was very inexpensive—too much so. We will come out all right, probably, but we learned something from this experience in low-budget comedies and the next comedy we do will probably be in color, with plusher setting and backgrounds and perhaps a strong cast in support of the principals."

Color! That's it. If *The Rookie* had been in color it would have been funny. It would have been funny, and it would have made a lot of money.

Having learned their lesson, Fox tripled the budget on Noonan's and Marshall's next comedy offering, *Double Trouble*. And it was in color! Since the studio was referring the comedy team as "the new Abbott and Costello," it was only fitting that A&C director Charles Barton was asked to helm the picture. There's nothing like a little laugh insurance to get a project off to a good start.

The screening for the bigwigs was a disaster. *Double Trouble* was double-dull. Noonan and Marshall had no chemistry and Charles Barton had apparently lost whatever comic timing he may have had. The studio gave Lippert $150,000 to fix it, as if a little duct tape could shore up the hole in the Titanic. What could possibly save an unfunny comedy?

Music! That's what the damn movie needed to get it on its feet!

Songs were added and the title was changed to something hip and with it: *Swingin' Along* (1961). With a mere $150,000, Lippert had successfully turned a colorful disaster into a colorful disaster with songs.

Before they had even finished shooting the picture, Marshall and Noonan had decided to call it quits for the second and last time.

While the Marshall-Noonan comedies were not anything that Lippert could crow about, he was justifiably proud of *A Dog of Flanders* (1959), released as a Fox film. It was the fourth screen version of Ouida's 1872 novel and was a hit with the critics and the public, winning the Golden Lion (the first prize in the children's film category) at the Venice Film Festival. It starred Golden Globe Award-winner David Ladd under the direction of James B. Clark. They'd previously worked together on another Lippert movie, *The Sad Horse* (1959), which went out as an API film and was a flop.

In 1960, Lippert made three bigger-budgeted Fox features—*The Third Voice, Murder, Inc.,* and *Desire in the Dust*. The latter film, based on a lurid paperback novel by Harry Whittington, turned out to be the sleeper of the fall movie season, — a mix of *The Long Hot Summer, Tobacco Road,* and *Grapes of Wrath*—and Fox was pleased.

At the same time that Lippert was making the medium budget pictures, he still had to deliver the $100,000 cheapies that Fox needed to fill out their television packages. Everyone came to the conclusion that the only way to make pictures at that price was to keep everything in house; consequently, Harry Spalding wrote all of the scripts and Maury Dexter directed them. They were making six pictures a year, cranking them out so fast that Skouras told Lippert to put the brakes on. The studio didn't have enough A-pictures to package them with.

Finally, after eight long years, Lippert's feud with the Screen Actors Guild came to an end on September 28, 1960. Lippert agreed to pay a lump sum to their pension and welfare benefit packages on the condition that the Guild did not ask for residual payments. This covered every film Lippert had produced between 1948 and 1959. Anything after that date, Lippert had to pay an amount equal to 5% of the actors' total earnings, with a limitation of $100,000 per actor per picture.

At long last, he could put his name on the pictures again. This was a big deal for Lippert, almost like a comeback, and he wanted to

Tommy Noonan, Julie Newmar and Peter Marshall from the laugh-free comedy The Rookie *(1959).*

come out strong with something special and dramatically different that audiences and critics, alike, would applaud.

The Fly was still on the drawing boards when Kurt Neumann told Buddy Adler he wanted to remake Robert Wiene's classic horror drama of the subconscious (both Freudian and political), *The Cabinet of Dr. Caligari* (1919). When Neumann died, the project was shelved or forgotten. However, something brought it to life because Lippert paid $50,000 for the rights, which included a sequel, *Return of Caligari*, written by choreographer Ernest Matray and his wife, dancer Maria Solveg. Anyone other than Lippert might have been worried about biting off more than he could chew when it came to remaking a movie that influenced a decade of movie-making, with its stylized sets, costumes, acting, and camera work. His only concern was whether audiences would rather see a faithful remake or a completely new version. Exhibitors, fans, and everyone on his staff begged him not to make either one.

The Cabinet of Caligari (1962) had its world premier at New York's Victoria Theatre. It ran two hours. "From our screening in New York we found the tempo somewhat on the slow side, especially in the early portion, and by very judicious re-editing we eliminated eleven minutes and achieved what we were looking for," Lippert told Herbert Luft at *Films in Review*.

The critic for *the Citizen News* called it "one of the best pictures so far this year." *The Los Angeles Times* critic said it was "an extraordinary film shocker." The most shocking voice of support came from Richard Griffith, the Curator of the Film Library of the Museum of Modern Art. He wrote a letter to Spyros Skouras which the studio happily reprinted in the April 11th issue of *Variety*:

> "Dear Mr. Skouras:
>
> When I first heard of it, I hated the idea of a remake of Caligari. Remakes usually lack the vitality of the originals, and this particularly old master seemed especially impossible to resurrect today! I don't think I have ever been so surprised in my life as I was at Monday's screening. Your Caligari is entirely true to the basic idea and spirit of the old picture, but it is in itself an independent work of art, and one of the most strikingly original uses of the medium that I have seen in a lifetime of looking at movies. In writing, direction, performances and most especially in lighting and the use of the space provided by CinemaScope, it is as stunning and as stylish as can be imagined. Best of all, everything in it *works*, rings true, and contributed to the vast surprise of the ending. Not to go on and on, it is a brilliant job and one on which I heartily congratulate you and your associates."

One cannot help but wonder if Mr. Griffith had taken leave of his senses. Outraged by his conduct, one critic publicly reminded him that Museum officials represent an institution and are, therefore, careful not to lend their corporate voices to promotion. If Griffith was so taken with the movie, why would he not write his letter to the film's director instead of Skouras, who had nothing to do with the picture?

Most of the critics did not share Griffith's enthusiasm. *Cue* magazine said: "[*Caligari*] is an alternately interesting and disconcerting problem melodrama, marred by illogicalities of script, performance, direction and cutting." *The Daily News* described it as "jumbled and garbled...a mere skeleton of what was once a great film." *Films and Filming* said it was ruined by "the appalling crudity of the writing." *The Hollywood Reporter*, in an attempt to say something positive,

Cute and perky Anne Helm plays a supporting role in the steamy and melodramatic Desire in the Dust *(1960).*

Poster for the suspense thriller The 3rd Voice *(1960).*

Peter Falk, May Britt and Stuart Whitman are at odds in Murder, Inc. *(1960).*

claimed it was "one of the most talked about pictures of the year," a remark wide open to interpretation. Harry Spalding summed it up when he said it was as if Roger Corman had decided to remake *Citizen Kane* (1941).

In a bold marketing scheme, Alfred Hitchcock had convinced the exhibitors not to allow anyone to enter the theater once *Psycho* (1960) was in progress. The ads for *Caligari* read: NO ONE permitted OUT or IN during the last 13 nerve-shattering minutes! Did the exhibitors really lock the doors? Would that not be kidnapping or, at the very least, a violation of the fire laws? Perhaps the ads should have read: NO ONE WILL BE PERMITTED TO ENTER THE THEATRE DURING THE ENGAGEMENT OF THIS PICTURE.

The picture had finished its run when Lippert addressed a group of drama students from USC, UCLA, LACC, and Loyola at a 20th Century-Fox seminar. "You don't face an easy road. Hollywood is traditionally a hard nut to crack, because of the great rewards and consequent competition," he told them. "Today you face added hurdles in lessened movie employment due to overseas production and consequent self-protective policies of union membership. But talent persistence will make a place for you. Get any practical experience you can, even if it's not in your chosen path."[1]

Lippert's days as a motion picture producer were numbered when he gave that address. For the next three years most of his movies were made in England with the help of a producer named

Glynnis Johns is terrified by the goings on in The Cabinet of Caligari *(1962).*

Jack Parsons. Once again, Lippert was taking advantage of that Eady money and seemed to be getting more bang for his buck than he did in Hollywood. He also negotiated a co-production deal with a Spanish production company to make a western, *Outlaw from Red River*. Lippert loved the title because the words "outlaw" and "Red River" had been associated with Westerns for over 35 years, though the title had nothing whatsoever to do with the film's plot. Harry Spalding wrote the script and Maury Dexter was the director.

"Bob told me he was going to put Margia Dean in the leading female role and asked me to call her to say it was my idea," Maury Dexter recalled. "I told him in no uncertain terms that I would not call her and would not direct if she even came on the set. He knew how I felt about her and up to that time had never pressed me to use her."[2]

Outlaw from Red River became *Django the Condemned* (1965). Margia Dean was not in it, and Lippert withdrew from the project. It received a limited theatrical release in Spain and went straight to television in the U.S.

One of the scandal magazines threatened to expose Lippert's affair with Margia Dean. Lippert wasn't interested in that kind of a headache and thought that the best way to avoid it was to retire from

Dan O'Herlihy plays a dual role in Lippert's remake of The Cabinet of Caligari *(1962).*

the business. Nobody knew who he was anyway. If he wasn't still part of the business, he wouldn't be much of a story.

He had made so many contacts in England that for a short time he considered living there. In the end he and Ruth moved back to northern California instead, settling in Alameda. Lippert spent the next ten years doubling the size of his theater chain. He was on a vacation at Lake Tahoe in 1974 when he suffered his first heart attack. Two years later, on November 10, a second heart attack took his life. His secretary phoned Margia Dean. "Mr. Lippert wanted you to be the first to know," the secretary told her.

Ruth lived another eight years.

Notes:

1. *Boxoffice*, Feb 4, 1963, page 28.
2. Maury Dexter didn't believe that Lippert fired Bill Magginetti for stealing from the company. He is convinced Margia Dean told Lippert to fire him because Magginetti told Lippert that she cheapened the movies and damaged the company's reputation. Margia Dean said she didn't know Magginetti and had no say in what Lippert did or did not do.

EPILOGUE

When Robert Lippert, Jr. quit the film business he moved to La Habra in Orange County where he built duplexes and triplexes for low income families. Not surprisingly, he couldn't stay in one spot for too long. After a few years he moved to Palm Springs where he built the first Thunderbird Motor Hotel, which he nursed into a chain that he sold to Hyatt Hotels. He used some of that money to build Bob Lippert's Steak House on South Palm Canyon Drive.

"My dad came once to my restaurant in Palm Springs. Only once," Junior recalled. "He came with Spyros Skouras. But he sent people down and he said: 'Just put it on my account.' Which he never paid!"

After a lot of drinking, and hitting as many massage parlors as he could (Annie's Bath House was his favorite), Junior sold the restaurant, divorced his high school sweetheart (Jacqueline Miller) and began traveling by freighters to almost every known island in the Pacific Ocean.

"He'd get married every year," Lippert III recalled, "come back with new ladies from the orient. Drove grandma nuts."

The marriages would last about a month. Junior would get bored and if the women didn't want to leave he got abusive. But when he couldn't get rid of a young lady named Hong Sook, and became abusive with her, she got the better of him, sobered him up and straightened him out.

News of his father's death brought Junior back to the Bay Area. He took over the management of the theater and concession operation for Lippert Affiliated and Transcontinental Theaters. Faced with a large inheritance tax of approximately $25 million, Junior sold the theaters and moved to Pebble Beach where, in 1990, he established the Robert L. Lippert Foundation, a trust for charitable or educational activities to benefit the citizens of the city of Alameda. Fifteen years later the foundation had given slightly more than $600,000 to three primary charities: Alameda Boys Club, Boy Scots Council and Alameda Meals on Wheels. Each year the foundation gives nine college scholarships of up to $2,000 to three students each from Alameda High School, Encinal High School, and St. Joseph Notre Dame High School. The Alameda Civic Light Opera also enjoys the foundation's support.

At the age of 83 Lippert Jr. died peacefully in his Pebble Beach home on September 29, 2011, survived by his wife, Hong Sook, his daughter, Stacy Lytle, his son Bob Lippert III, and his granddaughter, Amanda Lytle. Lippert III was instrumental in establishing a permanent display about his Granddad in the Alameda Museum, a display that contains posters, pictures, articles, theater programs, and two original movie projectors Lippert used at the Lincoln Bay Street and Times theaters in Alameda in the 30s and 40s.

APPENDIX ONE
FILMOGRAPHY

In his Screen Guild days, Robert Lippert purchased or leased a number of older movies for reissue to theaters and television, often giving them new titles. It would be a stretch to call these films "Lippert movies," yet to ignore them altogether doesn't seem right; so, I have chosen to simply list the titles without any additional information and call it a day. They are as follows: *Argentine Nights (1940)*, *Bar 20 Justice* (1938), *Border Vigilantes* (1941), *Borderland* (1937), *Call It Murder* aka *Midnight* (1934) , *Captain Kidd* (1945), *Cassidy of Bar 20* (1938), *Chu Chin Chow* (1934), *Convicts at Large* (1938), *The Duke of West Point* (1938), *Flames* aka *Fire Alarm* (1932), *Flirting with Fate* (1938), *The Frontiersman* (1938), *The Girl from Calgary* (1932), *Heart of Arizona* (1938), *Hell Harbor* re-edited (1930), *Red Salute* re-edited and reissued as *Her Enlisted Man* (1935), *Hidden Gold* (1940), *Hills of Old Wyoming* (1937), *Hopalong Cassidy Enters* aka *Hop-a-long Cassidy* (1935), *Hopalong Cassidy Returns* (1936), *Hopalong Cassidy Rides Again* (1937), *In Old Mexico* (1938), *The Iron Mask* (1929), *King of the Turf* (1939), *Law of the Pampas* (1939), *Law of the Sea* (1931), *Babes in Toyland* re-edited and reissued as *March of the Wooden Soldiers* (1934), *Miss Annie Rooney* (1942), *Mr. Robinson Crusoe* (1932), *North of the Rio Grande* (1937), *Outlaws in the Desert* (1941), *Pirates on Horseback* (1941), *Police Court* (1932), *Pride of the West* (1938), *People's Enemy* (1935) reissued as *Racketeers*, *Pittsburgh* (1942), *Range War* (1938), *Renegade Trail* (1939), *Riders of the Timberline* (1941), *Runaway Daughter* aka *Red Salute* (1935), *Rustler's Valley* (1937), *Santa Fe Marshal* (1940), *Secret of the Wastelands* (1941), *Silver on the Sage* (1939), *Sin Town* (1942), *Stagecoach War* (1940), *Stick to Your Guns* (1941), *Sunset Trail* (1939), *Texas Trail* (1937), *That's My Boy* (1932), *Three Men from Texas* (1940), *Trail Dust* (1936), and *Wide Open Town* (1941).

What follows is a list of the movies made or released by Lippert through the Screen Guild, Lippert Pictures, Inc., United Artists, Associated Film Releasing Corporation, 20th Century-Fox, American-International, Warner Bros., and Paramount. All titles are listed alphabetically under the company that released them. An asterisk (*) in front of a title indicates that the movie was a pick-up and not a production generated by Lippert. According to the American Film

Institute, Lippert produced some "additional material" for the independently made movie *Five Minutes to Live* (1961), which was later released as *Door-to-Door Maniac* (1966) by American International. The AFI usually knows what it is talking about, but since the information is vague, I did not include the title in the filmography.

Many of the Lippert Pictures, Inc. titles are available from VCI Entertainment. Some of the Fox titles are available from 20th Century-Fox, Olive Films and Image Entertainment.

SCREEN GUILD

ARSON, INC. (Working titles: **FIREBUG SQUAD** and **THREE-ALARM FIRE** 1949) B&W 63 min. Written by Maurice Tombragel from a story by Arthur Caesar; Produced by William Stephens; Directed by William Berke. Cast: Robert Lowery, Anne Gwynn, Edward Brophy, Marcia Mae Jones, and Douglas Fowley.
Tidbits: Shot in seven days for $60,000.
Critics: "...a strong example of program entertainment on a low budget."—*Variety*; "...convincing stock footage and a semi-documentary approach elevate this fast-moving cops-and-robbers melodrama several steps above the status indicated by its budget."—*Boxoffice*.
Exhibitors: "Pay day and I couldn't get more than a below average crowd in. Things are just as tough now as during the strike and the mines are starting to close again because of the coal surplus."—Ralph Raspa, WV; "This picture is a little weak to stand alone. I would recommend this on a double feature."—L. Brazil, Jr., AR.

THE BELLS OF SAN FERNANDO (1947) B&W 74 min. Written by Jack DeWitt and Duncan Renault (Renaldo); Produced by James S. Burkett; Directed by Terry O. Morse. Cast: Donald Woods, Gloria Warren, Byron Foulger, Shirley O'Hara, and Anthony Ward.
Critics: "So much attention and footage were devoted to creating atmosphere for this story...there remained scant time for action..."—*Boxoffice*.
Exhibitors: "O.K. for midweek dates."—Abe H. Kaufman, IN.

Robert L. Lippert.

*BOY! WHAT A GIRL! (1947) B&W 73 min. Harold Pictures; Written by Vincent Valentini; Produced by Jack Goldberg; Directed by Arthur Leonard. Cast: Tim Moore, Betti Mays, Elwood Smith, Duke Williams, and Sheila Guyse.

Tidbits: This was the first of eleven films produced by Jack Goldberg for the newly formed Herald Pictures. Goldberg had fought slip-shod methods in all-Negro productions for over twenty years and made this film to prove all-Negro motion pictures could play in any theater in the country, not just the ones that catered strictly to all-Negro audiences. It was the only movie to feature vaudeville comedian Tim Moore, who later became known as the "Kingfish" on the *Amos 'n Andy* television series.

Boy! What a Girl! was shot at the Fox Movietone Studios in New York City and on location in Harlem. Gene Krupa, the famous drummer, stopped by the set to visit drummer Sid Catlett, one of the actors in the film, and ended up playing a part in the picture, the only white member of the cast.

Critics: "So-called hep-cats will really go for this..."—*Film Daily*; "... should provide sufficient playing time on the south end of double-header."—*Variety*; "...made to order for the Negro film theaters. Elsewhere, it may serve as a supporting feature..."—*Boxoffice*.

*BUFFALO BILL RIDES AGAIN aka **RETURN OF BUFFALO BILL** (1947) B&W 69 min. Jack Schwartz Productions; Written by Frank Gilbert and Barney Sarecky; Produced by Jack Shwartz; Directed by Bernard B. Ray. Cast: Richard Arlen, Jennifer Holt, Lee Shumway, John Dexter, and Gil Patrick.
Critics: "Dialog is loaded with clichés."—*Variety*; "Even in the western field, excuse cannot be found for exhibits as poor as this one."—*Hollywood Reporter*; "...plenty of gunplay, chases, fisticuffs and other ingredients standard to westerns but their presentation is so inexpert that only the juveniles and most ardent sagebrush fans will take them seriously."—*Boxoffice*.
Exhibitors: "This is an average western that will attract kids and keep away adults."—Ralph Raspa, WV; "This is okay for actions lovers...We double-billed but the icy roads and bad weather were too much."—Harland Rankin, Canada; "It barely got by here—far below average."—Pat W. Murphy, TX.

*THE BURNING CROSS aka **THEY RIDE BY NIGHT** (1947) B&W 73 min. Somerset Pictures Corp.; Written by Aubrey Wisberg; Produced and Directed by Walter Colmes. Cast: Henry Daniels Jr., Virginia Patton, Dick Rich, Betty Roadman, and Raymond Bond.
Tidbits: This movie was based on facts gathered about the Ku Klux Klan by Jack Cartwright, a Colorado newspaper reporter. Every bank in the country refused to finance it. The Breen Office insisted on changes in the script. The "black characters" should not be too subservient and their dialogue had to be grammatically correct. The Virginia Board of Censors, fearing that the film might arouse animosity between the races, banned it. Lippert sued the Board; outcome unknown.
Critics: "[As] entertainment it is only fair..."—*Harrison's Reports*; "[Has] all the earmarks of a low-budgeted, amateurish production, including static script and inept acting and direction."—*Variety*.
Exhibitors: "It will hold your patrons from start to finish."—Carl F. Neitzel, WI; "I received many good comments on this picture. Should have done big business, but I failed to exploit it properly."—Ralph Raspa, WV.

BUSH PILOT (1947) B&W 60 min. Written by W. Scott Darling; Produced by Larry Cromien; Directed by Sterling Campbell. Cast: Rochelle Hudson, Jack La Rue, Austin Willis, Frank Perry, and Joe Carr.

Tidbits: Actor Austin Willis and businessman Larry Cromien were behind this "comeback" film for actress Rochelle Hudson which, unfortunately, backfired. The film became a running joke in Canada for years.

Exhibitors: "...it fills the bill and pleases the patron. Which is more than I can say for many of the reported million dollar productions."—Rahl and Hanson, CA.

*CALL OF THE FOREST (Working titles: **UNTAMED** and **THE FLAMING FOREST** 1949) B&W 56 min. Adventure Pictures, Inc.; Written by Craig Burns; Produced by Edward Finney; Directed by John F. Link. Cast: Robert Lowery, Ken Curtis, Chief Thundercloud, Black Diamond, and Charlie Hughes (debut).

Tidbits: *The Hollywood Reporter* said that Lippert added some scenes to this movie. The horse featured in the film was Black Diamond, soon to be the star of his own television series, *Fury*, on NBC from 1955 to 1960.

Exhibitors: "This is the kind of a call I like—one that is good enough and loud enough to bring in an average crowd."—Ralph Raspa, WV; "Comments and business on it was good."—L. Brazil Jr., AR; "I can say one thing—if Bob Lippert makes many more of these clinkers, they won't play this spot. I had so many walkouts that I finally went out, too."—George Pace, SD.

THE CASE OF THE BABY SITTER (1947) B&W 41 min. Written by Charles K. Hittleman and Andy Lamb; Produced by Charles K. Hittleman; Directed by Lambert Hillyer. Cast: Tom Neal, Pamela Blake, Allen Jenkins, Virginia Sale, and Keith Richards.

Tidbits: Filmed back-to-back with *The Hat Box Mystery*. In spite of what the exhibitor from California said below, these extremely short movies were not called Streamliners. Hal Roach coined that term to describe a series of service comedies that he made.

Critics: "Pic has been crudely assembled with deficient light, inferior camerawork, and bare settings framing a weak screenplay."—*Variety*.

Exhibitors: "They call this series 'Streamliners.' They would be properly labeled "Deadheads.'"—Jack Hammond, CA; "This proved O.K. If they would only outlaw Kenos and Bingos it would help."—Harland Rankin, Canada.

*DEAD MAN'S GOLD (1948) B&W 57 min. Western Adventure Productions, Inc.; Written by Ron Ormond and Ira Webb; Produced by Ron Ormond; Directed by Ray Taylor. Cast: Lash La Rue, Fuzzy St. John, Peggy Stewart, Terry Frost, and John Carson.
Exhibitors: "This series is very pleasing to my Western fans!"—Robert H. Perkins, KY; "If you are looking for some tough, two-fisted action for your avid westerns fans, brother, play this one. This Lash LaRue really hits them with fist and whip. Al St. John's comedy antics add to the loud whoops of the audience. It's a natural."—Philip Cohnstein, FL.

DEATH VALLEY (1946) Cinecolor 72 min. Written by Doris Schroeder; Produced by William David; Directed by Lew Landers. Cast: Robert Lowery, Helen Gilbert, Nat Pendleton, Sterling Holloway, and Russell Simpson.
Exhibitors: "Business was above average and it seemed to please our patrons."—V.H. Freeman, NC; "We did something unusual by playing this picture single bill on a weekend. Believe it or not we did O.K."—Harland Rankin, Canada; "A very poor trailer [for this film] hurt our usual Sunday business."—Jean Roberts, MI; "The story and color are good—slightly better than average draw."—L. Brazil, Jr., AR; "This is an Oklahoma picture, the kind people want around these parts."—Barney T. Holt, OK; "This was exceptionally well done with beautiful scenery and the best Cinecolor in many a moon."—Dinkel and Lemaster, KY.

*DRAGNET (Working titles: **DARK BULLET** and **SHOT IN THE DARK** 1947) B&W 71 min. Fortune Film Corp.; Written by Barbara Worth and Harry Essex; Produced by Maurice H. Conn; Directed by Leslie Goodwins. Cast: Henry Wilcoxon, Mary Brian (her last film), Douglas Dumbrille, Virginia Dale, and Douglas Blakely.
Critics: "...enough action and skullduggery to prove okay as a supporting feature."—*Variety*; "A worthy offering with suspense,

mystery and thrill-of-the hunt entertainment."—*Showman's Trade Review*; "One of the best the New York theatre has ever shown."— *New York Daily News*.

FLIGHT TO NOWHERE (1946) B&W 65 min. Written by Arthur V. Jones; Produced by William B. David; Directed by William Rowland. Cast: Alan Curtis, Evelyn Ankers, Micheline Cheirel, Jack Holt, and Jerome Cowan.
Critics: "As the title indicates, it flew for 65 minutes, leaving the customers wondering why."—*Variety*. "*Flight to Nowhere* is just that."—*Hollywood Reporter*.
Exhibitors: "...nothing exceptional...did only average business..."— Charles H. Corns, Canada; "This was used on a weekend double bill with negative results."—A.C. Edwards, CA; "This is a nice picture that will make a nice weekend double bill."—T.C. Norris, TX.

*FRONTIER REVENGE (1948) B&W 58 min. Western Adventure Productions, Inc.; Produced by Ron Ormond; Written and Directed by Ray Taylor. Cast: Lash La Rue, Al St. John, Peggy Stewart, Jim Bannon, and Ray Bennett.
Tidbits: Actress Peggy Stewart liked working with Lash LaRue. "I thought he was a good actor and underrated," she said. "He could have gone further if he'd gotten the chance. Lash would have made a fine character actor."[1]
Critics: "...should please armchair lead slingers."—*Variety*; "...a pattern familiar and happily accepted by most western fans."—*Motion Picture Herald*; "...routine story with no fresh twists..."—*Hollywood Reporter*.
Exhibitors: "Business was poor the first night but held up well the second night."—Ralph Raspa, WV; "[It] drew better than average weekend business."—P.B. Williams, VA; "These kinds of westerns always do good here."—Pat Fleming, AR.

GOD'S COUNTRY (1946) Cinecolor 64 min. Produced by William B. David; Written and Directed by Robert Tansey. Cast: Robert Lowery, Helen Gilbert, William Barnum, Buster Keaton, and Stanley Andrews.
Exhibitors: "Make no mistake on this one—you'll build business and have a lot of comments."—Harland Rankin, Canada; "I wish we

could get more of these."—Bill McDowell, GA; "Box office good."—Jack Hammond, CA; "...tailor-made picture for this town. Business good."—J.R. Hayworth, NC; "Nice color, good story and good crowds. Priced right."—C.W. Ritenour, IL; "Here is a natural for small towns. I could not get everyone into the theater...This feature set a new house record for a week night."—Bill Cosby, TX; "This has everything in it to make it a hit in a small town but the grosses were only average due to the coal strike."—Ralph Raspa, WV; "Play this outdoor action picture and make some money. The price was a little steep, but we showed a nice profit, so what?"—Mayne P. Musselman, KS.

GRAND CANYON (1949) Sepiatone 65 min. Written by Jack Harvey and Milton Luban from a story by Carl K. Hittleman; Produced by Carl K. Hittleman; Directed by Paul Landres. Cast: Richard Arlen, Mary Beth Hughes, Reed Hadley, James Millican, and Margia Dean.

Tidbits: During the opening credits, all of the people were thanked who made it possible to shoot this movie at the Grand Canyon National Park. Yet, in a prologue, (which may have been cut from the film; I have not seen it) Bob Lippert, who plays the part of the producer in the movie, tells Murray Lerner that bad weather has forced them to make the movie elsewhere. "True, we do see a bit of the Grand Canyon," wrote John Howard Reid in his book, *Westerns for a Rainy Day*, "but mainly through stock and second unit shots, as well as the ever-ready back projection."
A fist-fight that takes place during a dream sequence was lifted from Lippert's *The Return of Wildfire*.

Critics: "...numerous mild laugh-provoking situations through-out."—*Harrison's Reports*; "...a poorly contrived satire on horse operas....often borders on tedium."—*Variety*; "...acceptable support-ing fare."—*Boxoffice*.

Exhibitors: "Doubled with *Radar Secret Service* to make a nice bill. The two of them were well done, and the later especially inter-esting. Business was below average though."—D.W. Trisko, AZ; "I played this with a Columbia picture, *Smoky Mountain Melody*, and did better than any Sun., Mon., Tues. we've had for six months. You can buy this one right and it will play anywhere on a double bill."—C.J. Briggs, OR.

*HARPOON (1948) B&W 84 min. Danches Bros. Productions; Written by Ewing Scott and Paul Girard Smith; Produced by Georges Danches and Ewing Scott; Directed by Ewing Scott. Cast: John Bromfield, Alyce Lewis, James Cardwell, Holly Bane, and Grant Means.

Tidbits: Producer Ewing Scott was going to make this movie for $400,000 at Universal-International. When the studio backed out of the project, he convinced the Danches Brothers to back it for a lot less money. The brothers bought an old Army patrol craft to serve as a floating studio, and Scott spent a month filming scenes with whales in the Bering Strait and walrus hunts in Russian waters; scenes that, according to the cutting continuity, were not used. Actor Ernest Mitchens was injured when he fell through a rotting stairway and had to be replaced. All of the interior scenes were shot in a saloon in Skagway and a Klondike museum. They returned to California and filmed some pick-up shots in Catalina.

Critics: "...it lacks construction continuity and offers itself more as a series of sketches than a continuous story."—*Variety*; "...directed and acted in such a painfully amateurish way that the best thing a generous reviewer can do is look the other way."— *New York Times*.

Exhibitors: "The action fans turned out for it and it seemed to please, although much of the acting is definitely amateurish."—Walt Rasmussen, IA; "Doubled with *S.O.S. Submarine* for a first run at the Roxy for well over average business...We had favorable comments on both and a well-pleased boxoffice."—Jim Dunbar, KS.

THE HAT BOX MYSTERY (1947) B&W 44 min. Written and Produced by Carl K. Hittleman; Directed by Lambert Hillyer. Cast: Tom Neal, Pamela Blake, Allen Jenkins, Virginia Sale, and Leonard Penn.

Critics: "...somewhat marred by the unnecessary end, in which there's a round of explanations for what is already obvious to the audience."—*Variety*.

HIGHWAY 13 (1948) B&W 58 min. Written by John Wilster; Produced by William Stephens; Directed by William Berke. Cast: Robert Lowery, Pamela Blake, Michael Whalen, Hank Wilson and, Clem Bevans.

Pamela Blake is featured in these two production stills from Highway 13 (1948). She's with Robert Lowery on top and Michael Whalen on the bottom.

Tidbits: This 58 minute movie, shot in and around Gorham, took 58 hours to make.

Critics: "...a sure winner."—*Hollywood Reporter*; "...fast-moving programmer, gets a lot out of a small budget and goes about its thrill-making in a forthright fashion."—*Variety*.

Exhibitors: "…a humdinger. This company has some good little features…and I have found their terms to be fair…"—I. Roche, FL; "Screen Guild did a nice job on this picture. Better than average draw."—L. Brazil, Jr., AR; "Can't go wrong with this one."—Mrs. Denzil Hildebrand, MO; "Made expenses during the County Fair, so I was more than satisfied."—Ralph Raspa, WV; "A good little action picture which should do well in any small town."—Pat Fleming, AR.

Newspaper advertisement for Highway 13.

***HOLLYWOOD BARN DANCE** (Shooting title: **WESTERN BARN DANCE** 1947) B&W 72 min. Jack Schwarz Productions, Inc.; Written by Dorothy Knox Martin; Produced by Jack Schwarz; Directed by Bernard B. Ray. Cast: Ernest Tubb, Jimmie Short, Leon Short, Jack T. Drake, and "Red" Harrison.

Tidbits: "Hollywood Barn Dance" was a 30-minute, variety radio program created and hosted by Cottonseed Clark. It aired on CBS from 1943-1948. Clark wrote a movie script based on his show and sold it, and the right to use the show's name, to Oscar Davis who was Ernest Tubb's manager. Tubb was a major country music star when this picture was made and had engagements in Bakersfield and Oakland the night before this movie went into production. It premiered at the Rialto Theater in Dallas.

Critics: "[Those] who go for this type of entertainment will be more than satisfied."—*Variety*. **Exhibitors**: "…crude in production (corn is the word), crude in acting—but your rural family trade will eat it up…SRO on Saturday night, so what can we say but good for it!"—Ken Christianson, ND; "[My] patrons really got a bang out of this clunk."—Jack Hammond, CA; "We had the best crowd we ever had on Friday and over average business on Saturday. This is really the best corn we ever played, so don't pass it up."—V. Austin, MO; "Outgrossed any previous Sunday and Monday business."—Robert H. Perkins, KY; "A picture panned by the so-called critics, who don't seem to know that the boys and girls are buying Ernest Tubb records. If you live in the Midwest buy it."—T.A. Spurgin, MO; "The people really ate this one up and all the comments from our patrons were good ones...Screen Guild did right on the price."—Kalad Hindy, OH; "No walkouts, no bad comments. Business very good."—Art V. Phillips, KY; "All week long I was kicking myself in the pants for putting this on my 'bread-an'-butter nights. I was right about the picture—it was corny, but oh how I love that corn when it does the swell business this one did!"—Ralph Raspa, Canada; "If your patrons enjoy good hillbilly music, you can't go wrong playing this one."—R. D. Gibbons, AL; "I advertised this as mostly corn, but I didn't know how corny it really was! I have never been so ashamed of a picture in my life."—Fred G. Weppler, IL; "Don't run it unless you get paid plenty for it, as it will cost you dearly in bad publicity."—Max S. Slaughter, SD; "Our boxoffice returns were the largest in several weeks. My wife sang all the way home after checking up the first night!"—L. E. Wolcott, TX.

I SHOT JESSE JAMES (Shooting title: **I KILLED JESSE JAMES** 1949) B&W 81 min. Produced by Carl K. Hittleman; Written by Sam Fuller, suggested by an *American Weekly* short story by Homer Croy; Directed by Sam Fuller. Cast: Barbara Britton, Preston Foster, John Ireland, Reed Hadley, and J. Edward Bromberg.
Tidbits: First-time director Sam Fuller surprised his crew on the first day of filming at Republic Studios when, instead of calling for action, he shot off a gun, earning him the nickname "two-gun Sammy."
Critics: "When it stays on course, it is a story with moments of surprising power and drama."—*L.A. Weekly*; "John Ireland is type perfect for the Bob Ford Role, and does an excellent acting job."—*Los Angeles Tribune*; "...a very mild pretense at being entertainment."—*New York Times*; "Film fits more in the adult bracket than for kiddie audiences, but title and exploitable angles will give it enough push to attract younger ticket-buyers."—*Variety*.
Exhibitors: "...best weekend business in a coon's age...Thanks, Lippert, for a bread-and-butter picture."—Ken Christianson, ND;

"Don't be fooled by this one...It is definitely too boring for a west-ern—and our patrons thought so, too."—Ray Engle, MI; "It is tops for small town or action houses. We did over 200 per cent with it."—L. E. Blair, CA; "As good as the best—better than most. Play it single."—J. Knowles, NC; "Buy this picture while it is hot."—A. Spurgin, MO; "...well worth giving your best playing time."—George Kelloff, CO; "Well done, with a good cast that for some reason failed us miserably."—Jack Hammond, CO; "This unusual small-budget film from Lippert we played quite late. Yet we had our second largest gross for a Friday, due mostly to the fact that we had a small drawing for two hams. Comment on the film was not favorable—our fans insist on more action."—Tom S. Graff, CA; "This is not the shoot-'em-up type that the title might impart, but rather is well produced with a historical background. It will please."—Leo W. Smith, SD; "The few who came were free with their complaints. Nobody gave a hoot what happened to Bob Ford—they thought they'd see some Jesse James action and were disappointed. I was more than disappointed—I was sick. I paid top price and grossed about 50 percent."—Mrs. Pat Murphy, TX; "This was our second time to play this picture, with worthwhile results."—Harland Rankin; "Next to a good A&C picture, *Jesse James* broke all boxoffice records for us."—Ira Haaven, MN; "I would have bet my bottom dollar that this show would have packed the house. We had very poor attendance though several were surprised at the good enter-tainment in it."—Ralph Raspa, WV; "A very well-made picture, no overdone heroics, intelligently directed and plausible throughout—very good acting...This will please and do business, though some of the women patrons won't care too much for it."—Walt Rasmussen, IA; "It was nice to see a crowd in the theater on midweek and this brought them in. A dandy picture for a small town."—E. C. Holt, KY.

JUNGLE GODDESS (1948) Sepiatone 62 min. Written by Joseph Pagano from an idea by William Stephens; Produced by William Stephens; Directed by Lewis D. Collins. Cast: George Reeves, Ralph Byrd, Wanda McKay, Armida Smoki Whitfield, and Dolores Castle.
Critics: "This film is barely adequate, even for a budgeter."—*Hollywood Reporter*; "Had [it] been not quite so tragic, film might have possibly have registered as a comedy."—*Variety*.

Top and Bottom: Wanda McKay, George Reeves, and Ralph Byrd in two scenes from the studio-bound jungle adventure Jungle Goddess *(1948).*

Exhibitors: "This is a good up-to-date jungle picture and has better than average audience draw."—L. Brazil, Jr., AR; "Some of the supposedly tense and serious scenes were actually humorous due to the ineffectiveness of the meek looking cast of native cannibals."—Robert H. Perkins, KY; "Good weekend material, as are most this company's product."—Ralph Raspa, WV; "I hardly paid the electricity expense."—Pat Fleming, AR; "...it did nice business for us. Our patrons go for action pictures. No sophisticated stuff for them. We wish we could get more of these little jungle pictures."—Lois and Ira Haaven, MN; "This is obviously a weak production with poor acting, but in spite of that, it is interesting. However, it drew only average business here."—Mrs. Pat Murphy.

*KILLER DILL (1947) B&W 71 min. Nivel Pictures Corp.; Written by John O'Dea; Produced by Max M. King; Directed by Lewis D. Collins. Cast: Stu Erwin, Anne Gwynne, Frank Albertson, Mike Mazurki, and Milburn Stone.
Critics: "Plot goes overboard and there are a number of script holes that faster direction would have skipped over."—*Variety*; "...a broad burlesque of gangster epics..."—*Boxoffice*.
Exhibitors: "The comedy in this picture is meant mostly for the children but the adults went for it, too."—Ralph Raspa, WV; "... there are enough laughs and action to keep everyone happy."—F.C. Leavens, Canada; "Pictures like this we can get along without."—Malcolm Blohn, OR.

THE LAST OF THE WILD HORSES (1948) Sepiatone 86 min. Written by Jack Harvey; Produced by Carl K. Hittleman; Directed by Robert L. Lippert and Paul Landres (not credited). Cast: James Ellison, Mary Beth Hughes, Jane Frazee, Douglas Dumbrille, and James Millican.
Tidbits: Lippert movies were never more than seven reels in length except for this one, but since Lippert intended to direct this particular picture he allowed himself eight reels. After three days Lippert realized he'd never finish the picture on time so he let his editor take over. The movie was eventually cut to seven reels.
Critics: "[The] story is more substantial than either of the other two wild horse stories that [Lippert] has produced."—*Harrison's Reports*; "...takes a bit too much footage to tell its story, but otherwise measures up as a good western..."—*Variety*.
Exhibitors: "[Business] was good and customers had no complaints."—Pat Murphy, TX; "[Business] was poor."—Ralph Raspa, WV; "An excellent outdoor picture with romance, comedy and action similar to *Northwest Stampede*. Comments good."—L. Brazil,

Jr., AR; "Seems as if Screen Guild is coming to the top for features that the small town needs."—Mrs. Denzil Hildebrand, MO; "It was doubled with *My Dog Shep* for a nice bill that failed at the boxoffice."—Ken Christianson, ND; "The brown color in it was okay for the people who like it but ugh, how I hate it. The kids all liked it and with the kids we made enough to pay for the show."—Theron A. Pollard, UT; "They still love westerns and horses in our community."—Harland Rankin, Canada.

*MARK OF THE LASH (1948) B&W 57 min. Western Adventure Productions, Inc.; Written and Produced by Ron Ormond; Directed by Ray Taylor. Cast: Lash La Rue, Al St. John, Suzi Crandall, Marshall Reed, and Tom London.
Tidbits: The budgets for this series were so minimal, producer Ron Ormond could not afford to hire stuntmen. La Rue made sure his hat always came off during the fight scenes so the audience could see it was actually him.
Exhibitors: "I received plenty of good comments on this...Business was average but it could have been terrific if times had been normal."—Ralph Raspa, WV; "'Fuzzy' St. John has a drawing power in these smaller towns that usually exceeds that of the so-called stars he plays with."—L.D. Montgomery, TX; "Lash is always a good drawing card for us."—P.B. Williams, VA; "Any time Fuzzy St. John doesn't draw the customers in here something is wrong."—Pat Fleming, AR

*MIRACLE IN HARLEM (1948) B&W 70 min. Herald Pictures Inc.; Written by Vincent Valentini; Produced by Jack Goldberg; Directed by Jack Kemp. Cast: Hilda Offley, Sheila Guyse, Kenneth Freeman, William Greaves, and Sybyl Lewis.
Tidbits: This is considered to be one of the best of the "race movies" that was made in the 30s and 40s. It is a musical murder mystery, and it premiered at the legendary Apollo Theater in Harlem. For years it was a lost film until a print was found in 1983 in a warehouse in Tyler, Texas.
Critics: "...little more than a rudimentary mystery melodrama..."—*New York Times*; "Particularly appalling is the story line which drags religious themes into a routine murder yarn."—*Variety*.

*THE MOZART STORY (1948) B&W 91 min. Patrician Pictures, Inc.; Written by Richard Billinger and Arthur St. Claire; Produced by Abrasha Hamson; Directed by Karl Hartl. Cast: Hans Holt, William Vedder, Rene Dalgen, Wilton Graff, and Curd (Curt) Jergens (debut).

Tidbits: Producer Abrasha Hamson and director Frank Wisbar purchased this 1939 Austrian movie and took over a year to dub it. They also added twenty-two minutes of new footage, mostly involving a new frame story.

Critics: "The additional footage intended to explain more fully why Mozart's genius was so little appreciated in his lifetime not only runs too long but looks like the padding that it is.'—*Variety*.

MY DOG SHEP (1946) B&W 62 min. Written by Ford Beebe and Gertrude Walker; Produced by William B. David; Directed by Ford Beebe. Cast: "Flame," Tom Neal, William Farnum, Lanny Rees, and Russell Simpson.

Tidbits: This movie was shot in 9 days at Warner's Ranch, Iverson's Ranch and Corriganville. The hero of the film, Flame, had a stunt double for the attack scenes. The animal's trainer, Frank Barnes, developed a good relationship with young Lanny Reed and delighted in sneaking up behind the boy to growl in his ear as he grabbed his shoulders. Rees recalled that when they shot the scene of lonely William Farnum walking into the distance down a long and dusty road, even the most hard-bitten member of the crew was in tears. "This picture was well accepted by the public at the time it was released," Rees reported, "but remember—that was 60 years ago."

Exhibitors: "This is a good little program picture for the kids which we coupled with *Rolling Home* to nice business."—Harland Rankin, Canada; "This is a swell dog story that the small town goes for."—Barney Holt, OK; "Screen Guild really makes the pictures for the small towns."—Albert Heffernan, MI; "I couldn't ask for more."—Joe R. Hayworth, NC; "Here was a grand little picture from a company that is really going places—that is, with a few more pictures like this. The price was a little high but it left a better feeling in all who saw it."—Dinkel and Lemaster, KY.

'NEATH CANADIAN SKIES (1946) B&W 40 min. Written by Arthur V. Jones; Produced by William B. David; Directed by B. Reeves Eason. Cast: Russell Hayden, Inez Cooper, Douglas Fowley, Cliff Nazzarro, and E. Stanford Jolly.

Tidbits: This was the first of four mountie-movies starring Russell Hayden. Some of the loose ends in this picture are tied up in the follow-up film, *North of the Border*, released the same year. The other two titles in the series are *Where the North Begins* and *Trail of the Mounties* (both 1947) and all of them were about 42 minutes in length.

Exhibitors: "Hope they make a lot of these with the same running time."—S. T. Jackson, AL; "The local high school played their first game of the county tournament this night, which probably accounts for the low gross."—Fred G. Weppler, IL; "This did okay business but was not up to par, owing to our cold spell."—Harland Rankin, Canada; .

NORTH OF THE BORDER (1946) B&W 42 min. Written by Arthur V. Jones; Produced by William B. David; Directed by B. Reeves Eason. Cast: Russell Hayden, Inez Cooper, Douglas Fowley, Lyle Talbot, and E. Stanford Jolly.

Exhibitors: "Prints from this company are terrible."—D.W. Trisko, AZ; "The picture did not do so well. The actors are poor and there is very little action." Leroy Standberg, MN; "You can't expect too much from these forty-minute Westerns except that they are an excellent co-feature for a long show."—Ralph Raspa, WV.

NORTHWEST TRAIL (1945) Cinecolor 66 min. Written by Harvey Gates with additional dialogue by L. J. Swabacher; Produced by William B. David and Max M. King; Directed by Derwin Abrahams. Cast: Bob Steele, Joan Woodbury, John Litel, Madge Bellamy, and George Meeker.

Exhibitors: "It's in Cinecolor and it drew them in."—Harland Rankin, Canada; "Corny acting, under- exposure on many shots, but they ate it up so why should I worry?"—Johnnie Hunes, SD; "Business was good." Ralph Raspa, WV; "Play it and you will be satisfied."—Dow B. Summers, MO; "[It] seemed to please our patrons."—Melvin Lipnick, MS; "This one will do okay on weekends or Saturday—play it."—Arthur King, SC; "...will stand alone, but we doubled it with

Bob Steele and John Litel from the Cinecolor Mountie movie, Northwest Trail *(1945).*

Trigger Trails to above average weekend business—after four poor ones."—Barney T. Holt, OK; "With blue Cinecolor woods and a new roadster housing the final clinch, Steele romps through this ticket-pulling dualer like Errol Flynn through the masts."—Gray Barker, WV; "The outdoor scenes, which are in color, are very beautiful, although the acting was ordinary—but my customers kept coming."—Norris Kemp, OR.

*OMOO, OMOO, THE SHARK GOD (1949) B&W 58 min. Esla Pictures, Inc.; Written by George Green, based (supposedly) on Herman Melville's semi-autobiographical novel *Omoo*; Produced by Leonard S. Picker; Directed by Leon Leonard. Cast: Ron Randell, Devera Burton, Trevor Bardette, Pedro de Cordoba, and Michael Whalen.
Critics: "...pretty sorry stuff for the average ticket-buyer."—*Boxoffice*; "...an unpretentious jungle picture...merely something to round out a double bill."—*Variety*.

Exhibitors: "A good little picture."—Mrs. Denzil Hildebrand, MO; "This is a fair south sea island picture with some jungle scenes—ideal for a double feature."—L. Brazil, Jr., AR; "Your patrons will wonder at the title but they'll come out pleased at what they saw."—Ray Engle, MI; "This used to be my dream type of show, but it did terrible business for the weekend, even with a Lash LaRue."—Ralph Raspa, WV.

*OUTLAW COUNTRY (1949) B&W 72 min. Western Adventure Productions, Inc.; Written by Ron Ormond and Ira Webb; Produced by Ron Ormond; Directed by Ray Taylor. Cast: Lash La Rue, Fuzzy St. John, Dan White, John Merton, and Nancy Saunders.
Tidbits: Once the Lash La Rue series had run its course at Lippert, Ron Ormond convinced Jack Broder at Realart that there was still money to be made off the whip-wielding western star. The movies Ormond made for Realart were the cheapest of the lot, with scripts fashioned to make the maximum use of the action scenes from the Screen Guild features. A large chunk of this film was used for an extended flashback in the final Realart entry, *Frontier Phantom* (1952).
Critics: "One of the better Lash La Rue oaters."—*Variety*.
Exhibitors: "La Rue is fast coming to be my best western attraction on the weekend."—J.C. Balkcom, GA; "This is probably the best Western of the Lash LaRue series. We had a good crowd despite the rainy weather."—Pat Fleming, AR; "This is the second of these that we have played and we had a very good audience reaction, so this is going to become one of our regulars. Once a good series like this clicks, each succeeding picture is money in the bank."—L. D. Montgomery, TX.

*THE PRAIRIE (1947) B&W 80 min. Edward F. Finney Productions; Written by Arthur St. Claire based on the novel by James Fenimore Cooper; Produced by Edward Finney; Directed by Frank Wisbar. Cast: Lenore Aubert, Alan Baxter, Russ Vincent, Jack Mitchum, and Charles Evans.
Tidbits: "This is an interesting, desperate attempt to break the deadlock on independent production," producer Frank Wisbar told Philip K. Scheuer from the *Los Angeles Times*. Wisbar, a frail

man with grey hair, chose to make Cooper's story because it was low on action and it was in the public domain.

With only $120,000 to spend, Wisbar decided to make sure he did not have any weather problems by filming the entire movie on a 250 foot sound stage covered with buffalo grass.

"On the cyclorama we are projecting clouds—clouds painted on glass!—that will actually change with the feeling of the story, that will convey a mood of despair when our pioneers are starving, of ominous menace when a buffalo stampede is approaching, and so on," Wisbar said.

Critics: "It's good frontier fare, a bit more adult than the general run of westerns..."—*Variety*; "...more darkly stylized than convincing."—*Los Angeles Times*; "[It] has many weaknesses and only a few good points."—*Los Angeles Examiner*; "...a rather slow moving yarn..."—*Boxoffice*.

Exhibitors: "I was disappointed with this film and so was my audience."—Robert H. Perkins, KY; "Three 'love-starved men' fighting for one 'ravishing woman' was too much for our patrons."—Jack Hammond, CA; "Not worth the time I gave it."—Ralph Raspa, WV

QUEEN OF THE AMAZONS (1947) B&W 61 min. Written by Roger Merton; Produced and Directed by Edward Finney. Cast: Robert Lowery, Patricia Morrison, J. Edward Bromberg, John Miljan, and Amira Moustafa.

Exhibitors: "It seems that any jungle show goes fair here."—D.W. Trisko, AZ; "Another Screen Guild attraction that made an excellent double feature program."—James C. Balkcom, GA; "A very corny plot, but one that succeeded in filling the house..."—Jack Hammond, CA; "Doubled with *Gay Blades*. *Amazons* carried the load and brought in what we did get."—Community Amusement Co., AK.

RENEGADE GIRL (1946) B&W 65 min. Written by Edwin K. Westrate; Produced and Directed by William Berke. Cast: Ann Savage, Alan Curtis, Russell Wade, Jack Holt, and Edward Brophy.

Tidbits: Ann Savage loved the *Renegade Girl* script but had some misgivings about a role that required a lot of horseback riding. Assuming a little practice would put her at ease, director William Berke took her to the stables at Griffith Park. The horse that was

Ann Savage is the Renegade Girl *(1946), a rebel spy in love with Union soldier Alan Curtis.*

chosen for her seemed gentle enough, but to her surprise and horror it took off, ran through the gate and into the traffic on Alameda Boulevard. Berke and one of the stable hands came to her rescue.

Savage was ready to back away from the project but her agent, Bert D'Armand, whom she later married, convinced her that she could do it. He came to the set to give her moral support, but he could see that Berke felt undermined by his presence. "The director doesn't want me here," he told her, and after a few days he took off[2] but he made sure they would get a double for the more difficult scenes with the horse.

Critics: "...entertaining and fast-moving..."—*Boxoffice*.

Exhibitors: "Very good for a double feature."—James C. Balkcom, GA; "I've been playing too many westerns too close together and it sort of knocked this one for a loop."—Ralph Raspa, WV; "A good little programmer we double-billed to satisfaction."—Harland Rankin, Canada; "It has possibilities in certain situations if you can buy it right."—Mervin D. Pitts, NE; "[It] pleased our Saturday night crowd."—R.W. Hailey, TX; "Very good melodrama from an up-and-coming company, Screen Guild."—R.V. Dinkel, KY.

THE RETURN OF WILDFIRE (1948) Sepiatone 83 min. Written by Elizabeth (Betty) Burbridge and Carl K. Hittleman; Produced by Carl K. Hittleman; Directed by Ray Taylor. Cast: Richard Arlen, Patricia Morrison, Mary Beth Hughes, James Millican, and Reed Hadley.

Critics: "A very good picture..."—*Harrison's Reports*; "[It is] beautifully lensed in Sepiatone and story has been given twists that lift it above the usual western filmfare."—*Variety*.

Exhibitors: "This is a very good western with an exciting climax, but it failed to do business because Christmas shopping kept my patrons away."—Ralph Raspa, WV; "The only good thing about this feature was the print."—W.D. Edwards, VA; "Played with a cartoon festival to above average gross during rain, sleet and a ferocious wind...You could have knocked me over with a feather."—Fred G. Weppler, IL; "They never seem to tire of a horse picture here. This one in Sepiatone was well received, but the general comment was that Mary Beth Hughes should have played the lead."—Mrs. Pat Murphy; "...brought them out in spite of the adverse weather. Well liked by a weekend crowd."—Jack Hammond, CA; "Comments were good...Our business was off at this time, due to the fact that the sawmill burned down here and threw about 75 people out of work."—L. Brazil, Jr., AR; "Another dandy horse picture that paid off at the boxoffice. This is excellent for a small town and pleased everyone."—E. C. Holt, KY; "Played with *Shep Comes Home*...if you haven't played them and really want to do business and stand in the lobby when the show breaks and be complemented by your patrons, play them together like we did. They did okay in a small town with rural drawing area, against the competition of a new theater."—Richard C. Welch, VT.

RIMFIRE (1949) B&W 64 min. Written and Produced by Ron Ormond; Directed by B. Reeves Eason. Cast: James Millican, Mary Beth Hughes, Reed Hadley, Henry Hull, and Fuzzy Knight. **Critics**: "When it is telling a straight western action story, *Rimfire* packs a wallop..."—*Variety*; "...several notches above the conventional program western..."—*Boxoffice*.

Exhibitors: "With this western I booked another Lippert, *Shep Comes Home*, for an unsatisfactory weekend business."—Jim Dunbar, KS; "Good for any day of the week."—L. Brazil, Jr., AR;

James Millican, Mary Beth Hughes, and Reed Hadley from the film noir western Rimfire *(1949), one of Lippert's better pictures.*

"This is a pretty good western with a different twist. We had only average attendance but no complaints."—Mrs. Pat Murphy

RINGSIDE (1949) B&W 62 min. Written by Daniel Ullman from a story by Ron Ormond; Produced by Ron Ormond; Directed by Frank McDonald. Cast: Don Barry, Tom Brown, Sheila Ryan, Margia Dean, and Joey Adams.

Tidbits: This marked screenwriter Dan Ullman's debut. He wrote several scripts for Lippert before graduating to Allied Artists, where he became the studio's go-to guy for western screenplays. He would return to Lippert for the opportunity to produce and direct his own western, *Badlands of Montana* (1957) and continued to have a successful career as a writer for television.

Critics: "...should please action fans..."—*Motion Picture Herald*; "...an exceedingly routine prize-fight film."—*New York Times*; "Although quickly and cheaply made, its production values stand up, the pace is fast and the story consistent enough to sustain interest."—*Variety*; "...endowed [with] a dramatic wallop and entertainment values which greatly transcends its budgetary niche..."—*Boxoffice*.

Exhibitors: "[With] two dances and several school events we had our poorest Saturday to date. Comment was very good. Also, I find that on the whole Mr. Lippert's deal is hard to beat."—Tom S. Graff, CA; "This is the best boxing picture we have shown in a year."—L. Brazil, Jr., AR.

*ROAD TO THE BIG HOUSE aka **THE DARK ROAD** (1947) 73 min. Somerset Pictures Corp.; Written by Aubrey Wisberg; Produced and Directed by Walter Colmes. Cast: John Shelton, Ann Doran, Guinn Williams, Richard Bailey, and Joseph Allen.
Critics: "...adheres to standard situations found in previous films dealing with durance vile."—*Boxoffice*.

ROLLING HOME (1946) B&W 71 min. Written by Edwin Victor Westrate; Produced and Directed by William Berke. Cast: Harry Carey, Jr. (debut), Jean Parker, Russell Hayden, Raymond Hatton, and Pamela Blake.
Exhibitors: "A natural for very small towns. My patrons ate this up."—Joe B. Hayworth, NC; "Good family picture with lots of laughs."—Charles L. Jones, IA; "I would suggest you play it."—Charles H. Corns, Canada; "It pleased 100 per cent and the second day's business was built up by the first."—Joe R. Hayworth, NC; "Doubled with *Hat Box Mystery* to above average gross on a midweek."—Fred G. Weppler, IL; "I could use about three of these a week."—Ralph Raspa, W.VA; "...we played this picture before its scheduled release date of November 1, which might have caused the small crowd, due to lack of magazine publicity."—V.H. Freeman, NC; "A bit corny in spots but altogether seemed to please the customers and did average business."—R. W. Hailey, TX;

*S.O.S. SUBMARINE (UOMINI SUI FONDO 1948) B&W 71 min. Scalera Film; Produced by C. Zanetti; Written and Directed by Francesco De Roberts. Cast: Antonio Gandusio, Cesarina Gherald, Vittorio Mattiussi, and Tito Sango.
Tidbits: This 1941 Italian film concerns the safety measures surrounding Italy's underwater fleet. It is a drama and not a documentary as the *Variety* review suggests.
Critics: "An interesting documentary...off the beaten path."—*Variety*.

SCARED TO DEATH (1947) Cinecolor 65 min. Written by W. J. Abbott; Produced by William B. David; Directed by Christy Cabanne. Cast: Bela Lugosi, George Zucco, Nat Pendleton, Molly Lamont, and Joyce Compton.

Tidbits: Stage director-turned-writer Frank Orsino wrote a three-act play called *Murder on the Operating Table*, based on the 1933 Chicago murder case involving a 62-year old physician and feminist named Dr. Alice Wynekoop.

On the evening of November 21, Dr. Wynekoop said she found the naked body of her daughter-in-law, Rheta, on the antique operating table in her basement office. She had been chloroformed and shot. Wynekoop's gun lay beside her. The doctor told the police that she had been robbed several times, and that it was probably the work of some thief looking for drugs. Then it came to light that Dr. Wynekoop, who was in debt, had recently insured Rheta for $5,000 with the New York Life Insurance company. The policy had a double indemnity clause in case of death by violence.

Wynekoop was found guilty of murder and sentenced to 25 years in prison, though there were many people who believed that Rheta's husband may have actually killed her. He did, in fact, confess to the murder. Orsino's play, written under the pseudonym Bill Heedle, opened the same day that Wynekoop went on trial. Later, using the name Walter Abbott, Orsino adapted his play for the screen with a new title, *Accent on Horror*, the shooting title of *Scared to Death*. It is a miserable movie and nowhere near as interesting or creepy as the actual event on which it was based. Were it not for Bela Lugosi's presence, it would have probably fallen into obscurity decades ago.

The movie enjoyed its most successful engagement at the Million Dollar Theatre in Los Angeles, California when the Mills Brothers, a popular singing group, were part of the program that week.

Critics: "[A] preposterous and overplayed shocker..."—*Cleveland Plain Dealer*; "It's a dull, poorly put together melodrama that fails to generate goose pimples expected by a Bela Lugosi vehicle."—*Variety*.

Exhibitors: "It has a screwy story, poor color, and failed even to scare the kids."—Ralph Raspa, WV; "We doubled this with *Hazard* on a midnight show and had average business."—Harland Rankin, Canada.

*SEPIA CINDERELLA (1947) B&W 70 min. Herald Pictures, Inc.; Written by Vincent Valentini; Produced by Jack Goldberg; Directed by Arthur Leonard. Cast: Sheila Guyse, Billy Daniels, Tondaleyo, Hilda Offley Thompson, and Rubie Blakey.
Tidbits: This is one of the last of the impoverished "race movies," made exclusively for black audiences. The only note of interest, besides Freddie Bartholomew's inclusion in the cast, is that it was the first screen appearance of future Oscar-winner Sidney Poitier.
Critics: "...is worth its keep in the Negro houses, having marquee lure with well-known colored performers and offering a fair degree of entertainment."—*Variety.*
Exhibitors: "This should be played in a town like ours where a big percentage of the population is colored. There is no draw for white patrons."—W.S. Funk, SC.

SHEP COMES HOME (1948) B&W 60 min. Produced by Ron Ormond; Written and Directed by Ford Beebe. Cast: Robert Lowery, Billy Kimbley, Margia Dean, Martin Garraloga, and Sheldon Leonard.
Tidbits: Producer Ormond shot most of this film on Jack Ingram's Ranch in Woodland Hills. He was warned not to "give offense to the sensibilities of our Latin-American neighbors" and was told not use the expression "nuts to you."

Newspaper advertisement for Shep Comes Home (1948).

Actress Margia Dean recalled that the dog, Flame, "always did it right on the first take, but the actors kept goofing up. That's probably why they say actors don't like working with animals."
Exhibitors: "Doubled with a good Western to good business against strong competition. Picture is fair."—Ralph Raspa, WV.

*SHOOT TO KILL (Working title: **POLICE REPORTER** 1947) B&W 63 min. Screen Art Pictures Corp.; Written by Edwin V. Westrate; Produced and Directed by William Berke. Cast: Russell Wade, Susan (Luana) Walters, Edmund MacDonald, Robert Kent, and Vince Barnett.

Critics: "It has been well cast, except for femme lead, the production gloss gets the best from a small budget, and telling of its story leaves no loose ends."—*Variety*; "...sets a fast pace which it maintains throughout."—*Boxoffice*.

Exhibitors: "They were killed before entering—by the title—so I played to an empty house."—Ralph Raspa, WV.

Newspaper advertisement for Sky Liner (1949).

SKY LINER (1949) B&W 60 min. Written by Maurice Tombragel; Produced by William Stephens; Directed by William Berke. Cast: Richard Travis, Pamela Blake, Rochelle Hudson, Steven Geray, and Greg McClure.

"**Critics**: "Although it is purely a coincidence, the recent conviction on espionage charges of a gal employed by the state department gives this suspenseful drama a topical twist..."—*Boxoffice*; "William Berke's direction keeps the pot boiling at a good clip before bringing on the gun blazing climax..."—*Variety*.

Exhibitors: "This is an average murder mystery that failed to do any business. It will take several months before the coal miners will be back on their feet with enough 'luxury' money to take in the movies regularly."—Ralph Raspa, WV.

*SON OF A BAD MAN (Shooting title: **SON OF A GUN MAN** 1949) B&W 64 min. Western Adventure Productions, Inc.; Written by Ron Ormond and Ira Webb; Produced by Ron Ormond; Directed by Ray Taylor. Cast: Lash La Rue, Al St. John, Noel Neill, Michael Whalen, and Zon Murray.
Critics: "...one to please the fans."—*Motion Picture Herald*.
Exhibitors: "[Lash] LaRue and Fuzzy St. John have now made themselves my favorite pair of Western stars..."—James C. Balkcom, GA; "Most of the time I usually need a 'house stretcher' to take care of the Western addicts who come to see Fuzzy St. John."—Pat Fleming, AR; "There were too many long rides with not enough action. My people were disappointed as the other Lash LaRue pictures I have played were liked by all."—L. E. Wolcott, TX.

*SON OF BILLY THE KID (1949) B&W 64 min. Western Adventure Productions, Inc.; Written by Ron Ormond and Ira Webb; Produced by Ron Ormond; Directed by Ray Taylor. Cast: Lash La Rue, Al St. John, Marion Colby, Jane Carr, and George Baxter.
Critics: "...a routine oater grooved strictly for the action audience."—*Variety*.
Exhibitors: "La Rue and St. John can't be beat. They hold their own against Rex Allen, Roy Rogers and all the other cowboy stars."—Audrey Thompson, AR; "Perhaps the westerns may not do well in some towns, but here they're my best Saturday night insurance policy."—Pat Fleming, AR; "La Rue and Fuzzy always please my weekend patrons."—James C. Balkcom, GA.

SQUARE DANCE JUBILEE (1949) B&W 79 min. Written by Ron Ormond and Daniel B. Ullman; Produced by June Carr; Directed by Paul Landres. Cast: Don Barry, Mary Beth Hughes, Spade Cooley, Max Terhune, and Thurston Hall.
Critics: "[It] will undoubtedly prove to be a 'sleeper'..."—*Harrison's Reports*; "...several components of the film, television device, Western plot and a bagful of songs and acts take on such crowded form that each loses a certain amount of identity and sometimes detracts from the effect."—*Motion Picture Herald*; "Because of the current, nationwide popularity of square dancing, here's a picture which titlewise is as topical as tomorrow's newspaper and should be just as easy to sell in highly profitable volume."—*Boxoffice*.

Exhibitors: "I had a house full the first night and would not have been able to take care of the crowd the second night if a snow-storm had not hit. Action pictures and hillbilly pictures are the means of keeping me in business."—L.B. Fuqua, KY; "That hillbilly corn will get them, no matter how bad the picture is...We had the best Tuesday night in months."—Ralph Raspa, WV; "We doubled this with *Bandit Queen* and they liked this combination very much."—Harold Rankin, Canada; "This is a show that will do okay where a western goes...It failed to draw here." D.W. Trisko, AZ; "The farmers got in on this one, and during some of the music I could hear them stamping their feet; besides, they smiled on the way out, so I guess they had a good time. I did too, and although too many like this would kill me, it would be a pleasant way to die, with the coin machine jingling merrily."—Carl P. Neitzel, WI; "We need more like this one for small town shows."—Edwin A. Falk, OK; "This is strictly corn from beginning to end. Since this is what our patrons seem to like (after checking the boxoffice!), why should we complain?"—C. L. Summers, MO; "This is corn—and I mean corn, but it sure put money in the boxoffice! We ran to full houses both nights. This will do well at any town where there is a square dance club."—L. E. Wolcott, TX.

THUNDER IN THE PINES (1948) Sepiatone 62 min. Written by Maurice Tombragel; Produced by William Stephens; Directed by Robert Edwards. Cast: George Reeves, Ralph Byrd, Greg McClure, Michael Whalen, and Denise Darcel.
Critics: "...a cut or so above the usual low-budget program-mer."—*Variety*; "[An] excellent balance of action, comedy, and dialogue."—*Hollywood Reporter*.
Exhibitors: "[A] sure-fire crowd-pleaser for the small town trade. I wish there were more like this."—L.D. Montgomery, TX; "[A] good action story enjoyed by everyone."—Jack Hammond, CA; "Very poor in my opinion. So was business."—Ralph Raspa, WV; "Some said it was a cute little picture, but I can't make a living on cute pictures here."—Pat Fleming, AR; "I doubled this with *Dead Man's Gold* and did better than business on the weekend. Both pics are good."—E. C. Holt, KY.

TRAIL OF THE MOUNTIES (1947) B&W 42 min. Written by
Elizabeth (Betty) Burbridge; Produced by Carl K. Hittleman;
Directed by Howard Bretherton. Cast: Russell Hayden, Jennifer
Holt, Emmett Lynn, Terry Frost, and Harry Cording.
Critics: "Yarn is listlessly played by the small cast."—*Variety.*
Exhibitors: "Lots of laughs and a bit of corn, but then we like corn
up here."—Jack Hammond, CA; "They loved this and turned out
nicely to see it."—Harland Rankin, Canada.

THE TREASURE OF MONTE CRISTO (1949) B&W 68 min.
Written by Jack Pollexfen and Aubrey Wisberg; Produced by
Leonard S. Picker; Directed by William Berke. Cast: Glenn Langan,
Adele Jergens, Steve Brodie, Robert Jordan, and Margia Dean.
Critics: "...a blood and thunder actioner..."—*Boxoffice*; "Script could
have been more clear cut and less wordy, but players take the
action on the run and turn in sound performances..."—*Variety.*
Exhibitors: "I think some of the Lippert Productions rate above the
majors with their modest but interesting budgets...With additional
money, this Lippert could make the pictures for me any day."—
Jim Dunbar, KS; "Picture was only fair and a bit too long."—Ralph
Raspa, WV.

WHERE THE NORTH BEGINS (1947) B&W 41 min. Written by
Elizabeth (Betty) Burbridge; Produced by Carl K, Hittleman;
Directed by Howard Bretherton. Cast: Russell Hayden, Jennifer
Holt, Tristram Coffin, Denver Pyle, and Steven Barclay.
Exhibitors: "For a forty-minute show it will pass."—Ralph Raspa, WV.

WILDFIRE, THE STORY OF A HORSE (1945) Cinecolor 57 min.
Written by Frances Kavanaugh; Produced by William B. David;
Directed by Robert Tansey. Cast: Bob Steele, Sterling Holloway,
John Miljan, Eddie Dean, and Virginia Farnum.
Critics: "[The] low-budgeted oater is slow moving, despite its 59
mins, with a minimum of action."—*Variety.*
Exhibitors: "If you never heard of this picture, brethren of small
town situations, grab on to it. There are dollars in them thar
hills."—Harland Rankin, Canada; "Nothing to brag about."—M.W.
Hughes, IL; "Only average business done, mostly due to polio."—
Stiegelmeier and Fiedler, SD; "[They] walked out by the dozens...

and I don't blame them."—Glen A. Bilyeu, CA; "The trailer was full of action and really drew them in."—Melvin Lipnick, MS; "We had a number of walkouts."—Newman R. Robinson, VT; "I had a good house Friday and would have had a good house Saturday but the power line failed out of town which left us in darkness."—K. Walshaw, Canada; "If your patrons go for horse pictures they will go for this one. The only thing wrong was that it was in Cinecolor— yes, I know that's always my complaint."—George MacKenzie, MS; "The whole thing seemed more or less patched up."—J. E. Rougeau, MT; "It will outdraw most of the super-dupers from the major companies. Play it."—E.M. Freiburger, OK.

Notes:
1. Magers, Boyd and Michael G. Fitzgerald, *Westerns Women*, McFarland and Co. Inc., Jefferson, NC, 1999, page 220.
2. Muller, Eddie, *Dark City Dames: The Wicked Women of Film Noir*, Harper Entertainment, New York, 2001, page 165.

LIPPERT PICTURES, INC.

*THE ADVENTURES OF MR. WONDERBIRD (1952) aka **THE CURIOUS ADVENTURES OF MR. WONDERBIRD** Technicolor 62 min. Written by Paul Grimault and Jacques Prevert; Produced by Andre Sarrut; Directed by Paul Grimault. Voices: Peter Ustinov, Pierre Brasseur, Anouk Aimee, Serge Reggiani, and Claire Bloom.
Tidbits: Loosely based on Hans Christian Andersen's *The Shepherdess and the Chimney Sweep*, production on this feature-length cartoon began in 1948. The producer ran out of money and licensed the incomplete film to Lippert for a limited theatrical run. Audio Film Center owned the non-theatrical distribution rights in the early 60s. In 1967 the director, Paul Grimault, got possession of the film and spent a decade finishing it. It was finally released in 1980, using 42 minutes of the 1952 version, and is considered by many to be one of the best animated features of all time.
Critics: "First half abounds in imagination and solid whimsy... Second half bogs down with too much attempted poetry that backfires."—*Variety*; "...a not very good film."—*New Yorker*.

AIR STRIKE (1955) B&W 67 min. Screenplay, Produced and Directed by Cy Roth. Cast: Richard Denning, Gloria Jean, Don Haggerty, William Hudson, and Alan Wells.
Critics: "[An] uphill climb with cliché-ridden dialogue..."—*Motion Picture Herald*; "...a programmer lacking in just about every element of entertainment."—*Variety*.

APACHE CHIEF (1949) B&W 60 min. Written by George D. Green and Leonard Picker; Produced by George D. Green; Directed by Frank McDonald. Cast: Alan Curtis, Tom Neal, Russell Hayden, Carol Thurston, and Fuzzy Knight.
Critics: "[A] heap poor injun picture."—*Variety*; "[The] performances, direction and dialogue [run] at routine levels throughout."—*Motion Picture Herald*; "Even the productional legerdemain which heretofore has caused most of this outfit's action dramas to transcend their budgetary classification was helpless in this attempt to make an inexpensive cavalry-and-Indians drama without story, cast or proper attention to atmosphere, dialog and technical details."—*Boxoffice*.

Exhibitors: "It stood alone here, but it wobbled a little!"—Pat Murphy, TX; "Many thanks again to Lippert for supplying my bread and butter features.—Ralph Raspa, WV. Note: Fuzzy Knight made an appearance at a nearby first-run house to promote his latest Screen Guild release. Hoping to take advantage of the advertising, Ralph wrote to SG and asked the company if it were possible to get a Fuzzy Knight feature quick. Said Ralph: "The company showed its cooperation by offering me several Fuzzy Knight features."

William Tracy and Joe Sawyer revive the "Doubleday" series with As You Were *(1951).*

AS YOU WERE (1951) B&W 57 min. Screenplay by Edward E. Seabrook; Produced by Hal Roach Jr.; Directed by Bernard Gerard. Cast: William Tracy, Joe Sawyer, Russell Hicks, John Ridgeley, and Sondra Rodgers.

Tidbits: This was an attempt by Hal Roach, Jr. to revive his father's successful Doubleday comedy series. As a way to trim production costs, Roach Sr. made 40 to 50 minute features he called "streamliners" which were designed for double bills. The success of Universal's *Buck Privates* (1941) persuaded United Artists to bankroll Roach's first Doubleday comedy, *Tanks a Million* (1941). William

Tracy and Joe Sawyer were in the roles that had initially been concocted for Laurel and Hardy. "The show is a solid howl and a sure hit attraction on any bill," raved *The Hollywood Reporter*. The series came to an end two years later after six pictures.

Roach Jr. used footage from *Tanks a Million* in *As You Were*.

Critics: "Sawyer plays it broad, Tracy more reserved, with result dove-tailing for good effect."—*Variety*; "...surprisingly good fun."—*Hollywood Reporter*.

Exhibitors: "...far-fetched, but nonetheless funny."—Pearce Parkhurst, MI; "Swell comedy about the Army that pleased all."—Ralph Raspa, WV.

*BACHELOR IN PARIS (British title: **SONG OF PARIS** 1952) B&W 83 min. Roger Proudlock Productions; Written by Allan MacKinnon; Produced by Roger Proudlock; Directed by John Guillermin. Cast: Dennis Price, Anne Vernon, Mischa Auer, Hermione Baddeley, and Joan Kenny.

Critics: "...the picture has good atmosphere and director John Guillermin keeps his principals dancing about to create the illusion of action."—*Boxoffice*.

Exhibitors: "Positively the worst piece of cheese that I have tossed to my customers in years."—Lloyd Hutchins, AR.

BAD BLONDE (British title: **THE FLANAGAN BOY** 1953) B&W 81 min. Written by Guy Elmes based on the Max Catto (Finkell) novel; Produced by Anthony Hinds; Directed by Reginald LeBorg. Cast: Barbara Payton, Frederick Valk, John Slater, Sidney James, and Tony Wright.

Tidbits: A year before this movie was made, Barbara Payton was at the center of a notorious scandal. Her two lovers, Tom Neal and Franchot Tone, got into a fight and Tone ended up in the hospital in a coma. While she was making this movie, Payton and Neal were living together in a flat in the ritzy section of London. Their relationship had always been a stormy one, and it was not long before they quarreled; Neal moved out. When he learned that she had taken another lover, he broke into her apartment and found her in the altogether with nightclub owner Siegi Sessler. Neal threw Sessler out of the apartment then proceeded to slap Payton. She said she enjoyed every minute of it.

Above: Barbara Payton wants Tony Wright to kill her husband in Bad Blonde *(1953). Below: Poster for* Bad Blonde.

Critics: "...an inane melodrama...has all the subtlety of an atom bomb."—*Hollywood Reporter*; "[A] hodge-podge of trite melodrama, unbelievable dialogue and poor thesping."—*Variety*; "A lurid little melodrama..."—*Monthly Bulletin*; "[This] rag-bone-'n'-hank-o'-hair murder story has much to recommend it."—*Boxoffice*.

BANDIT ISLAND (1953) B&W/3-D 25 min. Written by Orville H. Hampton; Produced and Directed by Robert L. Lippert, Jr. Cast: Glenn Langan, Lon Chaney, Jim Davis, and Jay Lawrence.
Tidbits: At the beginning of the first 3-D craze, which lasted from 1953 to 1955, Lippert told his son to make a 27-minute all-action short in 3-D. There was never a script; Junior and the actors made it up as they went along.

To get a shot of Jim Davis and Jay Lawrence racing across the railroad track seconds ahead of a passing train, Lippert Jr. had the conductor run the train backwards. The actors also ran backwards. The lab printed the film in reverse, making it appear as if the actors had just missed being hit by the train.

The total cost of production, according to Junior, was $30,000. This sounds excessive for a silent, B&W 25 minute movie. The 3-D version has been lost, but the flat version was used as the climax of *The Big Chase*.

BANDIT QUEEN (1950) 71 min. Written by Budd Lesser, Victor West and Orville H. Hampton; Produced by William Berke, Jack Leewood and Murray Lerner; Directed by William Berke. Cast: Barbara Britton, Philip Reed, Willard Parker, Barton MacLane, and Victor Kilian.
Tidbits: Actress Martha Vickers was originally cast in the lead but bowed out on the advice of her doctor. She had recently had a baby and was ten pounds underweight. The doctor said she needed to rest; however, it was probably husband Mickey Rooney who forced her to withdraw from the project. He wanted her to stay home with their new baby.
Critics: "...several notches above previous routine westerns made by the Lippert organization—or any other."—*Boxoffice*; "Had the makers of this one tried to be a bit less pretentious they would have come up with a better actioner for the Lippert market."—*Variety*.
Exhibitors: "Excellent small town show...Play it for sure."—Buck Renfro, Jr., AR; "Here is the company that makes the movies that move...We played to a fairly good house and nobody was

disappointed."—Dave S. Klein, Africa; "This picture is a dandy. I had two good nights and almost filled my house on Saturday night."—R. B. Kerbow, TX; "The plot differs from the dumb westerns I've seen lately. The title drew 'em in."—Frank E. Sabin, MT; "It is better than *Renegade Girl*. Comment was good and so was its draw."—L. Brazil, Jr., AR.

THE BARON OF ARIZONA (1950) B&W 93 min. Produced by Carl K. Hittleman and Robert L. Lippert; Written by Sam Fuller based on an *American Weekly* article by Homer Croy; Directed by Sam Fuller. Cast: Vincent Price, Ellen Drew, Vladimir Sokoloff, Beulah Bondi, and Reed Hadley.

Tidbits: Surprisingly, James Wong Howe, one of the greatest cameramen in the business, told Sam Fuller that he wanted to work on this picture. Fuller thought he was crazy. The budget for the whole thing wouldn't pay his salary. Yet, seven months later when the movie went into production at the Sam Goldwyn Studio, Howe was behind the camera, working for a fraction of his salary, giving Fuller the dark, Gothic look he wanted.

"I had a nice cameo in it—a showy part, a love scene with Vincent Price," Margia Dean told Mike Fitzgerald. "I like myself in it. Sometimes I cringe when I see myself; other times I'm proud of what I did. Vincent was charming. We talked a lot on the set. He was cultured and educated. Years later, I was traveling in Italy and visited him on the set of the picture he was shooting. He was a gracious, nice gentleman."

This was an important picture for Lippert. He spent $100,000 to promote it. Ellen Drew, Donald O'Connor, Jackie Coogan, Murray Lerner, Jack Leewood, Marty Weiser, and a plane-load of press people were sent to the premier at the Paramount Orpheum Theatre in Phoenix, Arizona. The film was booked into 37 theaters in the state that week and was in 18 more theaters the following week.

Vincent Price made the trip by automobile, stopping in Arizona to schmooze with the exhibitors in Phoenix, Yuma, Prescott, Flagstaff, Globe, and Mesa.

The press was represented by: columnists George Fisher and Erskine Johnson, International News Service's Frank Neil, the *Los Angeles Mirror's* Florabel Muir, the *San Francisco Call-Bulletin's*

An angry mob wants to lynch Vincent Price in this scene from The Baron of
Arizona *(1950).*

Fred Johnson, Tom Brady from the *New York Times*, Nat Dallinger
from the King Features Syndicate, Howard Heym from the
Associated Press, the *Los Angeles Mirror's* Grant McDonald,
Frank Filan from World Wide Photos, Ezra Goodman, and Doris
Smith from the *Los Angeles Daily News*, Aline Mosby from the
United Press, and Wood Soanes of the *Oakland Tribune*. From the
trade press their was: Ivan Spear from *Boxoffice*, Ann Lewis from
Showman's Trade Review, Paul Manning from *The Exhibitor*, Bill
Weaver from the *Motion Picture Herald*, Larry Urbach from *The
Film Daily*, Milton Luban from the *Independent Film Journal* and
Chuck Daggett from *Variety*.

   The whole kit and caboodle was taken to the Flame Café
for lunch and then hustled to the Royal Palms in an entourage
escorted by two motorcycle cops, who used their sirens to breeze
through the red lights. It was not good enough for one reporter
who complained to one of the deputy sheriffs that a few more men
could have doubled their speed. With his tongue planted firmly
in his cheek, the deputy blandly replied: "Yeah, these lousy city
cops wouldn't help us out; said this was just a lousy commercial
promotion."

Governor Dan E. Garvey proclaimed the first of March as "Baron of Arizona" day. Kicking off the festivities was the selection of the queen of the annual Phoenix World Championship Rodeo. Vincent Price was the emcee. Ellen Drew and Robert Lippert were two of the six judges. KPHO, a Phoenix TV station, was on hand to cover the event.

Sam White, a producer-director of low budget movies, lodged a $90,000 damage suit in Federal Court against the Hearst Publishing Company, publishers of *American Weekly*. White insisted that he owned the copyright and all film, radio, and other rights to a story written by Tom Bailey and published in *True* magazine in 1943. That story was plagiarized by the *American Weekly* article that Fuller had written and then was sold by the Hearst firm on which *The Baron of Arizona* was based. I was unable to learn whether or not White emerged victorious, but the irony of the story is that Lippert had been the one to insist that the credits include the line "from an article first published in the *American Weekly*".

Critics: "Price seems too much aware of himself in playing the swindler character and less studied mannerisms would have helped..."—*Variety*; "The production is on an expansive scale, and the large cast is composed of able players."—*Motion Picture Herald*; "The story is labored and action less...the European sequences are frankly amateurish."—*Hollywood Reporter*; "[An] absorbing, beautifully acted, impressive film that would reflect credit on any studio."—*Independent Film Journal*; "[Fuller] and star Vincent Price make the Baron a brilliantly resourceful, fascinating fellow and his adventures absorbing."—*Los Angeles Times*.

Exhibitors: "All in all, it wasn't a bad flicker for its type but the price was far too high and business was below normal."—Jim Dunbar, KS; "...comments were poor and draw the same."—W. L. Stratton, ID; "There aren't many features made that are more entertaining and absorbing than this...yet, try as I would, I could not sell my rural trade on this feature."—Bob Walker, CO; "Without question the finest film I have seen from the Lippert organization. Our patrons went crazy over it."—Tom S. Graff, CA; "It was an excellent picture. The previews were misleading. Many figured it was a western and so many patrons didn't come—a poor crowd."—Earl Fleharty, MT; "The first night was only fair and the second night was pitiful."—Harland Rankin, Canada.

THE BIG CHASE (1954) B&W 60 min. Written by Fred Freiberger; Produced by Robert L. Lippert, Jr.; Directed by Arthur Hilton. Cast: Glenn Langan, Lon Chaney, Adele Jergens, Jim Davis, and Douglas Kennedy.

Alex Nicole and Eleanor Summerfield in the so-so mystery The Black Glove *(1954), a Hammer-Lippert co-production.*

THE BLACK GLOVE (British title: **FACE THE MUSIC** 1954) B&W 84 min. Written by Ernest Borneman from his novel; Produced by Michael Carreras; Directed by Terence Fisher. Cast: Alex Nicol, Eleanor Summerfield, John Salew, Paul Carpenter, and Geoffrey Keen.
Critics: "Another of those neat, efficiently made British thrillers..."—*Today's Cinema.*
Exhibitors: "Comments from patrons were favorable."—James Wiggs, Jr., NC.

THE BLACK PIRATES (EL PIRATA NEGRO 1954) AnscoColor 74 min. Written by Fred Freiberger and Al C. Ward; Produced by Robert L. Lippert Jr.; Directed by Allen H. Miner. Cast: Anthony Dexter, Martha Roth, Lon Chaney, Robert Clarke, and Victor Manuel Mendoza.
Tidbits: Just before the crew arrived in Guatemala to make this US-Mexico co-production, there was a major student

"Property of National Screen Service Corp. Licensed for display only in connection with the exhibition of this picture at your theatre. Must be returned immediately thereafter." "THE BLACK PIRATES" in Ansco Color, starring Anthony Dexter and Martha Roth co-starring Lon Chaney, Robert Clarke and Victor Manuel Mendoza. A Salvador Films Production. A Lippert Pictures Presentation. **54/509**

Above: Martha Roth, Robert Clarke, and Lon Chaney. Below: Lon Chaney, Martha Roth, and Anthony Dexter. Both stills are from The Black Pirates (1954)

demonstration near the Cathedral in the center of the city. Lippert Jr. and his cameraman, Gil Warrenton, were watching from a distance as the National Guard opened fire on the students. After that, Junior kept a gun with him at all times.

Two days before the start of production, the film's leading lady was invited to the home of an important army colonel. When she rejected his advances he had her thrown out of the country. Junior placed a frantic call to agent Hal Gefsky to get a replacement. Gefsky could not help him because the word was out about the revolution, and none of his clients would risk it. Mexican actress Martha Roth came to their rescue.

The cast and crew stayed in the village of Panchinmalco, about 40 minutes outside of the city of San Salvador. It rained every day at noon, turning what was supposed to be a three week shoot into a six week shoot. As if the rain and the tension created by the presence of the soldiers everywhere was not bad enough, their generator broke down, which brought the production to a standstill. Lon Chaney remembered the generator at the airport that was used to air condition the planes when they landed. Junior bribed one of the officials at the airport to give them access to the generator for two weeks.

Junior was sharing a room with the writer, Fred Freiberger, and every afternoon the two of them would make some excuse to go back to the hotel. After a nice hot shower they would take a nap. One afternoon there was a knock at the door. Junior went to answer it and stepped on a snake. His scream woke Freiberger, who took one look at the snake and jumped naked out of the window. Junior ran for the door, threw it open and saw Chaney and the rest of the crew laughing their asses off. Chaney had snuck into the room while they were sleeping and planted the dead snake.

"What I remember most about that picture," said Robert Clarke, "was that I came down with a bad case of dysentery. And I think I was the only one who did."

Exhibitors: "...has some pleasing color and the action is plentiful... "—I. Roche, FL.

BLACKOUT (British title: **MURDER BY PROXY**1954) B&W 87 minutes. Written by Richard Landau from the novel by Helen Hielsen; Produced by Michael Carreras; Directed by Terence Fisher. Cast: Dane Clark, Belinda Lee, Betty Ann Davies, Eleanor Summerfield, and Andrew Osborn.

Poster for Blackout *(1954)*.

Critics: "This readymade format is seldom compact or tingling under Terence Fisher's slack direction."—*New York Times*; "This is a gabby overlong import...Terence Fisher's direction is deliberate to the extreme, even for a British offering"—*Variety*; "Unnecessarily lengthy and, in spots, over-dialogued..."—*Boxoffice*.

BORDER RANGERS (1950) B&W 57 min. Written, Produced and Directed by William Berke.
Cast: Don Barry, Robert Lowery, Wally Vernon, Pamela Blake, and Lyle Talbot.
Critics: "[A] compact, fast-paced entry, complete with the pre-scribed dosages of hand-to-hand conflict, plenty of riding and gunplay, climaxed by a slam-bang finale."—*Boxoffice*; "A straight-line story clearly told, and with plenty of action..."—*Motion Picture Herald*; "A lot of plot is crowded into the 57 minutes of run-ning time, but players and direction keep it moving moderately well..."—*Variety*.
Exhibitors: "It is a little different but still very much an average western."—Audrey Thompson, AR.

COLORADO RANGER (TV title: **GUNS OF JUSTICE** 1950)
B&W 55 min. Written by Ron Ormond and Maurice Tombragel;
Produced by Ron Ormond; Directed by Thomas Carr. Cast: Jimmy
Ellison, Russell Hayden, Raymond Hatton Fuzzy Knight, and Betty
(Julie) Adams.
Critics: "[Slowed] up by a rather confused script and an attempt
to incorporate a few unusual comedy touches."—*Boxoffice*; "[The]
story is hard to follow..."—*Motion Picture Herald*.
Exhibitors: "Lippert did a nice thing when they filmed these for
the small towns. Try this...for some nice returns at the boxoffice."—
L. E. Wolcott, TX.

THE COWBOY (1954) Eastmancolor 69 min. Produced and
Directed by Elmo Williams. Narrators: Tex Ritter, Bill Conrad, John
Dehner, and Larry Dobkin. The Cowboys: Darrell Hawkins, Beau
Johnson, Robert Johnson, and Ross May.
Tidbits: Lippert had a screening of *High Noon* at his home, after
which he asked the film's editor, Elmo Williams, what his plans
were. Williams told him he wanted to capture the disappearing
legends of the old west on film. Lippert told him he'd grubstake
him if he could make the film cheap enough. Eastman Kodak
offered to give Williams a cut rate if he'd be their guinea pig for a
new color film stock. On their own, Williams and his wife, Lorraine,
spent the next three months in Arizona and New Mexico talking to
real cowboys about the life they lead. Final cost: $53,000. Williams
discusses the film at length in his autobiography.
Critics: "Arrestingly lensed documentary on the American cowboy
not quite qualifying as art house material."—*Variety*; "The general intention of the picture is to show how the cowboy's life has
changed from one of lonely trail-riding over the great, unlimited
range to one of cattle-tending on mile-square, wire-fenced plots,
while the cowboy himself has changed little in his behavior and
temperament...The picture is handsomely photographed and the
action is genuine and lively."—*New York Times*.

CROOKED RIVER (TV title: **THE LAST BULLET** 1950) B&W 55
min. Written by Ron Ormond and Maurice Tombragel; Produced
by Ron Ormond; Directed by Thomas Carr. Cast: James Ellison,
Russell Hayden, Betty (Julie) Adams, John L. Cason, and Raymond
Hatton.

Critics: "Pic follows cliché-ridden paths all the way with no imaginative touches to distinguish it..."—*Variety*.

Exhibitors: "This little western drew good business the first night, but almost an empty house the second night. As usual, these Lippert pictures have good trailers and advertising material, but that's all. The patrons are disappointed every time."—Pat Fleming, AR; "I have been disappointed with these 'Black Rider' series from Lippert."—Robert H. Perkins, KY.

THE DALTON GANG (Working title: **OUTLAW GANG** 1949) B&W 58 min. Produced by Ron Ormond; Written and Directed by Ford Beebe. Cast: Don Berry, Robert Lowery, James Millican, Greg McClure, and Betty (Julie) Adams.

Tidbits: When producer Ron Ormond asked Julie Adams if she could ride, she did what any hungry actor would do who did not know how to ride—she lied. "I learned on the job, eventually even doing camera-car rides—madly galloping along a road while the cameraman shot from a speeding car on one side," Miss Adams recalled in her autobiography, *The Lucky Southern Star*. The movie took six days to make.

Critics: "A turkey with very little stuffing was served at the Palace yesterday in the shape of a two-bit Western..."—*New York Times*; "The Saturday matinee crowds will find *The Dalton Gang* has a sufficiency of gunplay and hard riding."—*Variety*.

Exhibitors: "What other company can compare with this one when it comes to the features released that are playable at a small town theatre?"—Ralph Raspa, WV; "Another boost for television."—Pat Fleming, AR; "Don 'Red' Barry pleases my westerns fans and I played this on a Sunday with good results."—James C. Balkcom, GA; "You can't go wrong on this western for Friday and Saturday."—L. Brazil, Jr., AR; "I was surprised to find this western had some nice comic touches and held the interest throughout...I doubled with a strong picture, *Tarzan's Perils*, to 106 percent of normal business and had good comments from the action fans."—Carl F. Neitzel, WI.

THE FILMS OF ROBERT L. LIPPERT

DANGER ZONE (TV titles: **COME BE MY VICTIM** and **FLESH AND LEATHER** 1951) B&W 55 min. Written by Julian Harmon from two "Pat Novak for Hire" radio plays; Produced and Directed by William Berke. Cast: Hugh Beaumont, Edward Brophy, Richard Travis, Virginia Dale, and Ralph Sanford.
Critics: "High voltage in title but strictly low-juiced otherwise..."–*Variety*; "...it should convince a lot of people that TV and the motion picture theatre call for somewhat different production techniques."–*Hollywood Reporter*.

***A DAY IN THE COUNTRY** (Original title: **STEREO-LAFFS** 1953) 3-D/Color 15 min. Produced and Directed by Jack Ringer. Narrator: Joe Besser.
Critics: "Whatever progressive inventiveness was utilized for this crude, fly-by-night, cash-in on the current 3-D scramble, the staccato images are blurred often doubled, and the color is ghastly. The imbecilities of an exuberant 'man in the street' narrator are sufficient alone to provoke a splitting headache."–*New York Times*.
Exhibitors: "Played with *Tall Texan* and *I'll Get You*. Twice the usual Monday-Tuesday business."–Arden A. Richards, WV; "We packed them in and they went home laughing."–Bob Walker, CO.

Poster for Deadly Game *(1954).*

DEADLY GAME (British Title: **THIRD PARTY RISK** aka **THE BIG DEADLY GAME** 1954) B&W UK 71 min USA 63 min. Written by Daniel Birt and Robert Dunbar from Nicholas Bently's novel; Produced by Robert Dunbar; Directed by Daniel Birt. Cast: Lloyd Bridges, Finlay Currie, Maureen Swanson, Simone Silva, and Ferdy Mayne.
Critics: "...a flat, moderately-paced thriller."–*Monthly Film Bulletin*; "The trimmings accentuate rather than conceal its poverty of imagination."–*The Kinematograph Weekly*.

DEPUTY MARSHAL (1949) B&W 72 min. Written by William Berke and Charles Heckelmann; Produced by Robert L. Lippert; Directed by William Berke. Cast: Jon Hall, Frances Langford, Dick Foran, Julie Bishop, and Joe Sawyer.

Critics: "...further testimony to the Lippert organization's ability to endow westerns with impressive production mountings..."—*Boxoffice*; "The action is swift and steady [and] the picture stays well away from the ruts of routine from start to finish."—*Motion Picture Herald*; "[The] wisecracks seem a lot deadlier than the gunfire."—*New York Times*; "...the action is rough and ready in the best western tradition."—*Variety*.

Exhibitors: "Comments on this were good."—L. Brazil Jr., AR; "If you want a top western to fill your Fri.-Sat. needs, don't look any further. This is it—plus."—Bill Leonard, KS; "Business was excellent for a change."—Ralph Raspa, WV; "...stands head and shoulders above the epics usually released by Mr. Lippert...Excellent comments."—Tom S. Graff, CA.

EVERYBODY'S DANCIN' (1950) B&W 65 min. Written by Dorothy Raison from a story by Bob Nunes and Spade Cooley; Produced by Bob Nunes; Directed by Will Jason. Cast: Spade Cooley, Richard Lane, Barbara Woodell, Ginny Jackson, and Hal Darwin.

Critics: "For the hinterlands, where the 'fidlin' friend' is a record favorite, this one should go."—*Variety*. "...stacks up as a useful little item for breaking up the monotony of melodramas and formula westerns..."—*Motion Picture Herald*.

Exhibitors: "Played this with *Red Desert* to a fairly good turn-out, in spite of rain on both nights."—Ernest Le Valley, TX; "It helped bolster our weaker picture to only average mid-week business."—Harland Rankin, Canada; "I made an error, using the trailer on the co-feature *The Capture* (RKO) instead of this one. I suffered a heavy loss."—Ralph Raspa, WV.

EYES OF THE JUNGLE (1953) B&W 79 min. Written by Barry Shipman and Sherman L. Lowe; Produced by Rudolph C. Futhow; Directed by Paul Landres. Cast: Jon Hall, Ray Montgomery, Victor Millan, Merrill McCormick, and Frank Fenton.

FANGS OF THE WILD aka **FOLLOW THE HUNTER** (1954) B&W 71 min. Written by Orville H. Hampton based on a story by William Claxton; Produced by Robert L. Lippert, Jr.; Directed by William Claxton. Cast: Charles Chaplin, Jr., Onslow Stevens, Margia Dean, Fred Ridgeway, and Phil Tead.
Critics: "...is so statically handled that a good meller punch is lacking."—*Variety*; "...badly needing more drastic editing."—*Hollywood Reporter*.
Exhibitors: "I doubled this with *Monster from the Ocean Floor* from Lippert. The films were only fair but the advertising lured them inside."—Ralph Raspa, WV.

FAST ON THE DRAW (TV title: **SUDDEN DEATH** 1950) B&W 57 min. Written by Ron Ormond and Maurice Tombragel; Produced by Ron Ormond; Directed by Thomas Carr. Cast: James Ellison, Russell Hayden, Betty (Julie) Adams, Raymond Hatton, and Fuzzy Knight.
Critics: "Judging from the audience reaction to this product, cowboys and psychology do not mix."—*Motion Picture Herald*; "...so-so oater entertainment."—*Variety*.
Exhibitors: "This series has proven very popular with my trade."—Buck Renfro, Jr., AR; "Very good western from a small company that is giving the small town exhibitors what they want."—James C. Balkcom, GA.

FBI GIRL (1951) B&W 73 min. Written by Richard Landau and Dwight Babcock based on Rupert Hughes' 15-part story that ran from January 29 to April 9, 1950 in the New York *Sunday News*; Produced and Directed by William Berke. Cast: Cesar Romero, George Brent, Audrey Totter, Raymond Burr, and Margia Dean.
Tidbits: Audrey Totter had the lead role in this thriller about a politician who fears his checkered past is about to catch up with him. The three principals were offered the choice of taking a straight salary or a percentage of the profit. Totter took the salary. Fellow cast members George Brent and Cesar Romero told her she should have gone for the percentage. Years later, Totter ran into Romero at Edmond O'Brien's funeral. During the ceremony, Romero turned to her and peevishly said: "Sitting next to you reminds me that I never got a dime from *FBI Girl*."[1]

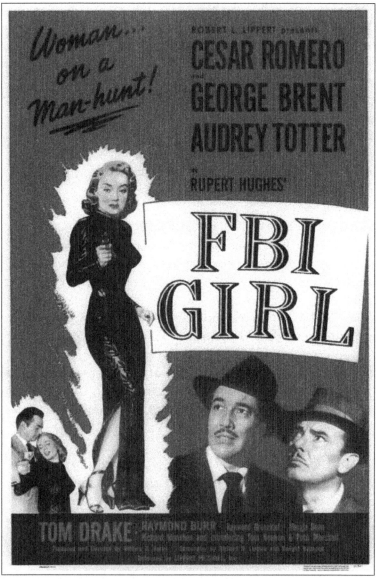

Poster for FBI Girl *(1951.)*

Critics: "[A] run of the mill cops and robbers that never quite comes off."—*Hollywood Reporter*; "Although the plot is rather tattered, good direction...makes this Lippert production a pretty fair action melodrama."—*L.A. Daily News*; "Producer-director William Berke keeps the story moving at a consistent pace..."—*Variety*; "[An] an expertly plotted picture packed with suspense and

Audrey Totter and Tom Drake from FBI Girl *(1951).*

action."—*Motion Picture Herald*; "[For] for a spy thriller, it is surprisingly dull."—*New York Times*.

Exhibitors: "The *Boxoffice* review said it was poor but others gave it a nice rating and I agree with them."—Frank E. Sabin, MT; "This is a great action feature from little Lippert."—Graham Yarnell, MI.

*THE FIGHTING MEN (1953) U.S. B&W 63 min. (1950) Italy 97 min. Compagnie Industrelle; Written by Lewis E. Cianelli and Gisela Mathess; Produced by Albert Salvatori and Alan Curtis; Directed by Camillo Mastrocinque. Cast: Rossano Brazzi, Claudine Dupuis, Eduardo Cianelli, Charles Vanel, and Giovanni Grasso.

FINGERPRINTS DON'T LIE (TV titles: **THE FINGERPRINTS** and **MISSING WITNESS** 1951) B&W 56 min. Written by Orville H. Hampton; Produced by Sigmund Neufeld; Directed by Sam Newfield. Cast: Richard Travis, Sheila Ryan, Sid Melton, Tom Neal, and Margia Dean.

Critics: "...holds one in suspense..."—*Harrison's Reports*; "...a bore."—*Variety*; "...a dull, lifeless concoction..."—*Hollywood Reporter*.

FOR MEN ONLY aka **THE TALL LIE** (1952) B&W 93 min. Written by Lou Morheim; Produced and Directed by Paul Henreid. Cast: Paul Henreid, Robert Sherman, Russell Johnson (debut), Margaret Field, and Kathleen Hughes.

Tidbits: Actor Paul Henreid and the Nassour Brothers co-produced this hard-hitting movie, shot at General Service Studios and on location at Los Angeles City College. Despite the enthusiastic response of the critics, box office returns were tepid, partly due to the fact a lot of women were put off by the title. Lippert changed the title to *The Tall Lie* and elevated Kathleen Hughes's billing to star status, but the damage had been done.

Critics: "...engrossing entertainment..."—*Boxoffice*; "...bound to stir emotions."—*Los Angeles Times*; "Powerful...noteworthy!"—*Los Angeles Examiner*; "Outstanding."—*Los Angeles Daily News*; "Strong...suspenseful!"—*Los Angeles Herald Express*; "...an example of the enterprise and ingenuity that are needed in the field of independent film."—*Hollywood Reporter*.

G.I JANE (1951) B&W 62 min. Written by Jan Jeffries (Henry Blankfort) based on a story by Murray Lerner; Produced by Murray Lerner; Directed by Reginald Le Borg. Cast: Harry Mancke, Jack Reitzen, Jean Porter, Tom Neal, and Iris Adrian.

Tidbits: The day after this picture was previewed at the Long Beach Veterans Hospital, the Pentagon issued a directive to all military personnel ordering them to refrain from using the term "G.I," an expression that had evolved from the legend "Government Issue" printed on military material. The Pentagon was aware that it had no control over the public at large, but expressed its hope that the public would follow suit. The Palladium Ballroom complied by scrapping an ad campaign describing Les Brown's orchestra as "The Favorite of GI's Coast-to-Coast." Lippert would have been happy to fall in line if the Pentagon wanted to spring for the cost of changing the titles on the film and advertising material which had already been printed.

Critics: "A fairly good musical comedy..."—*Harrison's Reports*; "...humorless..."—*Hollywood Reporter*; "...a pleasant, unpretentious musical programmer..."—*Variety*; "It's for laughs altogether, and gets a reasonable number of them."—*Motion Picture Herald*.

Exhibitors: "It is a lemon if I ever saw one."—Frank Sabin, MT.

THE GAMBLER AND THE LADY (British title: **IN THE MONEY**
1952) B&W 74 min. Produced by Anthony Hinds; Written and
Directed by Sam Newfield. Cast: Dane Clark, Kathleen Byron,
Naomi Chance, Meredith Edwards and Anthony Forwood.
Critics: 'Dane Clark deserved something rather better..."—*Monthly
Film Bulletin*; "...a dull, implausible melodrama..."—*Hollywood
Reporter*; "...packed with rather good melodramatic situation..."—
Los Angeles Times.

*****GHOST SHIP** (1952) B&W 69 min. Vernon Sewell Productions;
Written by Vernon Sewell and Philip Thornton; Produced by
Nat Cohen, Stuart Levy, and Vernon Sewell; Directed by Vernon
Sewell. Cast: Dermot Walsh, Hazel Court, Hugh Burden, John
Robinson, and Jose Ambler.
Critics: "...tends to place obstacles in the path of logical and fast-
paced development."—*Boxoffice*; "...there's a lot of talk and waste
motion before it goes into the suspense aspects."—*Variety*; "This
is a modern-times ghost story for grownups..."—*Motion Picture
Herald*.

THE GLASS TOMB (British title: **THE CLASS CAGE** aka **THE
OUTSIDERS** 1955) B&W 59 min. Written by Richard Landau based
on the novel by Archibald Edward Martin; Produced by Anthony
Hinds; Directed by Montgomery Tully. Cast: John Ireland, Honor
Blackman, Geoffrey Keen, Eric Pohlmann, and Sydney James.
Critics: "Naively handled..."—*Monthly Film Bulletin*; "...routine in
every respect."—*Boxoffice*; "[It] follows a stereotyped formula..."—
Motion Picture Herald.

*****THE GREAT ADVENTURE** (British title: **A FORTUNE IN
DIAMONDS** aka **THE ADVENTURERS** 1951) B&W 86 min (UK) 75
min (US). Mayflower Pictures Corp.; Written by Robert Westerby;
Produced by Aubrey Baring and Maxwell Setton; Directed by
David MacDonald. Cast: Jack Hawkins, Peter Hammond, Dennis
Price, Gregoire Aslan, and Charles Paton.
   Critics: "...it's a bad picture..."—*Boxoffice*; "...handicapped by its
slow pacing..."—*Variety*.

THE GREAT JESSE JAMES RAID (1953) AnscoColor 73 min.
Written by Richard Landau; Produced by Robert L. Lippert, Jr.;
Directed by Reginald Le Borg. Cast: Willard Parker, Barbara
Payton, Tom Neal, Wallace Ford, and James Anderson.

Tidbits: In this film Bob Ford and Sam Wells manage to find Jesse
James at 18 Lafayette Street, which is remarkable to say the least,
because Jesse's home was at 1318 Lafayette Street. Bob wants
Jesse to help Sam and him steal some gold from an abandoned
mine. They agree to meet again at Ford's saloon in Creede even
though Ford didn't own a saloon until after he killed Jesse James.
Historical lapses like these are to be expected even in films much
better than this one. If you're going to jerk history around, it
should be to make the story more exciting.

Critics: "...slow-paced western with few highlights and virtually no
climax."—*Variety*; "...inundated by pompous dialogue that gets in
the way of what little action there is."—*Hollywood Reporter*; "...ful-
fills the promise of the title adequately."—*Motion Picture Herald*; "...
above-average western with sufficient of the tried-and-true action
ingredients to satisfy the confirmed galloper addicts..."—*Boxoffice*.

Exhibitors: "This is what we wish for in every film we play.
Boxoffice 164 per cent."—James H. Hamilton, MS; "Did fair business...Color not too good."—D.W. Trisko, TX; "I did extra business
both nights."—James Hardy, IN.

GUNFIRE (Working titles: **JESSE JAMES RIDES AGAIN** and
DEAD RINGER 1950) B&W 59 min. Written by William Berke
and (uncredited) Victor West; Produced and Directed by William
Berke. Cast: Don Barry, Robert Lowery, Wally Vernon, Pamela
Blake, and Claude Stroud.

Critics: "...greatly transcends its budgetary classification..."—
Boxoffice; "...fast moving...makes a most actionful and credible hour
of melodrama..."—*Motion Picture Herald*.

Exhibitors: "...high above the heads of the usual series western.
Business was excellent..."—Ralph Raspa, WV.

HEAT WAVE (British title: **THE HOUSE ACROSS THE LAKE** 1954)
B&W 70 min. Produced by Anthony Hinds; Written and Directed
by Ken Hughes, based on his novel *High Wray*. Cast: Alex Nicol,
Hillary Brooke, Susan Stephen, Sidney James, and Alan Wheatley.

Critics: "An interesting yarn..."—*Motion Picture Exhibitor*; "Nicol and Miss Brooks give thoroughly competent portrayals." –*Los Angeles Times*; "...the material simply isn't interestingly presented."—*Variety*; "[It] promises much more than it delivers."—*Motion Picture Herald*.

*HELLGATE (1952) B&W 87 min. Commander Films Corp.; Produced by John C. Champion; Written and Directed by Charles Marquis Warren. Cast: Sterling Hayden, Joan Leslie, Ward Bond, James Arness and Peter Coe.
Tidbits: In 1949 Universal-International bought a story that was loosely based on John Ford's *The Prisoner of Shark Island* (1936). John C. Higgins and Sam Newman developed it and somehow writer-director Charles Marquis Warren ended up with it. He fashioned his own script for the Commander Films Corporation with the intention of shooting the film in Kanab, Utah, Lone Pine,

Hillary Brooke is not the woman featured on this poster from Heat Wave *(1954).*

California or New Mexico. Budget limitations forced Warren to scrap those plans. Instead he shot the film at a more convenient location, Bronson Canyon in Hollywood, California. Lloyd Bridges

Above: Sterling Hayden and Joan Leslie. Below: Sterling Hayden gets a taste of what happens to people who get out of line. Both scenes are from the gritty drama Hellgate *(1952).*

was set to play the lead but was replaced by Sterling Hayden who, like Bridges, was a victim of the Hollywood blacklist.

Critics: "...an unusual and grimly effective melodrama."—*Variety*; "...brilliantly directed, superbly acted thriller..."—*Hollywood Reporter*; "...a good suspense saga..."—*Hollywood Citizen News*; "... Performances are top-notch."—*Los Angeles Times*; "...stands out in

Bronson Canyon is the setting for Hellgate Prison in Charles Marquis Warren's Hellgate *(1952).*

production values that a far more expensive picture could envy."— *Los Angeles Examiner.*

Exhibitors: "Here's a big well-made western that's just too rough for family audiences. The trailer kept many away and the stouter-of-heart came out shuddering..."—Bob Walker, CO; "I make money on every Lippert picture and they treat me right."—Lloyd Hutchins, AR; "This is really one of the best pictures of the year...Better than average draw here."—L. Brazil, Jr., AR.

*HIGHLY DANGEROUS (1950) B&W 90 min. Written by Eric Ambler; Produced by Antony Darnborough; Directed by Roy Baker. Cast: Margaret Lockwood, Dane Clark, Marius Goring, Naunton Wayne, and Wilfred Hyde-White.
Critics: "...unremarkable..."—*Los Angeles Examiner;* "...there is little that is new in this espionage thriller..."—*Variety.*

HI-JACKED (1950) B&W 66 min. Written by Orville H. Hampton and Fred Myrton; Produced by Sigmund Newfeld; Directed by Sam Newfield. Cast: Jim Davis, Marsha James, Sid Melton, David Bruce, and Margia Dean.
Critics: "...it is somewhat ineptly dialogued which may account for the actors' inability to project themselves into convincing

performances..."—*Boxoffice*; "A surprisingly well produced 'B' melodrama."—*Harrison's Reports*; "...delivers nothing fresher than a couple of presumably authentic statistics..."—*Motion Picture Herald*; "Strictly a formula, low-budgeted actioner."—*Variety*.

HOLIDAY RHYTHM (1950) B&W 60 & 70 min. Written by Lee Wainer; Produced by Jack Leewood; Directed by Jack Scholl. Cast: Mary Beth Hughes, David Street, Wally Vernon, Donald McBride and Alan Harris.

Tidbits: Jack Leewood had been Lippert's publicity chief for years when he produced this variety show in three days for a cost of $45,000. "In my experience as an exhibitor," Lippert remarked, "I've often encountered situations in which a picture is meritorious enough to head a bill, but doesn't have sufficient length. In reverse, many times a film is ideally suited to fill out a program, but runs too long to use as a supporting feature without having the schedule run over-length. By making it optional to showmen as to whether the booking runs 60 or 70 minutes, we feel we are making [*Holiday Rhythm*] sufficiently flexible so that it can be used in either spot, depending upon the theatre and its booking problems."[2] Lippert hoped the flexibility factor would result in additional bookings.

Critics: "...this is a good picture of its kind..."—*Harrison's Reports*; "...easily the liveliest, fastest and brightest entertainment of its kind..."—*Motion Picture Herald*.

Exhibitors: "...OK for the lower half of the usual Fri.-Sat. double header. If you play it anywhere else you will be sorry."—I. Roche, FL; "A novel idea but 'tis a sad fact that it did not go over here. This is one time I feel that I did not get my money's worth from Lippert."—Tom S. Graff, CA; "It is just down-to-earth good music and comedy—no sobs or mush."—Bill Leonard, KS; "Just about the poorest picture of the year."—Ritz Amusements, Inc. IN; "I hope I never have to sweat out another feature that will disappoint as many as this one did. Business was poor and the walkouts many."—Ralph Raspa, WV; "...outgrossed pictures like *The Lawless*, *Desert Hawk*, *Geronimo* and *Trigger Jr*. I suggest you use a short western and advertise it well."—L. Brazil, Jr., AR.

*HOLLYWOOD THRILLMAKERS aka **MOVIE STUNTMEN**
(1954) B&W 53 min. B. B. Ray Productions; Written by Janet Clark;
Produced by Maurice Kosloff; Directed by Bernard B. Ray. Cast:
James Gleason, Bill Henry, Jean Holcombe, James Macklin, and
Theila Dean.
Critics: "...a crudely produced programmer..."—*Variety*.

HOLLYWOOD VARIETIES (1950) B&W 60 min. Written by Murray
Lerner; Produced by June Carr; Directed by Paul Landres. Cast:
Robert Alda, Hoosier Hot Shots, Shaw and Lee, 3 Rio Brothers, and
Glenn Vernon.
Tidbits: This picture was shot in two days at the Belasco Theatre in
Los Angeles, California.
Critics: "...has about everything one expects to see in a vaudeville
show..."—*Harrison's Reports*.
Exhibitors: "This is a good vaudeville show with no boxoffice draw.
Doubled with *The Dalton Gang* to below average gross."—D.W.
Trisko, AZ; "Personally, I liked it immensely, but of course I love
good vaudeville and this has many outstanding acts."—Jim Dunbar,
KS; "...business was very bad."—Ralph Raspa, WV.

HOSTILE COUNTRY (TV title: **OUTLAW FURY** 1950) B&W 60
min. Written by Ron Ormond and Maurice Tombragel; Produced
by Ron Ormond; Directed by Thomas Carr. Cast: Jimmy Ellison,
Russell Hayden, Raymond Hatton, Fuzzy Knight and Betty (Julie)
Adams.
Critics: "...an okay addition to the Saturday matinee market, featur-
ing a lot of riding, shooting and horseplay."—*Variety*. "[An] hour of
steadily sustained action..."—*Motion Picture Herald*.
Exhibitors: "Pleased young and old alike."—Tom S. Graff, CA; "It
gave our cowboy fans just what they wanted. Our print on this,
though, was in bad shape, with much of the dialog off synch."—
Jack Hammond, CA.

Poster for I'll Get You *(1952).*

I'LL GET YOU (Working titles: **ESCAPE ROUTE** and **THE BLACK PAWN** 1952) B&W 78 min. Written by John V. Baines with additional dialog by Nicholas Phipps; Produced by Ronald Kinnoch; Directed by Seymour Friedmann and Peter Graham Scott. Cast: George Raft, Sally Gray (final film), Frederick Piper, Reginald Tate, and Clifford Evans.

Tidbits: Michael David Productions financed this picture about FBI agent George Raft searching for a kidnapped scientist behind the Iron Curtain. Lippert was paid $2,246 to produce it and $8,061 in distribution fees and ultimately purchased the copyright from David for a mere $250.00.

Lowell Redelings reported in the *Citizen News* that actress Coleen Gray was "hopping" on a plane to England to co-star with George Raft in *I'll Get You.* She must have "hopped" on the wrong plane because she's not in the picture. Sally Gray was Raft's co-star, returning to the screen after a five year absence. "Locations are being shot all around London," she said. "George Raft is delighted with his role. I went out on location with him one day and exciting shots were made all around the blitzed areas and St. Paul's."[3]

As of August 27, 1955, the picture had grossed $46,425.16.

Critics: "[A] routine cloak and dagger melodrama."–*Variety*; "[A] slow moving, poorly contrived melodrama..."–*Hollywood Reporter*; "...best George Raft picture in a good while..."–*Motion Picture Herald*; "...is so mysterious indeed that the authors and actors very nearly succeed in keeping the story to themselves."–*Los Angeles Times*.

Exhibitors: "The general consensus of our audience...was, 'Well, the cartoon was good!' A trite story, poor acting, mediocre photography and ill-inspired direction will never add up to produce good film fare."–P. Rosenberg, Korea; "We were not expecting too much from this picture and we did not get it..."–Harold Bell, Canada.

I SHOT BILLY THE KID (1950) B&W 58 min. Written by Ford Beebe and Orville H. Hampton; Produced and Directed by William Berke. Cast: Don Barry, Robert Lowery, Wally Vernon, Tom Neal, and Wendy Lee.

Tidbits: Although the film's prologue claims that the picture "is based directly upon the true facts in the life of William H. Bonney," there is very little authenticity in *I Shot Billy the Kid*. There isn't enough hair-dye in the world to make 38-year old Don Barry look like the 21-year old Billy the Kid.

Critics: "...pretty fair stuff for most audiences, with some light touches of humor..."–*Variety*; "...a suitable booking wherever action fare is in demand."–*Boxoffice*.

Exhibitors: "It is a clinker and my patrons made no bones about letting me know about it. You won't make any friends playing it."–Donald Donohue, CA; "Both myself and my customers were very disappointed. This is one of the few times Lippert has really let us down."–Tom S. Graff, CA; "It is ideal for small towns on Fri., Sat."–L. Brazil, AR.

*JOHNNY THE GIANT KILLER (**Jeannot l'Intrepide** 1953) Technicolor 60 min. Jean Image Films; Written by Paul Colline; Directed by Jean Image and Charles Frank.

Tidbits: This 1950 French cartoon won the Venice Film Festival's Grand Prix for children's films. Lippert licensed it, trimmed 20 minutes out of it, and released it in America.

Critics: "...fails to tell a sustained fair story..."—*Boxoffice*; "...offers little for any but the very young ticket-buyers."—*Variety*; "...as fanciful, free and wish-full-filling as all the world's children would have it."—*Motion Picture Herald*.

Exhibitors: "Picture is not bad but business was terrible."—E.M. Freiburger, OK; "A few more so-called *cartoons* like this and every theatre in the country will close its doors."—Marcella Smith, OH.

THE JUNGLE (1952) Sepiatone 73 min. Written by Carroll Young, additional dialog Orville H. Hampton; Produced and Directed by William Berke. Cast: Rod Cameron, Cesar Romero, Marie Windsor, Sulochana, and M. N. Namblar.

Tidbits: William Berke was the one who came up with the idea of making a movie in India. He proposed a co-production deal in a letter he wrote to T. R. Sundaram, the owner of the Modern Theatres, Ltd. Studios in southern India. In exchange for the use of Sundaram's twenty-acre studio, its facilities, crew, and a supporting cast, Berke would furnish three stars, a screenplay, a cinematographer, and his services as a producer-director. Sundaram agreed to Berke's proposal in a single-page reply, which remained the only contract between them.

For a 60/40 split, Lippert agreed to distribute the picture and to pay Berke $250 a week for eight weeks.

Berke was surprised to learn that Sundaram's studio was in the jungle near Salem, nearly 1,000 miles from Calcutta and Bombay, the principal Indian films centers. He was even more surprised that it had everything he needed, including the trick camera dolly he had been trying to find in Hollywood for almost two years. Sundaram was kind enough to convert a large chunk of his studio into living quarters for the cast and the crew. The generous Maharajah of Mysore gave Berke access to his sister's 140 room palace, plus the loan of his personal guard of 100 cavalry and 100 infantry to use as extras in the movie.

Rod Cameron, Marie Windsor, and Cesar Romero were signed to play the leads. Windsor and Cameron had dated at one time, but now he was married to a part-Portuguese, part-Chinese woman who was fairly territorial. "The producer [Sundaram] offered to give me a monkey," Windsor told Mike Fitzgerald. "Rod's wife made such a fuss, because she wanted it, that I finally said

'Take it.' She had a terrible time getting it into the United States. And it messed up her house pretty bad."

Over 15,000 people came to watch Berke shoot a scene between Rod Cameron and Marie Windsor at beautiful Hogonikkal Falls. No matter which direction Berke angled his camera, he couldn't get all of the people out of the shot. So, he did what any resourceful director would have done; he incorporated them into the story. A similar thing happened during a scene where Cameron and Windsor found some stone idols in the middle of the jungle. They were told that no one was allowed within ten feet of the idols with their shoes on. "Marie and Rod removed their shoes and we moved in for close shots," the director told George Thomas from the *New York Times*. "Even though we were deep in the forest, a crowd of 700 soon gathered. We did a quick rewrite, changing an intimate scene to include spectators."

Two Indian versions of the movie were shot simultaneously, one in Hindustani, the other in Tamil, each running more than twice the length of Berke's 78-minute version. As an example, a dance that lasted forty seconds in the American version might run as long as four minutes in India.

Berke sold all rights to the movie to Lippert for $10,000.

In addition to their salaries, Rod Cameron and Cesar Romero were supposed to get 5% of the net profits. Ten years later MCA was curious as to why neither actor had received a statement for four years. After a little foot-dragging Lippert sent MCA a bunch of statements and a check for $200 to be divided equally between the two actors. As of March 31, 1959, the picture had grossed $160,742 from its theatrical run and another $32,170 from its sale to television.

Critics: "The elephant stampedes are rather tame and the mammoths ludicrous."—*Variety*; "...a choppy, confusing piece..."—*Hollywood Reporter*; "...far-fetched..."—*Hollywood Citizen News*; "...one of those off-the-cuff productions made precisely for the Saturday-afternoon youngster trade which goes in for fantastic action and silly improbabilities. This one had 'em all, from hand grenade-throwing monkeys to innocent old pachyderms with fur coats."—*New York Times*.

Exhibitors: "This is the third Lippert picture released by Fox in Quebec that we have played to no letdown."—Harold Bell, Canada.

KENTUCKY JUBILEE (1951) B&W 67 min. Written by Maurice Tombragel and Ron Ormond with special material by Harry Harris; Produced by Robert L. Lippert; Directed by Ron Ormond. Cast: Jerry Colonna, Jean Porter, James Ellison, Fritz Feld, and Margia Dean.
Critics: "Children should like it, but adults may find it too silly..."—*Harrison's Reports*; "[It] will be most enjoyed by the small-town trade."—*Hollywood Reporter*; "...for those who like hokum comedy, western talk and music."—*Variety*; "Oddly enjoyable..."—*Los Angeles Times*; "The story gets in the way of the vaudeville content...and stays there longer than is good for the project."—*Motion Picture Herald*.
Exhibitors: "As far as I'm concerned this is the biggest dish of corn in years, but as far as the boxoffice is concerned, it was the biggest in months..."—Paul Wood, FL; "This is simply awful...If you show it, make yourself scarce."—Frank E. Sabin, MT.

*****KING DINOSAUR** (1955) B&W 63 min. A Zimgor Production; Written by Tom Gries from the story "The Beast from Outer Space" by Bert Gordon and Al Zimbalist; Produced by Bert I. Gordon and Al Zimbalist; Directed by Bert I. Gordon (debut). Cast: Bill Bryant, Wanda Curtis, Douglas Henderson, Patricia Gallagher, and Marvin Miller (narrator).
Tidbits: In 1952, possibly inspired by the highly successful re-release of RKO's 1933 classic *King Kong*, Guy Reed Ritchie wrote a script called *King Dinosaur*. Producer Al Zimbalist bought the property the following year and bragged that it was going to be his biggest production to date. It was going to be filmed in a new anamorphic wide-screen process called Vistarama and Jack Rabin would be in charge of the special effects. Ritchie's script, Rabin's effects, and Vistarama were discarded when Zimbalist hooked up with newcomer Bert I. Gordon who co-wrote and directed the picture. He was also in charge of the not-so-special effects. Prior to this picture Gordon's only movie credit was *Serpent Island* (1954), a delightfully inept 16mm color feature which was sold directly to television. Tom Gries had directed that film. He wrote the screenplay *King Dinosaur*.

Patricia Gallagher, Douglas Henderson, Wanda Curtis and Bill Bryant are held at bay by King Dinosaur *(1955), the movie that taught everyone that the Tyrannosaur rex did not walk on two legs as we'd always been told but rather four.*

The entire film was shot in seven days in the Big Bear Mountains and the overworked Bronson Canyon for a cost of $15,000. All of the equipment was borrowed, and the four actors worked for deferred salaries. Rather than use stop-motion animation, or men-in-suits for his dinosaurs, Gordon took a cue from Hal Roach and used lizards.

"I had iguanas on a miniature set," Gordon recalled. "To make them appear to have size you have to overcrank the camera. You never know when an animal is going to move. I shot thousands of feet of film and the sons of bitches wouldn't move. They were like statues; like stone. Nothing would make them move and nothing would make them angry. So I finally ended up in the library and found a book with a chapter on iguanas that said they needed extreme heat to be active. So I bought a couple of heaters and blew hot air on them with fans."

Critics: "...the film's brief running time can be regarded as a programming asset."—*Boxoffice*. "The script limps along to a reasonably satisfactory ending…"—*Motion Picture Herald*; "…a mild science fiction yarn…"—*Variety*.

LEAVE IT TO THE MARINES (1951) B&W 65 min. Written by Orville H. Hampton; Produced by Sigmund Neufeld; Directed by Sam Newfield. Cast: Sid Melton, Mara Lynn, Gregg Martell, Ida Moore, Sam Flint, and Margia Dean.
Critics: "…a hokey little comedy…"—*Variety*.
Exhibitors: "Light and strictly for double feature houses."—Pearce Parkhurst, MI.

*LIFE WITH THE LYONS aka **FAMILY AFFAIR** (1956) B&W 78 min. A Hammer Film Production; Written by Robert Dunbar and Val Guest based on the BBC radio series; Produced by Robert Dunbar; Directed by Val Guest. Cast: Ben Lyon, Bebe Daniels, Barbara Lyon, Richard Lyon, and Hugh Morton.
Tidbits: Americans Ben and Barbara Lyon decided to make England their home during World War II where they had a popular radio show called *Hi Gang!* "Everyone wanted to make a film with them," said director Guest, "and they personally came to me to ask if I'd make it."[4] Guest incorporated three of their radio shows into his script and used some of the original cast. It was his first film for Hammer, and it was Hammer's first hit.
Critics: "A pleasant and unpretentious film…"—*The Monthly Film Bulletin*; "…expertly scripted, directed, and acted."—*The Kinematograph Weekly*.

*THE LIMPING MAN (1953) B&W 76 min. A Banner Films Ltd. production; Written by Ian Stuart Black and Reginald Long based on Anthony Verney's story "Death on the Tideway"; Produced by Donald Ginsberg; Directed by Charles De Lautour (Cy Endfield). Cast: Lloyd Bridges, Morra Lister, Alan Wheatley, Leslie Phillips, and Helen Cordet.
Tidbits: Rather than be questioned by the HUAC committee, director Cy Endfield moved to England and paid Charles De Lautour to front for him. Endfield and leading man Lloyd Bridges had previously worked together on the powerful film noir drama *Try and Get Me* (1950).

Critics: "...circuitous and illogical."—*Boxoffice*; "...well-made, tautly-told melodrama."—*Hollywood Reporter*; "...over-complicated plot..."—*Motion Picture Herald*; "The performances are adequate, the mood good and the pace leisurely British."—*Variety*.

LITTLE BIG HORN (Working title: **THE FIGHTING SEVENTH** 1951) B&W 86 min. Written by Charles Marquis Warren and Harold Shumate; Produced by Carl T. Hittleman; Directed by Charles Marquis Warren. Cast: Lloyd Bridges, John Ireland, Marie Windsor, Reed Hadley, and Jim Davis.

Tidbits: This picture cost a modest $183,849 to make, with a $15,000 deferred payment from DeLuxe Lab, and it grossed $521,260.12. However, the profit participators, who were looking forward to elevating their bank balances, were woefully disappointed. After Lippert deducted his distribution fee, the cost of the 250 release prints at $250.00 per print and other charges, the profit had successfully been whittled to a paltry $23,525.03. When it comes to making profits vanish, nobody does it better than Hollywood bookkeepers.

Critics: "You almost feel the agony, sweat and fear as these men push through the wild country stalked by hidden Indians."—*Los Angeles Evening Herald*; "The ending is to be expected, but never-the-less hair-raising."—*Hollywood Citizen News*; "...endless footage is expended upon views of men riding horses—men walking their horses—men mounting or dismounting their horses and—best of all—endless shots of horses' feet in close-ups."—*Los Angeles Examiner*.

Exhibitors: "Audience enjoyed every moment of this stirring western drama."—Buck Renfro, AR; "This is an extra good picture that will do well anywhere. Exhibitors take notice. Mr. Lippert sold to TV because the exhibitors would not help him stay in business by booking Lippert pictures."—John Lawing, NC; "So help me, Marie Windsor was only in the picture twice...Her name was used only to get people in. That did me more harm than anything."—Kenneth Clem, MD; "Use it on Fri., Sat. and give it plenty of help. Business was below average."—Don Donohue, CA; "...drew better than average business...but is definitely not for your best playing time."—Frank Sabin, MT.

Dorothy Hart and George Raft from Loan Shark *(1952), the best of the three movies that Raft made for Lippert. Hart replaced actresses Gail Russell and Mara Lynn, who were originally slated for the role.*

LOAN SHARK (1952) B&W 79 min. Written by Martin Rackin and Eugene Ling; Produced by Bernard Luber; Directed by Seymour Friedman. Cast: George Raft, Dorothy Hart, Paul Stewart, John Hoyt, and Margia Dean.

Tidbits: Lippert cut a deal with Charles Feldman and Ned Marin, the heads of a talent agency known as Famous Artists Corporation, to develop production deals for independently-made features. Writers, producers, and directors were promised greater freedom in selecting projects, exchanging salaries for profit participations, which they rarely received.

Lippert signed George Raft for two pictures—*Loan Shark* and *I'll Get You* (1953). He was paid $25,000 per picture plus 25% of the profits. Some sources have reported that Raft never saw a dime of his profit participation but, as astonishing as it may be, that simply isn't true. He received a final payment in the amount of $31,655.59 on December 30, 1960. It may not have been all of the money that he was entitled to, but it was more than anyone else ever saw.

The director of Raft's two features, Seymour Friedman, did not fare as well. Once he realized he wasn't going to get the money owed to him, he took Lippert to court, demanding $24,000 plus the right to look at the books. In the end, Lippert got the best of him. On August 13, 1954, Friedman signed a quit claim release for a paltry $1,000.

Critics: "Film has good pacing and sufficient plot punch to play satisfactorily as either to or bottom of the bill..."—*Variety*; "Raft acts well in a roll that was tailor-made for him."—*Harrison's Reports*; "Someday a movie racket-buster may be found who can moderate his voice differently through a love scene than facing the muzzle of the big boss's gun."—*New York Herald Tribune*; "[A] fast-moving, tense melodrama..."—*Hollywood Reporter*; "...exceptionally well-made..."—*Boxoffice*.

Exhibitors: "After playing this one we are willing to take anything Lippert has."—Harold Bell, Canada; "It's a good one from the up-and-coming small company."—Carey O. Fairbank, LA.

THE LONESOME TRAIL (1955) B&W 73 min. Written by Richard Bartlett and Ian MacDonald, based on Gordon D. Shirreff's short story "Silent Reckoning" that appeared in the December 1954 edition of *Real Western Stories*; Produced by Earle Lyon; Directed by Richard Bartlett. Cast: Wayne Morris, John Agar, Margia Dean, Edgar Buchanan, and Adele Jergens.

Critics: "...some good touches here and there."—Steven H. Scheuer; "...talky script and pedestrian direction..."—*Motion Picture Herald*.

Exhibitors: "...a class 'B' picture."—Harland Rankin, Canada.

LOST CONTINENT (1951) B&W (with green tinted sequence) 83 min. Written by Richard H. Landau; Produced by Sigmund Neufeld; Directed by Sam Newfield. Cast: Cesar Romero, Hillary Brooke, Chick Chandler, Hugh Beaumont, and John Hoyt.

Tidbits: Kurt Neumann's original idea for *Rocketship X-M* was to combine rocket ships with dinosaurs. Lippert felt it was an unbeatable combination, and even though Neumann's film ultimately abandoned the concept, Lippert still wanted to take advantage of it. He told Richard Landau to update Arthur Conan Doyle's *The Lost World*. Landau fashioned a scenario in which scientists and military people track a runaway atomic rocket to the top of a tropical plateau populated with prehistoric animals.

Special effects expert Ray Harryhausen read about the project in one of the trade magazines and thought there might be a job in it for him. He and his pal, Ray Bradbury, asked Lippert if he had thought about using stop-motion animation to create the dinosaurs. Harryhausen's last movie had been *Mighty Joe Young* (1949) for which he had done about 90 per cent of the stop motion work. The film won the Oscar for special effects, but it had not done much for Harryhausen's career. He had been looking for work ever since.

This is only speculation, but Lippert may have intended to use the same footage from *One Million B.C.* that Kurt Neumann had originally planned to use for *Rocketship X-M.* Harryhausen's visit may well have changed his mind. Since Lippert saw just about every movie ever made, there is no reason to believe he had not seen *King Kong* and *Mighty Joe Young.* Stop-motion sounded like the way to go, but when he told Harryhausen and Bradbury what he was willing to pay for the work, they were insulted and left his office in a huff. Undaunted, Lippert went looking for someone who *was* willing to work for the price he wanted to pay.

For years Edward Nassour had wanted to make a dinosaur movie. He and Walter Lantz (the creator of Woody Woodpecker) had made a reel of test footage for a Technicolor dinosaur film called *Lost Atlantis.* Columbia's Harry Cohn was interested in the project for a short time, but ultimately, the cost proved to be prohibitive.

Nassour had just sold his studio on Sunset Boulevard when he made the deal with Lippert to supply 750 feet of black-and-white footage of stop-motion dinosaurs. The *Los Angeles Daily News* reported that it took Nassour five months to complete his work. According to the article, there were motors inside the rubber puppets to make the animation "less jerky." Actually, the work was completed in six weeks and was accomplished without the use of motors or skill.

Special effects aside, *Lost Continent* is a decent little picture. It is well photographed and has a good cast—Cesar Romero, Hillary Brooke, Hugh Beaumont, Whit Bissell, John Hoyt, and Sid Melton. Sigmund Neufeld produced it, and his brother, Sam Newfield, directed it. They shot the picture in eighteen days at Sam Goldwyn Studios, "on the biggest stage they had there, because they actually built that mountain on the stage," Stanley Neufeld told historian Wheeler Dixon. "When they designed it, Sam was part of the process, because he had to shoot it all. They designed it so they could work their way around the mountain, going higher and higher as they shot the film. The damn thing went almost to the top of the stage. They designed it so they could just work their way around it without having to change the lighting throughout the shoot, and it worked very well."

"It was at least 60 feet high—big!—and there was nothing under us to catch us," Sid Melton told Tom Weaver. "But no one fell, thank God."

"I don't remember much about that one except that we took a long time to climb up that mountain," Whit Bissell recalled. "And I lost my balance or something and I fell. Well, I didn't actually fall, the stuntman did. He fell on a mattress or something. It was a pretty good scene if I remember."

At the Los Angeles premier of the film, Ray Bradbury ran into Lippert in the lobby and told him the picture wouldn't make a dime. **Critics**: "...the conversational marathon plus what must be the longest mountain climb ever recorded on film, will likely wear your nerves to a nub."—*Hollywood Citizen News*; "[It] doesn't pack enough entertainment power to hold up in any extended playdates..."—*Variety*; "...tells its preposterous story in comic strip terms, taking a considerable time over it."—*Monthly Film Bulletin*; "...a double-barreled exploitation picture for the dollar-minded showman..."—*Motion Picture Herald*.
Exhibitors: "It thrilled and scared the kids no end. Adults passed it up. That's the most I can say for it."—Frank Sabin, MT; "I think we'd have been better off if we had left it lost."—Edwin A. Faulk, OK; "... did fairly well on our weekend."—Harland Rankin, Canada; "This was too fanciful for us and our gross took a 25 per cent dive below normal."—R. G. Risch, MN.

MAN BAIT (British title: **THE LAST PAGE** aka **BLONDE BLACKMAIL** 1951) B&W (UK) 78 min. (US) 72 min. Written by Frederick Knott based on James Hadley Chase's play, *The Last Page*; Produced by Anthony Hinds; Directed by Terence Fisher. Cast: George Brent, Marguerite Chapman, Raymond Huntley, Peter Reynolds, and Diana Dors.

Marguerite Chapman and Diana Dors are at odds in the British-made melodrama Man Bait *(1951).*

Tidbits: The best thing about this picture is the talented and sexy Diana Dors, often called the British Marilyn Monroe. "I was the first home-grown sex symbol," she said, "rather like Britain's naughty seaside postcards." Rumor has it that Lippert offered her another picture but only if she would divorce her husband, Dennis Hamilton. Naturally, she told Lippert to get lost, although she did divorce Hamilton eight years later.

Critics: "Diana Dors gives a spirited performance..."— *Monthly Film Bulletin*; "Good for a certain amount of suspense..."— *Motion Picture Exhibitor*; "...a suspenseful story which never drags..."—*Variety*; "...average mystery story with solid suspense values..."—*Hollywood Reporter*.

THE MAN FROM CAIRO (Working titles: **ALGIERS AMBUSH** aka **MISSION TO ALGIERS** 1953) B&W 81 min. Written by Eugene Ling, Janet and Phillip Stevenson; Produced by Bernard Luber; Directed by Ray Enright (final film). Cast: George Raft, Gianna Maria Canale, Massimo Serato, Guido Celano, and Irene Pappas (American film debut).

Tidbits: This movie was shot on location in Rome. Producer Bernard Luber was frustrated by the fact that he could not get regular financial statements. Moneywise, he never knew where he stood. When he was told by a chap named Dr. Gazzi that they needed more money to finish the picture, Luber was flabber- gasted. "I took a hard swallow and swore like hell," Luber wrote in a letter to Lippert. "I also could see your face when I informed you we had to put up another thirty thousand." Luber took issue with most of the figures, and the battle over who owed what waged on for months. When the smoke cleared the picture cost $155,000 cash with an additional $80,000 in deferred payments.

The Man from Cairo marked George Raft's final appearance as a leading man.

Critics: "...takes all the prizes for inconsequential 'B' productions."—*Variety*; "...unexciting, uneventful confusion..."—Steven H. Scheuer; "It's an okay subject for the Raft crowd."—*Motion Picture Herald*; "...Story varies as little from its stock formula as Mr. Raft's dead panned expression."—*Cue*; "...adheres to the recently-overworked tendency of European whodunits to make the proceeding so involved that no one can begin to guess what's happening—and why—until the closing sequences."—*Boxoffice*.

MARSHAL OF HELDORADO (TV title: **BLAZING GUNS** 1950) B&W 55 min. Written by Ron Ormond and Maurice Tombragel; Produced by Ron Ormond; Directed by Thomas Carr. Cast: James Ellison, Russell Hayden, Betty (Julie) Adams, Raymond Hatton, and Fuzzy Knight.

Critics: "[It] won't churn up much reaction from actions fans one way or another."—*Variety*.

Exhibitors: "They try to be too funny to the point of boredom. They want action in 60 minute westerns—that's all."—Ralph Raspa, WV.

MASK OF THE DRAGON (TV titles: **DRAGON OF DEATH** and **THE ORIENTAL CLUE** 1951) B&W 53 min. Written by Orville H. Hampton; Produced by Sigmund Neufeld; Directed by Sam Newfield. Cast: Richard Travis, Sheila Ryan, Sid Melton, Michael Whalen, and Lyle Talbot.

Critics: "...the acting is good and Sam Newfield's direction fills it with pace and plenty of punch."—*Hollywood Reporter*; "...a pretty weak entry..."—*Motion Picture Herald*; "Attempting a combination of comedy and mystery, this entry fails to score in either department."—*Variety*.

Exhibitors: "Agreeably surprised to receive such favorable comment on this picture."—Z. Epstein, NJ.

*THE MONSTER FROM THE OCEAN FLOOR (1954) B&W 64 min. Written by William Danch; Produced by Roger Corman; Directed by Wyott Ordung. Cast: Anne Kimbell, Stuart Wade, Dick Pinner, Jack (Jonathan) Haze, and Wyott Ordung.

Tidbits: This was Roger Corman's first film as a producer. His office at the time was above the Cock 'n' Bull Restaurant on the Sunset Strip. Actually, it was the reception room of a fellow who was going bankrupt.

"I was working at a gas station at the time," remembered Corman veteran Jonathan Haze. "A funny little guy named Barney Ordung kept coming into the station, always talking about this movie he was going to make with a guy named Roger Corman. Everybody in Hollywood is going to make a movie so I didn't think much about it. Then one day he came in and said: 'We're gonna do it. We're finally gonna make the movie. Come on. I want you to meet the producer.'"

"There's a part for you," Corman told him. "A Mexican. But you'll have to grow a mustache. You'll also have to bring your own costumes, do your own stunts, and you won't be paid overtime. You still want it?"

Of course he did.

They filmed for six days at Malibu and Catalina in southern California.

"Barney was allergic to seagulls and every time one flew by he wanted to throw up," said Haze.

The trade papers at the time announced that the film was being shot in Ensenada, but that was a piece of misinformation that Corman deliberately fed to the press so that he could stay clear of the labor unions, a ploy that did not work. "It may have been the last day, or the next to the last day, that someone from the union found us shooting at the beach," Corman recalled. "I was driving the truck with all of the equipment. He was a good guy. He looked around and saw what a small operation we were and said to me:

Poster from Roger Corman's soggy science fiction effort The Monster From the Ocean Floor *(1954).*

'Next time hire a driver.' And that was it. He left and we never heard from him again."

A magazine article about a new one-man submarine developed by the Aerojet-General company inspired Corman to make the picture. "I called Aerojet and told them that if they would let me use it in the picture, it would give them a lot of free publicity. I then talked the writer into writing the script, raised six thousand dollars, and we made the picture for a total of twelve thousand, and six thousand deferred, as I recall."

When the title-monster made its first appearance on the screen at a sneak preview, someone in the audience yelled: "It looks like my wife's diaphragm." Corman went looking for someone to make him a new monster, something that was not laughable. The creature made by puppeteer Bob Baker looked like a one-eyed octopus rather than the giant amoeba described in the script, but at least it did not look like a diaphragm.

"I heard that Jim Nicholson, who I'd met a Realart, was looking for a movie to start his own releasing company. I arranged for Corman to meet with Jim and his wife, Sylvia. The four of us ate spareribs at the Cock 'n' Bull while Jim outlined his plan. He wanted to show the film to the sub-distributors, hoping they would buy the film at a profit and advance enough money to make a second picture. But Corman wanted a quicker return on his investment and passed on the deal. His brother, Gene, negotiated a pick-up deal with Lippert for $110,000.

"When Lippert got back to me with the contracts, he had changed the deal because he found out we had spent a lot less than $100,000 to make it," Gene remembered. "I reminded him that he had seen the film and agreed on the price, but in the end, we settled for $100,000, and everybody was happy."

Everybody but the film's director, Wyott Barney) Ordung, who claimed he never received the money that Corman had promised him. "Corman told me he'd sold 120 per cent of the picture by mistake so he could only give me 15 per cent," Ordung said. "I'd hocked my life insurance and my two-bedroom chicken coop in Sun Valley to raise $15,000 to make the picture. The guy that saved me was Leon Blender. He put a projector on top of the boxoffice at one of the downtown theaters and ran the trailer on a continuous loop. The picture grossed $850,000 and I got a check for the next 26 years."

In all fairness to Corman, Ordung was known to be a little reckless with the truth, so you can take his story for what it is worth.

Of course, Lippert came out of the deal just fine. He got a 50 percent distribution fee.

Corman retained ownership of the film and eventually sold it to Medallion TV. VCI Entertainment has recently released the film on a DVD that includes a few minutes of swimming footage of Anne Kimbell (yawn!) that was cut from the film as an extra.

Critics: "Good direction and performances..."—*Boxoffice*; "...it's a long way from a Grade-A product."—*Los Angeles Daily News*; "...a well-done quickie."—*Variety*; "...is distinguished by some magical undersea scenery, including swimmer Anne Kimbell..."—*Los Angeles Times*; "The monster in question resembles a huge, one-eyed octopus, but it is no more convincing than the plot."—*Los Angeles Examiner*.

Exhibitors: "It kept the kids running to the lobby during the movie's exciting scenes."—James Wiggs, Jr., NC.

MOTOR PATROL (1950) B&W 67 min. Written by Maurice Tombragel; Produced by Barney Sarecky; Directed by Sam Newfield. Cast: Don Castle, Jane Nigh, Reed Hadley, Bill Henry, and Margia Dean.

Tidbits: Writer, actor and publicist Jack Barron accused Lippert, Maurice Tombragel, and Lt. Louis Fuller, of the Los Angeles police department's motorcycle division, of ripping him off. Baron claimed that they had used material from his screen treatment, *Road Patrol*, which had been submitted to, and rejected by the Lippert organization the year before. Barron wanted $50,000 in damages, which was ridiculous. If Lippert had bought his treatment, he probably would not have paid more than $200 for it.

Critics: "...fast moving cops-and-robbers actioner..."—*Boxoffice*; "The direction is so good that one feels as if seeing a real-life occurrence."—*Harrison's Reports*; "...a brisk, competent and incidentally informative account of its 67 minutes on the screen."—*Motion Picture Herald*; "...an okay cops-and-robbers melodrama for secondary bookings in the smaller situations."—*Variety*.

Exhibitors: "You may never sell tickets on the merits of Lippert films, but there are very few patrons that are not satisfied."—Jim Dunbar, KS; "This little vehicle pleased and gave me an average crowd."—Ralph Raspa, WV.

Poster for Motor Patrol *(1950).*

William Tracy and Joe Sawyer star in the service comedy Mr. Walkie Talkie *(1952).*

MR. WALKIE TALKIE (1952) B&W 65 min. Written by C. Carleton Brown; Produced by Hal Roach, Jr.; Directed by Fred Guiol. Cast: William Tracy, Joe Sawyer, Margia Dean, Russell Hicks, and Robert Shayne.
Critics: "It is supposed to be a comedy, but only children may find it laugh-provok-ing."—*Harrison's Reports*; "A fairly amusing display of comedics..."—*Variety*.
Exhibitors: "Those who came liked it but business was below normal."—C. O. Taylor, AR; "They laughed all the way through it and the comments were good."—Lloyd Hutchins, AR; "Some thought it was as good as an Abbott and Costello show."—Leo W. Smith, SD.

***NAVAJO** (1951) B&W 70 min. Produced by Hal Bartlett; Directed by Norman Foster. Cast: Hal Bartlett, John Mitchell, Eloise Teller, Francis Teller, and Linda Teller.
Tidbits: This picture had its world premier at the Baronet Theatre in New York, and received a special award at the Edinburg film festival and endorsements from *Parents* and *Scholastic* magazines. Lippert's publicity department got behind it and, in the end, it was

Newspaper ad for Navajo *(1951).*

nominated for two Academy Awards—Best Documentary and Best Cinematography.

Critics: "...eloquent commentary and masterfully photo-graphed..."—*Boxoffice*; "...exquisite, pictorially beautiful and dramatically fascinating."—*Hollywood Reporter*; "Excellent, ranks with, if not topping, best of foreign award winner."—*Variety*; "Unusual and compassionate."—*New York Times*; "Moving and unusual."—*Newsweek*.

Exhibitors: "Maybe Lippert is working for television."—Harold Bell, Canada; "My folks didn't really care for it."—Frank Sabin, MT.

*NORMAN CONQUEST aka **PARK PLAZA 605** (1953) B&W 75 min. B&A Productions; Written by Bertram Ostrer, Albert Fennell and Bernard Knowles, from the novel by Berkeley Gray; Produced by Albert Fennell; Directed by Bernard Knowles. Cast: Tom Conway, Eva Bartok, Joy Shelton, Sid James, and Richard Wattis.

Tidbits: Norman Conquest (played by Tom Conway) was a charac-ter in a series of novels.

Critics: "...intriguing English who-dunit..."—*Los Angeles Times*.

Exhibitors: "Very good comments from patrons on this one."—Yves Legault, Canada.

OPERATION HAYLIFT (1950) B&W 74 min. Written by Dean Riesner and Joe Sawyer; Produced by Joe Sawyer; Directed by William Berke. Cast: Bill Williams, Ann Rutherford, Tom Brown, Jane Nigh, and Joe Sawyer.

Tidbits: Writers Dean Riesner and Joe Sawyer show how the cattle and sheep herds were saved by the U.S. Air Force during the bliz-zards of January 1949, when lack of feed threatened starvation for every head of stock in Nevada. The picture was filmed where it happened, in and around Ely, Nevada. The locals were used as extras and when the movie hit town it played to packed houses.

Critics: "A solid script on a comparatively topical subject..."—*Boxoffice*; "...it takes almost one-half hour before the main action is reached."—*Harrison's Reports*; "Fact and fiction are expertly inter-woven..."—*Motion Picture Herald*.

Exhibitors: "It is something different in entertainment. Business was a little better than what it has been..."—Ralph Raspa, WV; "My only regret was that more people were not here to view this very clever picture. Our weather was almost as poor as that shown in the film."—Tom S. Graff, CA.

*OUTLAW WOMEN
(1952) Cinecolor 75 min. Ron Ormond Productions; Written by Orville H. Hampton; Produced by Ron Ormond; Directed by Sam Newfield and Ron Ormond. Cast: Marie Windsor, Richard Rober, Alan Nixon, Carla Balenda, and Jacqueline Fontaine.
Tidbits: While director Sam Newfield was shooting all of the scenes with the women, Ron Ormond was shooting the scenes with the men. This was the first production of Howco International's Joy N. Houck and J. Frances White. "I was quite annoyed about the picture," Marie Windsor told Mike Fitzgerald. "Jacqueline Fontaine was the girlfriend of the producer or some big shot, and she got privileges she didn't deserve. Richard Rober, that poor guy, was killed in a car wreck before the picture was released."

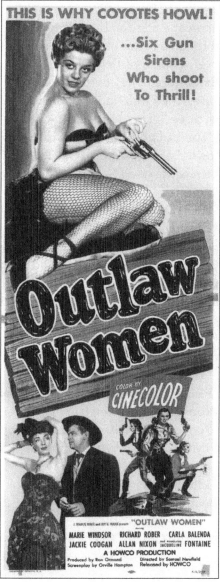

Poster for Ron Ormond's Cinecolor western Outlaw Women (1952)

Critics: "...a rather dull affair..."—*Variety*; "...more of a burlesque of the standard western formula than an action story."—*Hollywood Reporter*; "...a bevy of believable performances; surprisingly impressive production mountings; and deft trip hammer direction..."—*Boxoffice*; "It is probably the worst motion picture to open at a first-run Broadway house so far this year...The cast goes through a series of tired, meaningless motions that add up to nothing."—*New York Times*.

Exhibitors: "They certainly came for this one and we had no kicks. They were looking for legs, gals and action—and they got all three."—Lloyd Hutchins, AR; "The title, the gals, the color and Lippert's fair terms dictate that it will hold its own in most small towns."—Bob Walker, CO; "Color is fair and action is plentiful, all comments good."—James Wiggs, Jr., NC.

PAID TO KILL (British title: **FIVE DAYS** (1954) B&W 72 min. Written by Paul Tabori; Produced by Anthony Hinds; Directed by Montgomery Tully. Cast: Dane Clark, Paul Carpenter, Thea Gregory, Cecile Chevreau, and Anthony Forwood.

Critics: "The picture puts a considerable strain upon the credulity of its audience."—*The Kinematograph Weekly*; "It's a typical mystery-melodrama, fast, furious and slightly far-fetched."—*Motion Picture Herald*; "...scenes are put together with little sense of movement or continuity..."—*Monthly Film Bulletin*.

*PERILS OF THE JUNGLE (1953) B&W 61 min. Commodore Productions; Written by Frank Taussig and Robert T. Smith; Produced by Walter White Jr.; Directed by George Blair. Cast: Phyllis Coates, Clyde Beatty, Stanley Farrar, John Doucette, and Leonard Mudie.

Tidbits: This movie is comprised of stories adapted from the Clyde Beatty radio program.

*PHANTOM OF THE JUNGLE (1953) B&W 75 min. Written by Sherman L. Lowe and William Lively; Produced by Rudolph Flothow; Directed by Spencer Bennett. Cast: Jon Hall, Ray Montgomery, Anne Gwynne, Kenneth McDonald, and Carleton Young.

Tidbits: This feature was made from three episodes of the *Ramar of the Jungle* television series. In a 1953 interview, Jon Hall told Howard McClay: "None of our stories employ backgrounds, events or people that will date them. This makes the material good for many years." Ironically, the show was so racist, static, and cynically produced, it was dated almost as soon as it aired.

PIER 23 (TV titles: **PIER OF PERIL** and **THE LONG FALL** 1951) B&W 57 min. Written by Julie Harmon and Victor West based on two episodes of the *Pat Novak for Hire* radio program; Produced and Directed by William Berke. Cast: Hugh Beaumont, Ann Savage, Edward Brophy, Richard Travis and Margia Dean.
Critics: "...barely passable lowercase programmer."—*Variety*; "...good, thanks to William Berke's effective direction."—*Harrison's Reports*; "...moves along at a reasonably lively clip..."—*Boxoffice*; "Inevitably, the onlooker is confused, and when it comes to 'sum-up' scenes, so many names are mentioned in the course of a single speech that it sounds like a reading of the telephone directory."—*Hollywood Reporter*; "Whether audiences will accept the Lippert format with relish only time and test can tell."—*Motion Picture Herald*.
Exhibitors: "...as good as most of the product from the bigger companies..."—Audrey Thompson, AR.

*PIRATE SUBMARINE aka **CASABIANCA** (1951) B&W (France) 84 min. (US) 69 min. Written by Le Commandant Jean L'Herminier and Jane-Edith Saintenoy; Produced by H. Vincent Brechignac; Directed by Georges Peclet. Cast: Pierre Dudan, Gerard Landry, Jean Vilmont, Alain Terrane and Jean Vilar.
Critics: "...moves along at a good pace and has an air of authority..."—*Hollywood Reporter*; "...a listless approach to the subject..."—*Variety*.

*PROJECT MOON BASE (1953) B&W 63 min. Galaxy Productions; Written by Robert Heinlein and Jack Seaman; Produced by Jack Seaman; Directed by Richard Talmadge. Cast: Donna Martel, Hayden Rorke, Ross Ford, Larry Johns, and Herb Jacobs.
Tidbits: Noted sci-fi author Robert Heinlein wrote a pilot called "Ring Around the Moon" for Jack Seaman's proposed television series *The World Beyond*. Unable to secure a sponsor, Seaman added six minutes to his 57-minute pilot, changed the title to *Project Moon Base*, and sold it to Lippert as a feature. It has some surprisingly good special effects by Jacques Fresco, Howard Weeks and Jack R. Glass, but for all of its ambitions and good intentions it is pretty tough going.

Donna Martel and Ross Ford have to go to the moon to find romance in the dull and silly Project Moonbase *(1953).*

Donna Martel was offered a piece of the picture or a straight salary. Her agent told her take the salary and run, which was good advice.

The film's one highlight is when Hayden Rorke described the mechanics of his space station to a newspaper reporter. He struggled to remember his next line, tripping over words, obviously in trouble, and yet nobody would help him. They would neither cut the scene to let him try again, nor would they cut to another character so Rorke could simply read his lines. They simply hung the poor actor out to dry.

Critics: "...even the juveniles will not be hysterical about this offering..."—*Boxoffice*; "Character development upsets any semblance of credibility."—*Variety*; "By and large, it is pretty quiet stuff for its category."—*Motion Picture Herald*. "...complete ineptitude will make it an object for derision even from the Saturday matinee kid audience."—*Hollywood Reporter*; "...undoubtedly a quickly made affair."—*Los Angeles Times*.

*QUEEN OF SHEBA (LA REGINA DI SABA 1953) B&W 103 min. Oro Film; Written by Raoul De Sarro, Pietro Francisci, Girogio Graziosi, and Vittorio Nino Novarese; Produced by Mario Francisci; American Version Produced by William M. Pizor and Bernard Luber; Directed by Pietro Francisci. Cast: Eleonora Ruffo, Gino Leurini, Gino Cervi, Marina Berti, and Franco Silva.

Tidbits: Bernard Luber, producer of several movies for Lippert, and Bill Pizor, the head of Lippert's foreign sales division, purchased the rights to this picture for U.S. release. They took it to United Artists believing they would get a better deal from them than they would Bob Lippert; however, the deal fell through. Desperate, they convinced the manager of the Astor Theatre in New York to show the picture. After nine weeks of good boxoffice, Lippert agreed to take over the national distribution.
Critics: "Picture is a grand spectacle with impressive ceremonies, fierce battles..."–*Los Angeles Times*; "...a quartet of Italo scripters has not neglected to include every cliché of spectacle into the yarn."–*Variety*; "The sets are stupendous...but the story is weak, the writing weaker, and the performances by most all concerned are so inept as to be nearly funny." *Cue*' "[A] turgid and pompous costume drama..."–*New York Times*; "...well photographed, competently acted and directed..."–*Los Angeles Examiner*. "...the distributors might do better with it if they change the original date of issue to 1919, mention that a soundtrack has been added, and suggest that it has been reissued for historical purposes. Unethical, I guess, but I can't figure out how else they're going to sell this awful job."–*Saturday Review*; "...The story...has been conceived in routine fashion."–*Motion Picture Herald*.

RACE FOR LIFE (British title: **THE MASK OF DUST**) (1954) B&W (UK) 79 min. (US) 69 min. Written by Richard Landau based on the novel "Last Race" by Jon Manchip White; Produced by Mickey Delmar; Directed by Terence Fisher. Cast: Richard Conte, Mari Aldon, George Coulouris, Peter Illing, and Alex Mango.
Critics: "Skillful use of newsreel footage in the actual racing sequence raise the routine story slightly higher than average."–*Monthly Film Bulletin*; "The two stars struggle as best they can with cliché-filled roles, but it's colorless acting at best as directed by Terence Fisher."–*Variety*.

RADAR SECRET SERVICE (1950) B&W 60 min. Written by Beryl Sachs; Produced by Barney Sarecky; Directed by Sam Newfield. Cast: John Howard, Adele Jergens, Tom Neal, Myrna Dell, and Sid Melton.

Critics: "...imaginative little melodrama..."—*Motion Picture Herald*;
"Plot is transparent but wastes little time on dialog, so the pace
and action are good..."—*Variety*.
Exhibitors: "This is a fine action picture that is just right for a double-header on Fri., Sat."—Ed Vernon, FL.

RED DESERT (Working title: **TEXAS MANHUNT** 1949) B&W 60
min. Written by Ron Ormond and Daniel B. Ulman; Produced by
Ron Ormond; Directed by Ford Beebe. Cast: Don Berry, Tom Neal,
Jack Holt, Margia Dean, and Tom London.
Tidbits: "It was my first leading lady, but still a thankless part,"
Margia Dean told Mike Fitzgerald. "You go in early in the morning
for hair and makeup; then are driven a long ways to a dusty, hot,
sticky location. At dust, they take the leading lady's close-up—just
when she's grimy!"
Critics: "Interesting and suspenseful, the story makes a good
vehicle for Don Barry."—*Variety*; "...gets sufficiently away from sagebrush formulas make it considerably more interesting..."—*Boxoffice*.
Exhibitors: "Too much walking on the Red Desert spoiled this
would-be good Western. Average attendance."—Pat Fleming, AR;
"There is nothing good about this picture at all...We double billed it
with *Holiday Rhythm*...I'd have to say I wouldn't want any more like
these two, or I would have to lock my front door."—Virgil Anderson,
MO.

*THE RETURN OF GILBERT AND SULLIVAN (1952) Color 32
min. Irving Allen Productions; Written by William S. Gilbert and Sid
Kuller; Produced by Irving Allen; Directed by Irving Allen and Sid
Kuller. Cast: The Sportsman Quartet, Melville Cooper, Billy Gray,
Tudor Owen, and Dee Turnell.
Tidbits: This short subject began filming sometime in 1950 according to
notices in *The New York Times*, *Variety* and *Quick*. The plot: Gilbert and
Sullivan return to earth to protest the jazz treatment of their work. It was
shot in two days. The film is now in the public domain.

THE RETURN OF JESSE JAMES (Working title: **DEAD RINGER**
1950) B&W 75 min. Written by Jack Natteford; Produced by Carl
K. Hittleman; Directed by Arthur Hilton. Cast: John Ireland, Ann
Dvorak, Henry Jull, Reed Hadley, and Hugh O'Brien.

Critics: "Strictly off the beaten path for a Lippert oater..."—*Variety*; "Lippert Productions has turned out one of their better than usual western dramas..."—*Independent Film Journal*; "...a first-rate film..."— *Los Angeles Times*; "...plenty of action, new story-twists and fine performances by a well balanced cast."—*Film Daily*; "...fast, hard-hitting sagebrush saga."—*Cue*.

Exhibitors: "...too cheaply made to be good."—Pat Fleming, AR; "Comments weren't good on this but business was 125 per cent. *Square Dance Jubilee* billed with it was the one that drew them in and kept them happy."—Bob Walker, CO; "This was the worst Jesse James I ever ran."—Kenneth Clem, MD; "Very boring to sit through...Very poor business."—Raymond Fleming, LA; "This is a good western, cast and a story ideal for a small town. It had better than average draw here."—L. Brazil, Jr., AR; "It squeaked by on the bottom half."—Don Donohue, CA; "I missed seeing it but receipts were good."—Frank Sabin, MT; "This one broke all Saturday western records, bringing in the crowds. We really ate steak on this one."—R. D. Gibbins, AL.

*RIVER BEAT (1954) B&W 73 min. Victor Hanbrury Productions; Written by Rex Rientis; Produced by Victor Hanbrury; Directed by Guy Green (debut). Cast: Phyllis Kirk, John Bentley, Robert Ayres, Leonard White, and Evan Roberts.

Critics: "Okay lowercase thriller..."—*Variety*; "Its brightest asset is the performance of Phyllis Kirk..."—*Hollywood Reporter*; "...standard English melodrama..."—*Motion Picture Herald*.

ROARING CITY (Television titles: **SISTERS IN CRIME** and **JEWELS OF JEOPARDY** 1951) B&W 59 min. Written by Victor West from two episodes of the *Pat Novak for Hire* radio show; Produced and Directed by William Berke. Cast: Hugh Beaumont, Edward Brophy, Richard Travis, Joan Valerie, and Greg McClure.

Critics: "...strictly for the nabes."—*Variety*; "The plot becomes thicker and harder to understand...and just as you think you are getting somewhere, there is the fade out and the second story is underway."— *Los Angeles Times*.

ROCKETSHIP X-M (1950) B&W (red tinted sequence) 77 min.
Written by Kurt Neumann and Dalton Trumbo (no credit);
Produced and Directed by Kurt Neumann. Cast: Lloyd Bridges,
Osa Massen, John Emery, Noah Berry, Jr., and Hugh O'Brien.
Tidbits: This picture was rushed into production to cash in on
the publicity surrounding the making of George Pal's *Destination
Moon*. Jack Rabin was hired to do the special effects. His partner,
Irving Block, supplied the matte paintings that helped turn Death
Valley, Red Rock Canyon, and the Mohave Desert into a Martian
landscape. Lippert added a red tint to these scenes which helped
give the locations an alien feel, supported by the moody and eerie
camera work by Karl Struss.

"I used special lenses to create a distorted feeling in the
spaceship," Struss told *Hollywood Cameraman*, "and I had some
wonderful planetscapes in outer space, with fantastic cloudscapes;
I went hogwild with filters."

Struss won an Academy Award for *Sunrise* in 1929 and was nominated three more times for *Dr. Jekyll and Mr. Hyde* (1932), *The
Sign of the Cross* (1934), and *Aloma of the South Sea* (1942). He
and Neumann made several films together and his contribution to
Rocketship X-M was significant.

The cast that Neumann assembled was an unusually good one.
The underrated Lloyd Bridges was given the lead role. His co-star
was Danish-born Osa Massen who, at one time, was more interested in being a film editor than she was an actress. The rest of the
astronauts were played by Hugh O'Brien, John Emery, and Noah
Berry Jr. Each day these people were flown to the already mentioned desert locations. As there was no time to waste, they did
their own make-up en route, so that by the time the plane touched
ground they were in costume and ready to go.

Knowing that music can often make or break a movie, Lippert
hired Ferde Grofe', the composer of the "Mississippi Suite" and
the "Grand Canyon Suite," to score *Rocketship X-M*. Normally the
assignment would have gone to Albert Glasser, Lippert's resident
composer. Glasser was nothing if he wasn't prolific, and nobody
thought more highly of his scores than he did, but for this picture
Glasser was asked to simply orchestrate and conduct the music
that Grofe' had written. "No reflection on you, kid," Lippert told
him, "but I need to add a little class to this picture."

Lloyd Bridges told film historian Tom Weaver that he didn't know how much artistic value Lippert gave to the piece, "but he was crazy about motion pictures, and had seen just about every one that was ever made. Most of the things he did were the so-called B pictures of the day, but he made his impression on the business I think. With *Rocketship X-M* we did beat our competitor, *Destination Moon*. And they paid a lot more for their production. We kind of took advantage of the publicity they were putting out—people weren't quite sure whether they were seeing that picture or our picture."

Critics: "...carefully constructed, impressively cast and pro-duced."—*Boxoffice*; "For 77 minutes the auditor will be undergoing a bombardment of goose-pimples and cold sweat..."—*Variety*; "...box-office dynamite..."—*Hollywood Reporter*; "Karl Struss rates a cheer for his expert cinematography, as does Jack Rabin for his stunning special photographic effects."—*Hollywood Citizen News*.

Exhibitors: "This is a most unusual picture...We did nice business with it."—Harland Rankin, Canada; "Latch on to this one if you want to stay out of the red ink. Let's all help this little company. They have made some fine product for small theatres and this is one of the best with production values right up there with the majors."—Arthur Goldstein, CO; "...the lowest gross in five years."—W.L. Stratton, ID; "I bow before Mr. Lippert and his adventure into the unknown with a fine, first class feature."—Jim Dunbar, KS; "This one drew fair attendance, but pleased only the children."—Tom S. Graff, CA; "The comments were divided."—Ralph Raspa, WV; "...very entertaining and suspenseful, but here it proved to be a big disap-pointment."—Pat Fleming, AR; "It has that 'something different' quality and it will satisfy." Robert H. Perkins, KY; "They liked this better than *Destination Moon*; doubled with *Love Happy* to aver-age grosses."—Rene L. Garneau, VT; "Very good adventure-type picture."—A. P. Quesnel, Canada; "This was a big disappointment and certainly not worth a top price in any theater. Customers' comments were unfavorable and did not leave a feeling of being satisfied."—Virgil Anderson, MO.

SAVAGE DRUMS (1951) B&W 70 min. Written by Fenton Earnshaw; Produced and Directed by William Berke. Cast: Sabu, Lita Baron, H.B. Warner, Sid Melton, and Margia Dean.

Tidbits: This was mostly filmed at Baldwin Lake, California. *The Hollywood Reporter* stated that some of the footage was shot in India. This footage was probably lifted from *The Jungle*, another Berke/Lippert film.

Critics: "The story is synthetic and lacks human interest."—*Harrison's Reports*; "Performances throughout are definitely on the clumsy side..."—*Boxoffice*; "Self-conscious dialog and stereotyped situations..."—*Variety*; "...shallow melodrama...unevenly developed..."—*Motion Picture Herald*; "...far-fetched..."—*Hollywood Reporter*.

Exhibitors: "The title is right but the trailer and the picture weren't savage enough for our patrons."—James Wiggs, Jr., NC; "The dance scene in this brought down the house."—Buck Renfro, Jr., AR; "This is the poorest picture shown for months. You'll be sorry if you buy it...I had nothing but kicks from my audience."—Frank Sabin, MT.

SCOTLAND YARD INSPECTOR (British title: **LADY IN THE FOG**) 1952) B&W 82 min. Written by Orville H. Hampton from the 1947 BBC radio serial by Lester Powell; Produced by Anthony Hinds; Directed by Sam Newfield. Cast: Cesar Romero, Lois Maxwell, Bernadette O'Farrell, Geoffrey Keen, and Campbell Singer.

Tidbits: "I had just completed a film in India—*The Jungle*—for Lippert," Cesar Romero recalled, "and I stopped off in London on my way home. I was met at the airport by someone from Hammer who informed me that Lippert had made a deal for me while I was in the air!"[5]

Critics: "...fair crime melodrama."—Steven H. Scheuer; "...very minor, actionful thriller..."—*Product Digest*; "...an exciting story..."—*Hollywood Reporter*.

*THE SECRET PEOPLE (1952) B&W 96 min. Ealing Studios; Written, Produced and Directed by Thorold Dickinson. Cast: Valentina Cortese, Serge Reggiani, Charles Goldner, Audrey Hepburn, and Angela Foulds.

Tidbits: Director Dickenson's attempt to make an art house film, instead of an imitation Hollywood film, met with such hostility from the film critics that it was all but shelved. He was quite pleased with it, and decades later some critics have concluded his film was unfairly treated.

Critics: "It was all such an embarrassing mixture of pretentiousness and naivety I felt ashamed and wanted to look away."—*Daily Herald*; "...a mausoleum of good intentions."—*The Evening Standard*; "...one of the most disappointing efforts to come from Ealing Studios in some time."—*Variety*; "...a narrative link seems to have been left out."—*The Sunday Times*; "...muddled, inadequate and often inaudible..."—*The Observer*; "...the most boring film I have ever seen in my life."—*The Spectator*.

SHADOW MAN (British title: **STREET OF SHADOWS** 1953) B&W 76 min. Produced by William Nassour and William H. Williams; Written and Directed by Richard Vernon based on the novel *The Creaking Chair* by Laurence Mynell. Cast: Cesar Romero, Kay Kendall, Edward Underdown, Victor Maddern, and Simone Silva.
Critics: "...excellent characterizations..."—*Los Angeles Times*; "...mildly diverting..."—*Variety*; "...mildly interesting..."—*Hollywood Reporter*; "...is no better or worse than the average of recent lower-budgeted English whodunits to reach domestic screens."—*Boxoffice*.
Exhibitors: "...a bit slow but a good murder mystery."—James Wiggs, Jr., NC.

*THE SIEGE (Augustina de Aragon 1954) B&W 126 min. (Spain) 66 min. (U.S.) CIFESA; Written by Vicente Escrivia; Directed by Juan de Orduria. Cast: Fernando Aguirre, Valeriano Andres, Manuel Arbo, Maria Asquerino, and Francisco Bernal.

*SILENT RAIDERS Working title: **THREE MILES TO DAWN** (1954) B&W 65 min. L&B Productions; Produced by Earle Lyon; Written and Directed by Richard Bartlett. Cast: Richard Bartlett, Earle Lyon, Jeanette Bordeaux, Earl Hansen, and Robert Knapp.
Tidbits: This movie was based on a WWII operation involving Canada, New Zealand, and Australia known as The Dieppe Raid. Commando troops slipped into France to knock out a German communications center and to pave the way for an assault the following day.

Shot in 16 days with a crew of 45 technicians and 17 actors, it was filmed entirely on location near Malibu Beach for $65,000. "We started at the beach, filmed the landing and worked our way three and a half miles inland to the climax scene of the picture without having to backtrack once," producer Lyon told Vernon Scott of the *Los Angeles Daily News*. Striving for realism, Lyon and his partner, director Richard Bartlett, cast seven veterans of the invasion in their movie. "When we saw what a good picture we had, we decided to go all out on the music. It was worth it." They hired Elmer Bernstein who was one year away from making his mark as a major league composer with his score for *The Man with the Golden Arm* (1955). When Blake Owensmith saw the movie he turned pale. He worked for the Canadian Cooperation Project which was attached to The Breen Office. "It can't be done," he declared. "This picture shows Americans participating in the Dieppe Raid and there were none," he told *Variety*. In lieu of shooting new scenes Lyon and Bartlett made the necessary changes by dubbing new dialog into their film which altered the nationality of the characters. They also changed the lyrics to the song that permeates the movie.

Critics: "...low-wattage film fair..."—*Variety*.

THE SILVER STAR (1955) B&W 73 min. Written by Richard Bartlett and Ian MacDonald; Produced by Richard Bartlett and Earle Lyon; Directed by Richard Bartlett. Cast: Edgar Buchanan, Marie Windsor, Lon Chaney, Richard Bartlett, and Barton MacLane.

Tidbits: Edgar Buchanan had been a dentist in Pasadena who performed at the Pasadena Playhouse in his spare time. A Columbia scout was in the audience one evening, and the studio put Buchanan under contract. He never had a chance to practice dentistry again, but he never forgot his roots. On the first day of production on this film he walked up to Richard Bartlett, raised his lip, looked at his teeth and said: "I think you need a filling here."

Critics: "...depends too much on...a man's philosophy and not enough on action..."—*Variety*; "You could almost expect it when the hero says he's agin 'shootin' and killin.' He avoids them like the plague."— *Los Angeles Times*.

*SIMBA—MARK OF THE MAU MAU (1956) Eastman Color 99 min. Group Film Productions; Written by John V. Baines; Produced by Peter De Sarigny; Directed by Brian Desmond-Hurst. Cast: Dirk Bogarde, Donald Sinden, Virginia McKenna, Basil Sydney, and Marie Ney.

Tidbits: Lippert acquired the U.S. rights to this film for more money than he was used to paying because it had enjoyed some unusually enthusiastic reviews. But the initial engagements in San Francisco, San Diego, Oakland, and Las Vegas were disastrous. Lippert and publicity chief Marty Weiser concluded that the title was keeping people away. So they changed it to *Simba—Mark of the Mau Mau*. The advertising campaign was revised and the film went through the roof in Boston. After that, Lippert had a hit on his hands.

Critics: "...solidly written...excellent performances..."—*Boxoffice*. "One has the feeling that tensions have grown up in a vacuum. The native peoples never express any grievance against white, the implication being that through fear, ignorance and superstition, they have been influenced by a band of terrorists into believing they are a bad thing."—*Monthly Film Bulletin*; "Colonel Blimp is not actively present in the movie, but his shadow hovers over it."—*Saturday Review*; "...overly melodramatic and strained."—*Los Angeles Examiner*; "...a well-made adventure drama..."—*Mirror News*; "...briskly directed...expertly played..."—*Variety*; "...powerful and eloquent..."—*Hollywood Reporter*. "...it is doubtful whether racial tensions should be discussed at all in the form of popular entertainment."—*Financial Times*. "...compassionate and chilling..."—*New York Times*.

Exhibitors: "...this was one of our best second features—very acceptable to our action-mad audience."—Moz Burles, WA; "I had a lot of good comments on this picture and a lot of satisfied customers..."—F.I. Murray, Canada; "...pretty fair picture and well done."—David Pace, NE.

SINS OF JEZEBEL (1954) AnscoColor 75 min. Written by Richard Landau; Produced by Sigmund Neufeld; Directed by Reginald Le Borg. Cast: Paulette Goddard, George Nader, John Hoyt, Eduard Franz, and Margia Dean.

Paulette Goddard and John Shelton from Lippert's grossly underfunded Sins of Jezebel *(1954).*

Tidbits: The cheesy sets were built on a stage at KTTV television studio in Hollywood. Outdoor scenes were filmed in Chatsworth, making the Holy land look more like the Old West. If anyone had done their duty, Bert Shefter's derivative main title should have been replaced with the popular Frankie Laine song, "Jezebel,"

The picture was given the largest cooperative trade press, newspaper and TV campaign in Lippert's history. *Life* magazine carried a four page, two color illustrated tabloid. Five thousand Ansco Film dealers were supplied with window cards in a national tie-up to promote the movie and Ansco color. Other co-op deals included Ceil Chapman dresses and Sally Victor hats. All of the dealers were listed in the larger than usual pressbook which was the first Lippert pressbook in color. There was even a special set of Color-Glow stills.

Critics: "Good audience picture blends religious significance with sex."—*Film Daily*; "Critically, there is not likely to be any applause for the writing, direction or playing..."—*Variety*; "...not particularly outstanding in any respect."—*Citizen News*; "Paulette Goddard does not measure up...to the idea of the voluptuous, fiery, vengeful Jezebel..."—*Los Angeles Times*; "...presents no artistic challenge to *The Robe* or *Samson and Delilah*..."—*Motion Picture Herald*; "The production is not pretentious nor is the writing terribly inspired."—*Los Angeles*

Examiner; "...a none-too-successful effort to film a big biblical spectacle on a beer and skittles budget."—*Toledo Blade*; "...adequate, if slow-paced entertainment with a moral."—*Times Daily*; "...comes close to parodying its dimly scriptural source...As the hypnotic heroine, Miss Goddard fans her eyelashes, swings a bare midriff with pendulum precision and weights crises of religion and state as though a wad of gum were parked behind the royal tiara."—*New York Times*.

Exhibitors: "Although it does not contain any great luxurious scenes, the story makes up for that..."—Yves Legault, Canada; "It was thoroughly enjoyed by the patrons and would be perfect to tie in churches."—Maj. I. Jay Sadow, GA.

SKY HIGH aka **UP AND AT 'EM** (1951) B&W 60 min. Written by Orville H. Hampton; Produced by Sigmund Neufeld; Directed by Sam Newfield. Cast: Sid Melton, Mara Lynn, Sam Flint, Doug Evans, and Margia Dean.

Critics: "...comedy action becomes pretty sad and direction by Samuel Newfield doesn't help."—*Variety*; "...one of the unfunniest comedies of the season."—*Motion Picture Herald*. **Exhibitors**: "Below average."—Parker Parkhurst, MI.

*THE SLASHER (British title: **COSH BOY** aka **THE TOUGH GUY** 1953) B&W 75 min. Angel Productions; Written by Vernon Harris and Lewis Gilbert based on the play "Master Crook" by Bruce Walker; Produced by Daniel M. Angel; Directed by Lewis Gilbert. Cast: James Kenney, Joan Collins, Betty Ann Davis, Robert Ayres, and Hermione Baddeley.

Tidbits: This British import was released without a Production Code certificate.

Critics: "...unrelentingly sordid study of adolescent delinquency in the slums of London."—*Boxoffice*; "...bound to provoke undue controversy wherever it is screened."—*Variety*; "...may or may not be accurate but is completely convincing..."—*Motion Picture Herald*.

SPACEWAYS (1954) B&W 76 min. Written by Paul Tabori and Richard Landau based on a 1942 BBC radio program by Charles Eric Maine; Produced by Michael Carreras; Directed by Terence Fisher. Cast: Howard Duff, Eva Bartok, Andrew Osborn, Anthony Ireland, and Alan Wheatley.

The poster for the Hammer/Lippert co-production Spaceways (1954), a tepid sci-fi programmer to say the least. "This was really lunacy," declared its producer, Michael Carreras, "as the budget was the same as it would have been if it was about two people in bed—a domestic comedy type of thing."

Tidbits: The successful release of *Rocketship X-M* in England provoked Hammer Films to make their own science fiction space opera. Shooting began on November 17, 1952 in the hope of completing it by December 19. But leading lady Eva Bartok needed throat surgery so the schedule had to be extended another month. Cameraman Len Harris recalled that director Terence Fisher wanted some quick and cheap camera effects to indicate the rocket launch. "The only thing I could think of was to free float the camera and let Harry Oakes shake it while I tried to get *something* on film," he recalled. "Elaborate effects, Hammer style! Actually, it worked pretty well and didn't cost a thing."[6]

Critics: "A dull and shoddy affair..."—*Monthly Film Bulletin*; "On the slow side..."—*Motion Picture Exhibitor*; "...a mild, talky and overlengthy melodrama."—*Variety*; "Terence Fisher's megging is over-leisurely..."—*Hollywood Reporter*.

THE STEEL HELMET (1951) B&W 84 min. Written, Produced and Directed by Sam Fuller. Cast: Gene Evans, Steve Brodie, Robert Hutton, James Edwards, and Richard Loo.

Tidbits: There were two reasons why Fuller's edgy proposal for a war movie sounded good to Lippert. As far as Lippert knew, nobody else had a Korean War picture in the works. They would be first. Headline hot! Also, three of the top ten money-makers of 1949 had been war movies—MGM's *Battleground* ($4,550,000 gross), Republic's *Sands of Iwo Jima* ($3,900,000 gross), and 20th Century-Fox's *Twelve O'Clock High* ($3,225,000 gross). The only reservation Lippert had concerned the actor Fuller had hired to play his lead. Who the hell had ever heard of Gene Evans?

Fuller had been looking for a big man with a beard when Gene Evans walked into his office looking for a job. "Fortunately, he had a beard," Fuller told Ezra Goodman from *The Daily News*. "If you look at a man you have an instinct about him. That's what I went by."

Instincts were one thing, but exhibitors liked to have a recognizable name to put on the marquee, even if it was a has-been name. It gave the movie some legitimacy; some respectability. Lippert understood Fuller's concern about the expectations audiences placed on certain actors. With someone like John Wayne or Clark Gable people would expect a typical good guy/bad guy movie about the glory of war. Lippert understood all that well enough. Nevertheless, a name was still important.

In writing his script, Fuller drew on his three-year experience as a rifleman in the First Division of the 16th Infantry during WWII. The Breen Office, which did its level best to keep movies "moral" and free of anything that smacked of reality, was not happy with his script. They were not happy at all because it offended their sensibilities in a number of ways. They didn't like Fuller's negative depiction

Gene Evans, Robert Hutton, Sid Melton, Steve Brodie, Richard Loo, Richard
Monahan (?), and James Edwards are the rag-tag soldiers in Sam Fuller's
The Steel Helmet *(1951).*

of race relations in America. Why was there a need to revive that old business about the Japanese-American citizens being hustled off to internment camps during WWII? Why in blazes did he have to have that conversation about black people having to ride at the back of the bus? Why all of those racial slurs? These were the very things our enemies used as propaganda against us. In a letter to Lippert, the Breen Office urged him to muzzle Fuller on these issues. They also urged him to persuade Fuller not to show the wanton destruction of Buddhist religious icons. They also demanded that Lippert nix the scene where a Korean POW is killed in cold blood by a hot-tempered American soldier, a clear violation of the Geneva Convention. They weren't saying that it never happened; they simply didn't want anybody to know about it.

Lippert had no intention of caving in to their demands, but he thought it would be best if he gave the impression that he would. To that end, he had executive producer William Berke assure the folks at the Breen office that any damage done to the temple would be the result of enemy fire. Also, *if* they retained the scene with the POW, the soldier who shot him would be punished.

They were only a few days away from the start of production when Lippert heard that Larry Parks was being asked to testify before the House on Un-American Activities Committee. Parks had made a name for himself playing Al Jolson in a pair of highly fictionalized Columbia biographies. Lippert knew that if Parks ended up on the blacklist, he would be available for a more than reasonable price.[3] He told Berke to pay Evans off and send him home. At last, he had that "name" for the marquee. Parks wouldn't bring the kind of baggage to the role that some other actor might, which is why Lippert thought (or rather he hoped) that Fuller wouldn't raise any objections.

Lippert was lighting a fresh cigar when Fuller blew into his office like the blast of an atomic bomb. Fuller was outraged that Evans, who was waiting in Lippert's reception room, had been fired and wanted to know what the hell was going on. How could Lippert explain the situation with Fuller screaming at the top of his lungs? After a few heated exchanges, Fuller turned on his heels and left Lippert's office pretty much the way he had entered it. Had it been a scene in a movie, it would have ended with Fuller slamming the door. Instead, it was more like a scene out of one of Fuller's movies, which were always unconventional. He deliberately left the door open so he could be sure Lippert would hear him say to Evans: "Let's get the hell out of here. This place is history!"

It was one thing for Lippert to shout like that when he got hot under the collar—he did it all the time; he liked to "cast a long shadow," as someone once said of him—but, where did Fuller, or any of his employees for that matter, get off talking to *him* like that? Who the devil did Fuller think he was?

Lippert waited until they both had time to cool off before he called Fuller to patch things up. If it was all that important to him to have some "no name" actor nobody had ever heard of play the lead in the picture, then so be it. Fuller was making a mistake; Lippert was sure of that.

Fuller rounded up a couple of dozen film students, dressed them like enemy soldiers, and spent the first day and a half shooting on location in Griffith Park. After that, Fuller and his crew moved to the sound stage where the rest of the film took place. There were two sets—a Korean temple and the observation post on top of it.

Sculptor Yucca Salamunich created a 12-foot high Korean Buddha that figured very prominently in these scenes.

In what can only be described as a childish bit of weenie wagging, Fuller hung a sign on the stage door that read: NO ASSOCIATE PRODUCERS, CO-PRODUCERS, EXECUTIVE PRODUCERS OR ANY PRODUCERS ADMITTED HEREIN. It didn't keep Lippert out when he heard that Fuller was going into overtime on the last day of the shoot. Lippert made it a hard and fast rule that no one was ever allowed to go into overtime, and everyone who ever worked for him knew it. He threw the door open, and in a voice that was loud and clear, told Fuller that his picture was finished. He shut off the power and walked back out.

Fuller had one scene left to shoot, the destruction of the temple, which was the climax of the picture. Without it they had no picture. So he waited until he was sure that Lippert was gone, turned the power back on and finished the scene. In all probability, this is exactly what Lippert expected him to do and, even more to the point, what he wanted him to do. But if Lippert didn't pay lip service to his most sacred rule, then everyone might get the idea he could be pushed around. I could be wrong, but it seems to me that if Lippert really wanted Fuller to take him seriously, he would have waited until everyone had gone home. Then again, maybe I'm giving Lippert too much credit.

After hearing *The Steel Helmet* was doing phenomenal business, an anxious exhibitor in Detroit decided to heavily promote the film with a huge display. He sent one of his employees to National Screen Service to get more advertising material on the film. The exhibitor hastily wrote the title of the film on a note that read: *Stalmet*. The exhibitor became the laughingstock when the employee mistakenly promoted *Hamlet* instead.

Critics: "...a grim, hard-hitting tale that is excellently told."—*Variety*; "...as timely as today's front line dispatches, and is more informative..."—*Motion Picture Daily*; "Unfortunately, the texture of this picture, apparent in the staging and sets, is patently artificial."—*New York Times*; "It is more dynamic than a documentary, more authentic than 99 per cent of the fiction films founded on fact, and it is more, rather than less, powerfully effective because its cast contains no overwhelming stars to distract or distort the script or tip off its ending."—*Motion Picture Herald*; "...sets the mark at which Hollywood will be shooting for a long time to come."—*Los Angeles Times*.

Exhibitors: "This is a very timely picture and well received by our patrons. I seldom play return engagements but this did a splendid job for us both times."—H. H. Love, AR; "Another cheaply made picture, with high priced terms..."—Pat Fleming, AR; "We were proud to play this wonderful picture...Give it your best playing time."—Buck Renfro, Jr., AR; "If you have good results with war picture, by all means don't fail to book this one."—Harland Rankin, Canada; "It played to good houses with *Samson and Delilah* against us."—Dave S. Klein, Africa; "...it did record breaking business for me all three days...I was lucky enough to rent it first run, at a very fair price which Lippert always gives."—Paul Wood, FL; "This is a 'blood and guts' picture so be sure to play a comedy to help it out."—C. L. Strickland, GA; "This was an ambitious undertaking for Lippert but too bloody for the ladies."—Audrey Thompson, AR; "It drew above average due to intense interest in the Korean War."—D. W. Trisko, AZ; "We outgrossed *Battleground* on this picture."—L. Brazil, Jr., AR; "Maybe you'll have luck with it. I sure didn't."—Frank E. Sabin, MT.

STOLEN FACE (1952) B&W 72 min. Written by Martin Berkeley and Richard Landau; Produced by Anthony Hinds; Directed by Terence Fisher. Cast: Paul Henreid, Lizabeth Scott, Mary MacKenzie, Andrew Morell, and John Wood.

Tidbits: This was Hammer's biggest production at the time. It opened at the Plaza, a prestigious West End cinema which had never shown a Hammer film before. The stars of the film were Lizabeth Scott, on loan from producer Hal Wallis, and Paul Henreid, one of the stars of the classic *Casablanca* (1942). Henreid had become persona non grata for protesting the jailing of people who refused to testify before HUAC. Scott received $25,000 for her services. Henreid was paid $20,000 plus 15 percent of the net profit. As one might have predicted, according to the statements he received, the film never went into profit.

As a rule Lippert made two hundred copies of each of his films at a cost of $75 per print. He had to more than double that amount to accommodate the demand for *The Steel Helmet*, *Little Big Horn*, and *Stolen Face*. So how could it not have gone into profit?

Paul Henreid and Lizabeth Scott from the film noir melodrama Stolen Face *(1952).*

Henreid's agent, Ingo Preminger, smelled a rat. After looking at a list of the deductions charged against the film he cried foul, and for eight years he tried to get the monies owed to his client. Exhausted, he turned the matter over to the legal firm of Kaplan-Livingston, Goodman and Berkowitz. They told Lippert to pay Henreid $2,087.82 and to be quick about it because "the matter has dragged on for some time and the questions at issue seem quite clear."

Kaplan-Livingston, Goodman and Berkowitz didn't know who they were dealing with. After a lot of jaw-flapping, Lippert agreed to pay Henreid a lesser amount, $550, but Henreid had to sign away his profit participation to get it.

Critics: "The pacing is laborious."—*Variety*; "...virtually ruined by mallet-handed scripting and direction..."—*Boxoffice*; "...unconvincing and unpleasant."—*Harrison's Reports*; "...it takes some straining of the credulity to take it all in."—*Los Angeles Examiner*; "...it rarely becomes either believable or interesting."—*Hollywood Reporter*; "... more saleable than satisfying..."—*Motion Picture Herald*.

Exhibitors: "A nice little feature that was well-liked."—Harold Bell, Canada.

STOP THAT CAB (TV titles: **THE STREET IS MY BEAT, ON FOUR WHEELS,** and **FOLLOW THAT CAB** 1951) B&W 58 min. Written by Walter Abbott and Louella MacFarlane; Produced by Abrasha Haimson; Directed by Eugenio de Lignoro. Cast: Sid Melton, Iris Adrian, Marjorie Lord, Tom Neal, and Greg McClure.

Tidbits: Abrasha Haimson made two half hour comedies starring Sid Melton for a proposed TV series called *Hey, Taxi!* When Haimson was unable to sell his series to television, he sold the two pilots to Lippert. At Lippert's request, Sid Melton wrote fifteen minutes worth of additional material to bridge the two films. His payment was 10 percent of the net profits. Lippert put $27,000 into making a feature out of the thing and released it as *Stop That Cab*. The Screen Actors Guild cried foul. Haimson told the actors they were working on a TV pilot, which was why they had agreed to work for Guild for minimum wage. Though he felt it was Haimson's problem, Lippert gave SAG $1,330 to settle the matter.

Critics: "...misses its mark by the widest possible margin."—*Variety*; "...as lacking in professional touch as any feature to come out of Hollywood in a long time."—*Hollywood Reporter*.

*STRONGHOLD (1951) B&W 72 min. Written by Wells Root; Produced by Olallo Rubio Gandara; Directed by Steve Sekely. Cast: Veronica Lake, Zachary Scott, Arturo DeCórdova, Irene Ajay, and Alfonso Bedoya.

Tidbits: Veronica Lake pretty much summed up this US-Mexican co-production in two short words. She called it "a dog."

Critics: "...the actors go through their parts listlessly..."---*Harrison's Reports*; "Boasting some few action scenes, the film does little else to justify a thin plot."—*Hollywood Reporter*; "Developed at a slow pace with an overload of dialog..."—*Motion Picture Herald*; "...an overload of dialog and lack of suspense."—*Variety*.

Exhibitors: "Where you figure on playing this—don't. Walkouts a-plenty."—Dan Guest, TX.

Above: Jeff Corey, Phyllis Coates, George Reeves, and Walter Reed. Below:
Superman (George Reeves) needs to pull up his pants a little if he wants
Luke Benson (Jeff Corey) and his mob to take him seriously in Superman and
the Mole Men *(1951).*

SUPERMAN AND THE MOLE MEN (1951) B&W 58 min. Written by
Richard Fielding (Robert Maxwell and Whitney Ellsworth) based
on characters created by Jerry Siegel and Joe Schuster; Produced
by Robert Maxwell and Barney A. Sarecky; Directed by Lee
Sholem. Cast: George Reeves, Phyllis Coates, Jeff Corey, Walter
Reed, and J. Farrell MacDonald.
Tidbits: Whitney Ellsworth, the editorial director for National
Comics, wrote the outline and co-wrote the screenplay for this

film, using the pseudonym Richard Fielding. In their scenario reporters Clark Kent and Lois Lane come to the little town of Silsby to do a story on the world's deepest oil well. Strange little creatures emerge from the well and cause quite a panic. Everyone assumes they're evil and Superman has to stop a mob from killing them. After the picture was completed, Lippert's production supervisor, Betty Sinclair, went to work on the *Superman* TV series.
Critics: "Lee Sholem's direction keeps the Richard Fielding script running at a clicko pace."—*Variety*.

TALES OF ROBIN HOOD (1951) B&W 62 min. Written by Le Roy H. Zehren; Produced by Hal Roach, Jr.; Directed by James Tinling. Cast: Robert Clarke, Mary Hatcher, Paul Cavanagh, Whit Bissell, and Margia Dean.
Tidbits: "Looking back now, it's almost amazing what we were able to do," Robert Clarke said. "There was a lot of action in *Tales of Robin Hood*, and it's hard to get that amount of action on film in just four days."[8]
Critics: "...well-produced...boasts several bright performances."—*Variety*.

THE TALL TEXAN (1953) B&W 81 min. Written by Samuel Roeca and Elizabeth Reinhardt; Produced by T. C. Woods; Directed by Elmo Williams. Cast: Lloyd Bridges, Marie Windsor, Lee J. Cobb, Luther Adler, and Syd Saylor.
Tidbits: Having been a film editor for years, Elmo Williams wanted to direct and Lippert gave him his chance. "He was always looking for new talent that worked cheap," Williams said. Lippert gave him $102,000 and eight days to make a picture. If he could pull it off he'd get fifty percent of the profits.

Williams went to the small ranching community of Deming, New Mexico to scout locations. His brother, Skeeter, once co-owned a meat packing plant there. Thanks to the generosity of an old-time cattleman named Edgar May, Williams had access to cowboys, horses, food, and lodging at May's Spanish Stirrup Ranch. The cowboys worked for beer and beans but Williams had to pay for the use of the horses.

Williams knew he needed good actors who worked cheap to bring his film to life so he took a page out of Lippert's book and hired actors who were under the watchful eye of HUAC. Lloyd Bridges,

Marie Windsor and Lloyd Bridges from The Tall Texan *(1953).*

Lee J. Cobb, and Luther Adler were known liberals, and the three of them were represented by the same agent. The agent gave Williams a package deal and threw Marie Windsor into the bargain for good measure.

Meanwhile, one of Lippert's theater managers, Frank Woods, asked Lippert for a raise. Rather than give it to him, Lippert told him that he could produce the picture. Believing he knew what audiences wanted to see, and unbeknownst to anyone, Woods rewrote the script and gave it to the actors as they boarded the plane to New Mexico. As soon as they arrived, Windsor told Williams they wanted out. The script was nothing like the story he had told them. Williams begged them to reconsider; however, it was his wife who convinced them to stay, but it was on the condition that Elizabeth Reinhardt was allowed to rewrite the dialog. Williams phoned Lippert and told him he had better get Reinhardt there on the double, and whatever she cost, it had better not come out of his budget since his idiot producer had been the one to screw up everything.

In an interview with Mike Fitzgerald Marie Windsor said: "...the dust was so fine that when we drove out to location, we'd be covered in this fine dust, even if the windows were rolled up tight."

Each day Bill Magginetti drove the dailies to the airport in El Paso so the film could be flown to Los Angeles, where it was processed by Consolidated Lab. On the last day of the shoot he had all of the equipment, save one camera, shipped back to Hollywood to save a day's rental, which meant the film would come in on budget. Williams begged Lippert to let him keep some of the equipment so that he could shoot the final scene of the movie the way he had envisioned it. Lippert wouldn't budge and Williams cracked under the strain. He slid down the side of the phone booth and started to cry. "Now, listen, get hold of yourself," Lippert told him. "I can tell your upset. You've got a vision of an ending that you think I'm ruining. Tell you what. You remember Red River? It had a hell of an ending. It was simple. Just give me a tag like that and I'll be happy."[9]

One afternoon, as Lee Cobb was rehearsing a scene, one of the horses walked past him and let loose with a fart. "Even the horses are critics," Cobb remarked.

Critics: "Elmo Williams' direction is heavy-handed."—*Boxoffice*; "...the story is weak and the characters unpleasant."—*Harrison's Reports*; "On the basis of the poorly-developed script, the performances...have little credence"—*Variety*; "...does not lack for excitement."—*Los Angeles Examiner*; "...story lacks that final punch..."—*Hollywood Reporter*; "All of the performances are a cut above their material..."—*Newsweek*; "...this little horse opera amounts to nothing more than a feeble, contrived conversation piece on sun-baked rocks, lacking both the shoot-'em-up temp it pretends to scorn and the novelty it so pitifully tries to be."—*New York Times*.

Exhibitors: "I'm happy to report on this film...because it's from a company that has been extremely nice to me (and helpful) and whose product is improving all the time...All comments were good."—J.H. Hamilton, MS; "Better than average draw here."— L. Brazil, Jr., AR; "...there isn't enough action to keep the kids from getting restless, but it was good entertainment for adults... Business was good."—L. Hutchins, AR; "A really good little, inexpensive western. It has a story that is different from the average of its type. Doubled with *Masterminds* to round out a pretty good bill. A little shooting and a little comedy that were way above average."— Fred E. Tabor, CA.

*TERROR SHIP (British title: **DANGEROUS VOYAGE** 1954) B&W 72 min. Merton Park Studios; Written by Julian Ward; Produced by William H. Williams; Directed by Vernon Sewell. Cast: William Lundigan, Naomi Chance, Vincent Ball, John Warwick, and Jean Lodge.
Critics: "Average mystery film..."—*Monthly Film Bulletin*; "Above average..."—*The Cinema*.

TERROR STREET (British title: **36 HOURS** (1953) B&W 84 min. Written by Steve Fisher based on his novel; Produced by Anthony Hinds; Directed by Montgomery Tully. Cast: Dan Duryea, Elsy Albin, Ann Gudron, Eric Pohlmann and John Chandos.
Critics: "...leans rather toward the implausible."—*Boxoffice*; "...loses much of its interest simply because Dan Duryea has not the look of a sympathetic character..."—*Monthly Film Bulletin*; "Duryea manages to bolster up the show with good histrionics but gets little help from the others."—*Variety*; "...unevenly made..."—*Hollywood Reporter*; "...a well-made suspense story."—*Motion Picture Herald*.

THEY WERE SO YOUNG (1954) B&W 80 min. Written by Felix Lutzkendorf, Kurt Neumann, Dalton Trumbo (no credit) and Michael Wilson (no credit) based on an outline by Jacques Companeez; Produced and Directed by Kurt Neumann. Cast: Scott Brady, Johanna Matz (debut), Raymond Burr, Ingrid Stenn and Gisela Fakelday.
Tidbits: This was a US-German co-production with Corona-Film Productions, G.M.B.H., and Lippert in which Lippert got the ownership and most of the distribution rights. He also received a 20 percent commission for handling and distributing the picture.
   The working titles of this movie about white slavery, shot on location in Rome, Italy and Germany, were *Mannequins for Rio, Beautiful and the Damned, Mannequins, Party Girls for Sale,* and *Violated.* It was incorrectly listed in the trades as a romantic drama. Two versions were produced: one in English and one in German. Since the subject of white slavery was not permitted by the Production Code, the screenplay was rejected, and the film was released without a PCA certificate. New footage was later added to the film with Ian MacDonald explaining that Coltos (the character played by Raymond Burr) was a corrupt tycoon. This shifted

the focus from white slavery to racketeering as far as the PCA was concerned, and the film was awarded a certificate on May 6, 1955.
Critics: "...enlightening, engrossing and exciting drama."–
Boxoffice; "Adult entertainment with a special femme appeal."–*Film Daily*; "It is sexy all the way through...a high-class white slave picture!"–*Harrison's Reports*; "...picture deals with a very sensational theme, while avoiding anything censorable!"–*Hollywood Reporter*; "It's a drab and distressing story, and while it does not glamorize vice it is...questionable subject matter for theatrical exhibition."–*Motion Picture Herald*; "Its director and producer have combined good taste with the nominal excitement."–*Los Angeles Times*; "It's exploitable fare, and okay entertainment to boot."–*Variety*.

THREE DESPERATE MEN (Working titles: **THE DALTON'S LAST RAID** aka **THREE OUTLAWS** 1951) B&W 69 min. Written by Orville H. Hampton; Produced by Sigmund Neufeld; Directed by Sam Newfield. Cast: Preston Foster, Virginia Grey, Jim Davis, Ross Latimer (Kim Spalding), and William Haade.
Critics: "...standard..."–*Variety*; "...standard western..."–*Motion Picture Herald*; "The film's weakness lies in scripting..."–*Boxoffice*.
Exhibitors: "Three desperate men were my assistant, my operator and myself. Desperate about what to do to try to bring them in to see this very mediocre western."–Dave S. Klein, Africa; "Not a big one but a good picture. I made a little money on it."–E. M. Frieburger, OK; "Happy to report good business on this fast-moving action western. Everyone seemed satisfied."–I. Epstein, NJ; "Good picture and I had two good nights."–R. B. Kerbow, TX.

*THUNDER OVER SANGOLAND (1955) B&W 73 min. Arrow Productions Inc.; Written by Sherman L. Lowe; Produced by Rudolph C. Flothow; Directed by Sam Newfield. Cast: Jon Hall, Ray Montgomery, Marjorie Lord, House Peters, Jr., and Myron Healey.
Exhibitors: "From the way the boxoffice looked, everybody left town and even took their dogs with them."–Joe Meyer, PA.

THUNDER PASS (1954) B&W 76 min. William Broidy Productions. Written by Fred Eggers and Tom Hubbard; Produced by A. Robert Nunes; Directed by Frank MacDonald. Cast: Dane Clark, Dorothy Patrick, Andy Devine, Mary Ellen Kay, and Raymond Burr.

Critics: "...entertainment quotient isn't high enough to justify anything more than lukewarm reactions."—*Boxoffice*; "...routine western..."—*Hollywood Reporter*; "...78 minutes crammed with boredom."—*Variety*.

TOUGH ASSIGNMENT (1949) B&W 64 min. Written by Milton Lubin; Produced by Carl K. Hittleman; Directed by William Beaudine. Cast: Don Barry, Marjorie Steele, Steve Brodie, Marc Lawrence, and Iris Adrian.

Tidbits: Used as a selling point for this movie was the fact that it was shot with the new Garutso lens "for 3-Dimensional effect." This "new" extreme wide angle lens, in use since the 1930s, could be used with a large assortment of diopter filters to keep both the foreground and the background in perfect focus.

Critics: "Plot generates a modicum of interest but pace is not as fast as it should have been..."—*Variety*; "...tense suspense throughout."—*Harrison's Reports*; "The picture is ably made for the boxoffice level it seeks."—*Motion Picture Herald*; "...William Beaudine's direction...is a little ragged around the edges... probably attributable to [the producer's] efforts to make the picture look more substantially mounted than the bankroll provided."—*Boxoffice*.

Exhibitors: "It will take nine cartoons and two extra pictures to hold this thing up."—J. F. Hall, NM.

TRAIN TO TOMBSTONE (1950) B&W 56 min. Written by Orville H. Hampton (debut) and Victor West; Produced and Directed by William Berke. Cast: Don Barry, Robert Lowery, Wally Vernon, Tom Neal, and Judith Allen.

Tidbits: In the climax of this picture, the train is attacked by "blood-thirsty savages." Through the windows of the train, projected on a process screen, we see the Indians on horseback. Either these scenes were taken from some other movie, or the person who shot them hadn't the faintest idea what he was doing since the camera is placed too high, giving the impression that the train must be floating in the air. If that were not bad enough, the same scenes are shown over and over again; it is truly a terrible movie.

Critics: "...it's a long, talk-packed while before the first bullet is fired, so long that the danger doesn't seem very real by the time it arrives."—*Motion Picture Herald*; "...a poor excuse for a western."—*Variety*.

Exhibitors: "Anyone who thinks a picture like this is entertainment should have their heads examined. Practically 90% of the picture deals with a train ride to Tombstone, which destination is never reached. Many walkouts."—Pat Fleming, AR; "...it has most of the usual action and should please your 'dyed-in-the-wool' oat fans."—Robert H. Perkins, KY.

*TROMBA, THE TIGER MAN (1952) B&W 61 min. Titanus; Written by Helmut Weiss and Elisabeth Zimmermann; Directed by Helmut Weiss. Cast: Rene Deltgen, Angelika Haulf, Gustav Knurth, Hildre Wesner, and Grethe Weiser.

Critics: "...cliché-ridden screenplay and...inexpert direction..."—*Boxoffice*; "The English dubbing is poor, the editing bad and the story slow and talky."—*Hollywood Reporter*; "The original picture, before cutting, evidently had quite a few hot amatory sequences, but these obvious exploitation pegs have been sliced for the domestic market."—*Variety*.

Exhibitors: "Strictly junk."—Lloyd Hutchins, AR.

*TWILIGHT WOMEN (British title: **WOMEN OF TWILIGHT** aka **ANOTHER CHANCE** 1952) B&W 89 min. Angel Productions; Written by Anatole de Grumwald based on a play by Sylvia Ryan; Produced by Daniel M. Angel; Directed by Gordon Parry. Cast: Freda Jackson, Rene Ray, Lois Maxwell, Joan Dowling, and Dora Bryan.

Critics: "...isn't as naughty as tag and theme indicate."—*Boxoffice*; "...a frankly sordid story with no punches pulled."—*Variety*; "...overly melodramatic."—*Los Angeles Daily News*; "...a taut little drama..."—*Hollywood Reporter*; "...deals earnestly and bluntly with the subject of the unwed mother and the problems that surround her."—*Motion Picture Herald*.

*UNDERCOVER AGENT aka **COUNTERSPY** (1953) B&W 69 min. Merton Park Studios; Written by Guy Elmes and Gaston Lazare from the short story "Criss Cross Code" by Julian Symons; Produced by William H. Williams; Directed by Vernon Sewell. Cast: Dermot Walsh, Hazel Court, Hermione Baddeley, James Vivian, and Archie Duncan.

Critics: "...overall effect is unremarkable."—*Motion Picture Herald*; "So mysterious is this mystery that spectators will never know what it was all about. There is virtually nothing in the picture to recommend it to American audiences..."—*Boxoffice*; "...a nifty little programmer..."—*Variety*; "...sports lots of suspense, plenty of novelty and some excellent acting."—*The Independent Film Journal*; "...a mild, British-made cloak and dagger meller..."—*Hollywood Reporter*.

THE UNHOLY FOUR (British title: **THE STRANGER CAME HOME** 1954) B&W 80 min. Written and Produced by Michael Carreras based on George Sanders' novel; Directed by Terence Fisher. Cast: William Sylvester, Paulette Goddard (final film), Patrick Holt, Paul Carpenter, and Alvys Maben.
Critics: "...a competent job of screen story-telling..."—*Hollywood Reporter*; "...stacks up as a routine whodunit, slow-moving and heavy on plot."—*Variety*; "A few more fly-by-nights like this...and the still-shapely Miss Goddard may find herself collecting the pieces of her career."—*New York Times*; "By and large, the picture measures up snugly to the promise of its billing."—*Motion Picture Herald*.

*****UNKNOWN WORLD** (1951) B&W 74 min. J.R. Rabin-I.A. Block Productions; Written by Millard Kaufman; Produced by Jack Rabin, Irving Block and, some sources say, Philip Yordan; Directed by Terrell O. Morse. Cast: Victor Kilian (not billed because he was on the blacklist), Marilyn Nash, Bruce Kellogg, Otto Waldis, and Jim Bannon.
Tidbits: Producers Jack Rabin Irving Block told the trade magazines that they were making an outer space movie called *Night Without Stars*. Nothing more was said about the story or the setting, and everyone connected with this film about a journey to the center of the Earth was sworn to secrecy for fear that some other enterprising, low-budget producer would beat them to the punch. The film's leading lady, Marilyn Nash, told Tom Weaver: "I couldn't imagine how they became producers. I just thought that they didn't know what they were doing." Having worked with Charles Chaplin, Nash didn't realize that low budget films didn't allow for endless retakes. The fact of the matter is Rabin and Block knew exactly what they were doing.

William Sylvester and Paulette Goddard in the murder mystery The Unholy Four *(1954).*

"I spent only $500 on sets," Rabin said. "The rest were paintings."[10]

Most of the movie was shot in Bronson Canyon. Director Terry Morse supervised the editing at the Eagle Lion Studios where Rabin and Block were headquartered. When the film opened in Los Angeles, Nash was there. "As for the movie itself," she said, "it drags at the beginning. Then it finally picks up a little, about halfway through it, when the action starts. *Then* it becomes interesting. But before then, it's *nothing*—the beginning is a bloody bore!"

Some sources claim that Nash's husband, Phillip Yordan, had some money invested in the film which would explain her being cast in it.

Critics: "It is a routine set-up combining a contrived story, footage filmed in Carlsbad Caverns, and miniature shots."—*Variety*; "...unusually childish piece of science fiction..."—*Monthly Film Bulletin*; "Nothing about it rings true..."—*Hollywood Reporter*; "...great ingenuity has been employed in presenting the story!"—*Harrison's Reports*; "...spectacularly staged..."—*Los Angeles Examiner*; "...bogs down to a repetitious, boring pace..."—*Boxoffice*; "A sieve has fewer holes than the logic it offers..." *Citizen News*; "...impressively exciting..."—*Los Angeles Times*; "...the premise and the equipment are more credible than most..."—*Motion Picture Herald*.

Jim Banion, Marilyn Nash, Otto Waldis, Bruce Kellogg, and Victor Kilian (who didn't get screen credit because he was on the blacklist) take a long and tedious journey to the Unknown World (1951).

Exhibitors: "...in a small town you'll receive more favorable comments on this than on the Academy Award winner."—Ken Christianson, ND; "Doubled with *Fangs of the Wild* for, ugh, no business like show business."—Lew Bray Jr., TX; "This played TV but still made a little money on it...Buy it cheap and play it up."—Joe Meyer, CA.

*VALLEY OF THE EAGLES (1951) B&W 83 min. J. Arthur Rank; Produced by Nat A. Bronstein; Written and Directed by Terence Young. Cast: Jack Warner, Nadia Gray, John McCallum, Anthony Dawson, and Mary Laura Wood.
Tidbits: 35-year-old director Terence Young had heard that there were Laplanders who still hunted wolves with eagles, following a tradition handed down from their Siberian ancestors. Young and someone from J. Arthur Rank organized an expedition from London to the streets of Stockholm to the mountain village of Nystuen, 300 miles from the Arctic Circle. Young fashioned his script so that more than half of it was devoted to a long pursuit over the frozen tundra of the little-known icy region of Lapland. Eight weeks were spent on location. One week alone was spent on

a sequence in which the "eagle men" save the protagonists from converging wolf packs.

Lippert bought the rights to the film when it was still nothing more than a title on a Rank trade press product announcement. The film sat in his office for four days before he looked at it, then he spent the next ten nights screening it for his friends and local exhibitors. As with *The Steel Helmet* and *For Men Only*, he spent $3,000 to bombard seven local Los Angeles TV channels with one-minute trailers on the opening day of this movie, a promotion pitch devised by Marty Weiser, Lippert's advertising chief.

Critics: "...novel...exciting entertainment..."—*Boxoffice*; "...top enter-tainment."—*Los Angeles Daily News*; "...a science-adventure film that adults can enjoy wholeheartedly."—*Los Angeles Examiner*; "...one of the most off-beat films ever made!"—*Citizen News*; "...splen-didly-made film combining the best elements of natural history and melodrama."—*Motion Picture Herald*; "Not since *Brief Encounter* has effortless skill made so little into so much."—*Films in Review*.

Exhibitors: "Some customers will leave with a 'what-was-that-all-about' expression but the majority will okay it heartily."—Frank Sabin, MT; "Anyone who can't find enough selling angles in this one to do some old fashioned business is really having troubles."—Bob Walker, CO; "This pleased most of our patrons."—James Wiggs, Jr., NC.

VARIETIES ON PARADE (1951) B&W 54 min. Written, Produced and Directed by Ron Ormond. Cast: Jackie Coogan, Eddie Carr, Tom Neal, Eddie Dean, and Iris Adrian.
Critics: "...best suited for the nabe houses."—*Variety*; "...show is more 'family time' than big time."—*Hollywood Reporter*.

***WE WANT A CHILD** (1953) B&W 97 min. ASA Film; Written by Leck Fischer; Produced by Henning Karmark and Preben Philipsen; Directed by Alice O'Fredericks and Lau Lauritzen Jr. Cast: Maria Garland, Preben Lerdorff Rye, Grethe Thordahl, Ruth Brejnholm, and Jorgan Reenberg.
Tidbits: This picture was released in Denmark in 1949 and was one of the biggest grossing films in Europe. Lippert bought the U.S. distribution rights from Sol Lesser.

WEST OF THE BRAZOS (TV title: **RANGELAND EMPIRE** 1950) B&W 58 min. Written by Ron Ormond and Maurice Tombragel from a story by Forbes Parkhill; Produced by Ron Ormond; Directed by Thomas Carr. Cast: Jimmy Ellison, Russell Hayden, Betty (Julie) Adams, Raymond Hatton, and Fuzzy Knight.
Critics: "...for houses which specialize in such fare..."– *Boxoffice*; "[It] contains ample action and better-than-average acting."–*Variety*.
Exhibitors: "This is my first of this series and it went over well."– Ralph Raspa, VA.

WESTERN PACIFIC AGENT (1950) B&W 64 min. Written by Fred Myton; Produced by Sigmund Neufeld; Directed by Sam Newfield. Cast: Kent Taylor, Sheila Ryan, Robert Lowery, Mickey Knox, and Morris Carnovsky.
Tidbits: This picture was made in 6 days.
Critics: "...one of the all time best Bs ever offered by the ambitious Lippert organization."–*Boxoffice*; "...one of the best of its kind in many months..."–*Motion Picture Herald*; "Sparked by a fine performance by Mickey Knox..."–*Variety*; "...realistic and suspenseful..."–*Hollywood Reporter*; "Fast moving drama..."–*The Film Daily*; "...skillfully acted, tightly written and smooth directed..."– *Independent Film Journal*.
Exhibitors: "This is a pretty fair murder picture that failed to meet expenses because of the local fair."–Ralph Raspa, WV.

WHITE FIRE aka **THREE STEPS TO THE GALLOWS** (1953) B&W 62 min. Written by Paul Erickson; Produced by Robert S. Baker and Monty Berman; Directed by John Gilling. Cast: Scott Brady, Mary Castle, Gabrielle Brune, Ferdy Mayne, and Colin Topley.
Critics: "Production-wise, the picture can boast nary a bow."– *Boxoffice*; "Plot line becomes so involved it would take more than a Scotland Yard inspector...to unravel it."–*Variety*; "...ludicrous in its complete absence of logic."–*Motion Picture Herald*; "...it becomes hard to sift the accumulating evidence."–*New York Times*.

*THE WHITE GODDESS (1953) B&W 73 min. Arrow Productions Inc.; Written by Sherman L. Lowe and Eric Taylor; Produced by Rudolph Flothow; Directed by Wallace Fox. Cast: Jon Hall, Ray Montgomery, Ludwig Stossell, James Fairfax, and Milicent Patrick.
Tidbits: The movie's only point of interest is the appearance of Milicent Patrick in the cast, the woman who designed the Creature from the Black Lagoon.
Critics: "The usual stock shots of jungle flora and fauna are integrated in the footage, none of which is overwhelmingly original."—*Motion Picture Herald*.
Exhibitors: "Jungle films have done well at our boxoffice before but we lost money on this. Film is poor."—James H. Hamilton, MS.

WINGS OF DANGER (British Title: **DEAD ON COURSE** 1952) B&W 73 min. Written by John Gilling based on the novel by Mansell Black; Produced by Anthony Hinds; Directed by Terence Fisher. Cast: Zachary Scott, Robert Beatty, Kay Kendall, and Naomi Chance.
Tidbits: This was the second co-production between Hammer and Lippert. It starred Zachary Scott as a man who is trying to clear the name of his dead friend. Later, Scott discovers his friend faked his own death. It began shooting in September of 1951 in the seaside village of Rye with Lippert's chief supervisor, Jack Leewood, on hand to have a look at Hammer's production techniques. Lippert extended an invitation to producer Anthony Hinds (the son of Will Hinds) to come to America to observe American studio techniques, which he did.

Wings of Danger was double billed with Lippert's *FBI Girl* (1951) in the U.K. and did quite well at the boxoffice.
Critics: "Conventional in treatment and characterization but competently made."—*Today's Cinema*; "Uninspired, uninteresting plot ingredients hamper this weak British entry."—*Variety*; "...leaves the spectator as confused as the scripter apparently was..."—*Hollywood Reporter*.

YES SIR, MR. BONES (1951) B&W 54 min. Written, Produced and Directed by Ron Ormond. Cast: Cotton Watts, Chick Watts, Slim Williams, Ches Davis, and Scatman Crothers (debut).
Critics: "...a cut above the formula musicals of its type..."—*Boxoffice*; "...fails to take advantage of the subject."—*Hollywood Reporter*; "...a nice tribute to the by-gone days of the minstrel man."—*Motion Picture Herald*; "...Ormond has done an acceptable budget job."—*Variety*.
Exhibitors: "...there is not a thing wrong if you have a trade old enough to remember black-face minstrel shows. I am that old and got a kick out of it. However, the take was not too great."—Edwin A. Falk, OK.

Notes:

1: Muller, Eddie *Dark City Dames*, Harper Collins Publishers, Inc., New York, NY 2002, page 54.
2: *Boxoffice*, October 14, 1950, page 59.
3. Aaker, Everett *George Raft, The Films*, McFarland and Company, Jefferson, NC. 2013, page 154.
4. Johnson, Tom and Deborah Del Vecchio *Hammer Films, An Exhaustive Filmography*, McFarland and Company, N.C. 1996, page 91.
5. Ibid pages 73-74.
6. Ibid page 83.
7. When Parks admitted that he had been a member of the Party, his career was all but dead and he was forever tagged as the guy who played Al Jolson. The joke around Hollywood was that when Jolson died, they buried Larry Parks by mistake.
8. Clarke, Robert and Tom Weaver, *Robert Clarke, To "B" or Not to "B," A film Actor's Odyssey*, Midnight Marquee Press, Charleston, S.C. 1996, page 89.
9. Williams, Elmo *Elmo Williams*, McFarland and Co. Jefferson, N.C. 2006, page 96.
10. *Spokane Daily Chronicle*, March 24, 1951, page 15.

UNITED ARTISTS

THE CREEPING UNKNOWN (British Title: **THE QUATERMASS XPERIMENT** 1956) B&W (U.K) 82 min. (U.S.) 78 min. Written by Val Guest and Richard Landau, based on the 1953 BBC serial by Nigel Kneale; Produced by Anthony Hinds; Directed by Val Guest. Cast: Brian Donlevy, Jack Warner, Margia Dean, Richard Wordsworth, and David King Wood.

Richard Wordsworth has been infected by The Creeping Unknown (1956) in one of the best of the 1950s sci-fi thrillers.

Poster for Hammer's sci-fi classic The Creeping Unknown.

Tidbits: Lippert had been working on this deal since 1954, about the time he announced he was relinquishing his post as president of Lippert Pictures, Inc. At that time, the picture was called *Shock!* Lippert wanted to add another exclamation point to the title. He was the one who supplied Hammer with actor Brian Donlevy and screenwriter Richard Landau. Director Val Guest explained Landau's contribution to the project to Tom Weaver. "Exactly what

Dick Landau did was this: As we were working for the American market, when I had done my script, they would pass it to Dick and say, 'If there's anything you want to Americanize, do it.' So if I had put got, he would put gotten." Lippert also insisted that Hammer use Margia Dean. "She was a sweet girl, but she couldn't act!" Guest remarked.

Filming began on October 18, 1954. As most horror films in England received an "X-certificate", which meant that only adults could see it, they called the picture *The Quatermass Xperiment* to emphasize the "X" quality of the picture. It premiered the following year at the London Pavilion. Since no one in America was familiar with the Quatermass character, Lippert changed the title to *The Creeping Unknown*. Having divested himself of his company, Lippert shopped the film around to the various studios and finally sold it to United Artists for $125,000. It opened in U.S. theaters in June 1956 as a second feature to *The Black Sleep*, which it easily eclipsed. A nine-year old boy died of a ruptured artery during a showing of the film in Illinois, the only known case of someone dying of fright while watching a movie.

In his book, *Keep Watching the Skies*, author Bill Warren called *The Creeping Unknown* "an intelligent, taut and well-directed thriller" that's both "scary and exciting," and I agree.
Critics: "...an excellent programmer for fans who like science fiction, adventure, mystery and horror..."—*Boxoffice*; "Despite its obvious horror angles, production is crammed with incident and suspense."—*Variety*; "It remains very horrid and not quite coherent."—*Daily Telegraph*; "...never gets quite so unwholesome as to call for restriction to adult viewing but it might give the kiddies bad dreams."—*Motion Picture Herald*; "...a narrative style that quite neatly combines the horrific and the factual."—*The Manchester Guardian*; "...one of the best essays in science fiction to date."—*Today's Cinema*; "...a real chiller thriller but not for the kids."—*Daily Mirror*; "...exciting but distinctly nauseating."—*The Sunday Times*; "This is the best and nastiest horror film I have seen since the war."—*News Chronicle*; "...better than either *War of the Worlds* or *Them!*"—*New Statesman*; "...82 minutes of sick-making twaddle."—*Reynolds News*.
Exhibitors: "If your crowd likes horror, this is it...it did good business."—Terry Axley, AK.

ASSOCIATED FILM RELEASING CORPORATION

BLONDE BAIT (British title: **WOMEN WITHOUT MEN** 1956) B&W 73 min. (U.K.) 71 min. (U.S.). Written by Val Guest and Richard Landau; Produced by Anthony Hinds; Directed by Elmo Williams. Cast: Beverly Michaels, Jim Davis, Joan Rice, Richard Travers, and Paul Cavanagh.

Tidbits: Over lunch one afternoon, Bob Lippert and Michael Carreras decided to co-produce a women's prison movie. They kicked around a few titles—*Jailbirds, Bare Behind Bars, Gang Girls*, etc.—and came up with one that pleased them both: *Prison Girls*. In what proved to be little more than wishful thinking, the two men agreed to make a slightly classier movie than they had been making. Lippert was sure he could get Jan Sterling and Paul Douglas to star in it, and Carreras was equally certain that he could add Diana Dors and Dirk Bogarde to the cast.

Lippert asked Elmo Williams if he would like to direct the picture. Williams was ready to ask for a little more money than he had made on *The Tall Texan*, but Lippert was way ahead of him. Before the subject of money had a chance to surface, Lippert told him that his salary would be the same because he was giving Williams the opportunity to direct a class movie. To that end, writer Richard Landau was instructed to add more class than sleaze to his script. Landau and Williams were shipped off to England before Lippert had closed the deal with Jan Sterling's agent, the same agent who handled Paul Douglas. The agent wanted a five per cent bump in Sterling's salary. Lippert refused to pay it, assuming that when he called the agent back in a couple of days he would give in. In the meantime, Sterling was nominated for an Academy Award for her role in *The High and the Mighty* (1954). Lippert phoned the agent, congratulating him on his client's good fortune and said he was willing to pay the extra five percent. Only now the agent wanted *ten* percent. Lippert got sore and hung up. The agent called him back to remind him that without Sterling he wouldn't get Paul Douglas. It wasn't in Lippert's nature to give in, so he decided to look elsewhere for his two leads without saying anything to Carreras about it.

Robert Lippert and Elmo Williams.

Producer Anthony Hinds and director Williams were at the airport to meet their leading lady. Expecting to see Jan Sterling, they
were surprised to find Beverly Michaels, a little known actress who
had been in a couple of B-movies. Hinds phoned Carreras with
the news. But Carreras wasn't angry. He laughed. "That bugger,
Lippert," he said. "He thought he'd pull a fast one on me." Carreras
had a friend in Hollywood who had already told him the deal with
Sterling fell through so Carreras had already withdrawn his offer
for Dors and Bogarde. "I never did fully trust Lippert," Carreras
told Hinds.[1]

Once the film went into production, Tony Hinds locked himself in his office and didn't show his face until the last scene was
shot. Exclusive Films released the movie in England as *Women
Without Men*. Lippert shot some new footage which altered the
plot. His version eliminated some of the British performers and
replaced them with American actors. In the hustle and bustle of

cast switching, plot changing, fast writing and hastily built cramped sets one thing got lost—that class movie that Carreras and Lippert had set out to make.

Critics: "Stereotyped woman's prison drama..."—*Monthly Film Bulletin*; "It's an over-length, below-par British entry..."—*Variety*; "Too much talk and too little action."—*Motion Picture Exhibitor*.

Notes:
1. Williams, Elmo, *Elmo Williams*, McFarland and Company, Inc., Jefferson, N.C. 2006, page 120.
20TH CENTURY-FOX

20th CENTURY-FOX
(Regal Films and Associated Artists)

THE ABDUCTORS aka **SECRET SERVICE** (1957) B&W/Scope 80 min. Written and Produced by Ray Wander; Directed by Andrew McLaglen. Cast: Victor McLaglen (his last film), Gavin Muir, George Macready, Fay Spain, and Carl Thayer.

Tidbits: This movie was inspired by the antics of Chicago criminal James Kennally who, in 1876, hired a pair of grave-robbers to snatch the body of Abraham Lincoln from the Oak Ridge cemetery and take it to a hiding place along the shores of Lake Michigan.

Critics: "...talks more often than it moves, and walks more often than it runs."—*Motion Picture Herald*; "...the basis for the plot is really too skimpy for sustained attention."—*Hollywood Reporter*; "Plot is overlong...and slowed by an overage of dialog..."—*Variety*; "The film comes off—even if the plot does not..."—*Los Angeles Times*.

THE ABOMINABLE SNOWMAN OF THE HIMALAYAS (1957) B&W/Scope (U.S.) 85 minutes (UK) 91 min. Written by Nigel Kneale based on his teleplay *The Creature*; Produced by Aubrey Baring; Directed by Val Guest. Cast: Peter Cushing, Forrest Tucker, Maureen Connell, Richard Wattis, and Robert Brown.

Tidbits: "The claims that this is a Hammer film or a Regal film are completely wrong," explained Sam Sherman. "The film was originally made as a US British co-production between (US) Buzz Productions Inc. [Robert Lippert, William Pizor and his son, Irwin] and Clarion Films Ltd. [owned by James Carreras, an entity that was not legally part of Hammer] with Fox handling all world-wide distribution outside of the Clarion territories of UK and Japan, as the film was a UK quota financed film there, as released by Warners...In the Fox territories, the film was cut by several minutes and re-titled *Abominable Snowman of the Himalayas*. Videos here are from the British master and show the Warners logo and UK credits." Author Gary Smith, who knows a thing or two about Hammer Films, said this is a lot of hooey; it was a Hammer project from beginning to end.

According to John Brosnan's *Future Tense*, the film was a flop which director Guest felt was largely to the intelligence of the theme. "It was too subtle," Guest told Brosnan, "and I also think it had too much to say. No one was expecting films from Hammer that said anything, but this one did—it had a message." But it was boring.

Critics: "The cast is first rate..."—*Hollywood Reporter*; "...ordinary in most respects..."—*Citizen News*; "Unfoldment is logical and exciting at times."—*Variety*; "...in attempting to give some credence to the myth, the film defeats its own purpose and winds up absolutely nowhere."—*Los Angeles Times*; "It is among the best of British science fiction thrillers..."—*The Evening Standard*; "...played for weird mood and constantly mounting suspense..."—*Motion Picture Herald*; "...a disappointingly tame and ineffectual screen version of Nigel Kneale's intriguing TV play."—*Monthly Film Bulletin*.

Exhibitors: "Doubled with *Ghost Diver* for a very good program... the kinds of pictures that seem to jar loose a few who otherwise find something else to do."—B. Berglund, ND; "...I would not have been one bit upset if my patrons called me 'The Abominable Showman!' after seeing this."—Dave S. Klein, Africa.

AIR PATROL (1962) B&W/Scope 62 min. Written by Henry Cross (Harry Spaulding), Produced and Directed by Maury Dexter. Cast: Willard Parker, Merry Anders, Robert Dix, John Holland, and Russ Bender.

Tidbits: "I remember one scene where I was supposed to open the door and be accepting a delivery from the pizza man," recalled actress Merry Anders. "Instead, I found Willard with his tie askew, staggering against the door jam, and he just absolutely broke me up! They had that outtake on some film clip. It was such an uproar and it just surprised everybody."[1]

Critics: "...will make a neat and handy feature for double billing."—*Hollywood Reporter*; "...rather slow paced..."—*Product Digest*.

ALASKA PASSAGE (1959) B&W/Scope 71 min. Produced by Bernard Glasser; Written and Directed by Edward Bernds. Cast: Bill Williams, Nora Hayden, Leslie Bradley, Lyn Thomas, and Nick Dennis.
Critics: "First of the Associated Producers' action programmers... routine..."—*Boxoffice*; "...a well-done low-budgeter."—*Variety*; "...a fairly routine story."—*Motion Picture Herald*.
Exhibitors: "Can just make it for the bottom of a double bill and that's all."—W. G. Hall, NE.

THE ALLIGATOR PEOPLE (1959) B&W/Scope 74 min. Written by Orville H. Hampton; Produced by Jack Leewood; Directed by Roy Del Ruth. Cast: Beverly Garland, George Macready, Lon Chaney, Richard Crane, and Freda Inescort.
Tidbits: Beverly Garland recalled a couple of moments when something would strike her funny and make it impossible for her to finish a scene. At one point she walked into a roomful of alligator people. They're wrapped in bandages from toe to head, and the way their heads were covered made them look like urinals. "I took one look at all these men with urinals on their heads and I just cracked up," she said. "I think they finally just cut and let me go back to my dressing room." In another scene with her alligator husband, Richard Greene, Miss Garland tried to convince him she would love him no matter what he looked like. "I thought I'd die," she said. "It was easily the most difficult scene I had to do in the film. Hell, it may have been the most difficult scene I ever had to do. I don't remember how long it took, maybe an hour, maybe more."
Critics: "Equipped with well motivated lines, Miss Garland turns in a fine performance."—*Variety*. "...too much on the talky side for genuine suspense."—*Citizen News*; "...a better than average horror film..."—*Hollywood Reporter*; "...fairly well executed story..."—*Los Angeles Examiner*; "Script by Orville Hampton is half incoherent; Roy Del Ruth's directed is erratic. Save for the pro cast, this one is strictly from the swamp."—*Los Angeles Times*.

Beverly Garland is a little perplexed by the fact that her fiance, Richard Crane, is turning into an alligator in The Alligator People *(1959).*

Beverly Garland and friend from The Alligator People *(1959).*

AMBUSH AT CIMARRON PASS (1958) B&W 73 min. Written by Richard G. Taylor and John K. Butler; Produced by Herbert E. Mendelson; Directed by Jodie Copeland (debut). Cast: Scott Brady, Margia Dean, Clint Eastwood, Irving Bacon, and Frank Gerstle.

Tidbits: Margia Dean had problems with Scott Brady. She told Mike Fitzgerald: "We clashed and had a feud! He was very cocky and rude. He would tell smutty jokes on purpose, trying to shock you. I did know him socially, but he was not my cup of tea. He's pretty lousy. There was a scene in the film where he's carrying me off, all the while saying vile things to me as the camera rolled!" This was Clint Eastwood's first major role. He thought it was the worst movie ever made.

Critics: "...moves rather well within the limitations of its low budget."—*Variety*; "Pedestrian pace slow Regal oater."—*Hollywood Reporter*; "...a rather ambitious story vein, and by and large, they succeed..."—*Motion Picture Herald*.

APACHE WARRIOR aka **APACHE KID** aka **THE LONG KNIVES** aka **RED ARROW** (1957) B&W/Scope 74 min. Written by Kurt Neumann, Eric Norden and Carroll Young; Produced by Plato Skouras; Directed by Elmo Williams. Cast: Keith Larsen, Jim Davis, Rudolfo Acosta, and John Milijan.

Critics: "...follows none of the ruts worn deep by writers of Westerns over the long and prosperous record of mounted melodrama."—*Motion Picture Herald*; "...stands as an example of intelligence and skill applied to a modest budget."—*Variety*; "...out of date as a western, never giving more than superficial character-izations and those are stereo-typed."—*Hollywood Reporter*.

Exhibitors: "I'd rather have standard ratio color than Regalscope or CinemaScope in black and white."—S. T. Jackson, AL; "Too many Indians in titles lately. Business fair."—D. W. Trisko, TX.

BACK DOOR TO HELL (1964) B&W 79 min. Written by Richard A. Guttman and John Hackett; Produced by Fred Roos; Directed by Monte Hellman. Cast: Jimmy Rodgers, Jack Nicholson, John Hackett, Annabelle Huggins, and Conrad Maga.

BACK FROM THE DEAD (1957) B&W/Scope 79 min. Written by Catherine Turney from her novel *The Other One*; Produced by Robert Stabler; Directed by Charles Marquis Warren. Cast: Peggy Castle, Arthur Franz, Marsha Hunt, Don Haggerty, and Marianne Steward.

Tidbits: "[It's] certainly not a fine film. I don't think that I could even say it's a good film," said Marsha Hunt who was, nevertheless, grateful to be offered the role.[2] She had been blacklisted for speaking out against the blacklist and hadn't worked for some time.

Critics: "...lacking in suspense or thrills..."—*Motion Picture Herald*; "...achieves moments of suspense and horror."—*Hollywood Reporter*; "This is a laudable attempt, but only spasmodically successful, at an 'adult' horror story."—*Variety*.

BADLANDS OF MONTANA (1957) B&W 75 min. Written by Daniel B. Ullman; Produced by Daniel B. Ullman and Herbert E. Mendleson; Directed by Daniel B. Ullman. Cast: Rex Reason, Beverly Garland, Emile Meyer, Keith Larson, and Margia Dean.

Critics: "A good story, well-directed and played..."—*Variety*; "...Reason and Miss Garland make a good romantic couple..."—*Hollywood Reporter*; "...uninhibited script played out with gusto by a large and competent cast..."—*Motion Picture Herald*.

BATTLE OF BLOODY BEACH (1961) B&W/Scope 80 min. Written and Produced by Richard Maibaum; Directed by Herbert Coleman. Cast: Audie Murphy, Gary Crosby, Dolores Michaels, Alejandro Ray, and Marjorie Stapp.

Tidbits: The story called for Audie Murphy to hide in an old World War II vessel. Art director John Mansbridge found a stripped down, 100 foot Navy vessel in a scrap metal place. Lippert paid $2,000 for it. Mansbridge gutted it and had it toed to Catalina where the movie was shot. Two days before the start of production, high tide and strong surf broke the hull and sunk the ship. Fearing that it posed a hazard, the Coast Guard got a court order forcing Lippert to raise the ship at a cost of $8,000. "I don't know what all the fuss what about," Lippert said. "I would have raised it with or without the court order. I needed it for the movie."

Critics: "...a rather stereotyped story."—*Motion Picture Herald*; "...the movie never comes to grips with the central emotional situation."—*Limelight*; "Even allowing for its faults, there is nothing 'low budget' about the feel of this picture."—*Variety*.
Exhibitors: "Did only fair business on a double bill."—S. T. Jackson, AL.

THE BIG SHOW (1961) DeLuxe Color/Scope 113 min. Written by Ted Sherdeman; Produced by James B. Clark and Ted Sherdeman; Directed by James B. Clark. Cast: Esther Williams, Cliff Robertson, Nehemiah Persoff, Robert Vaughn, and Margia Dean.
Tidbits: Lippert knew that a spendthrift ex-husband had left Esther Williams owing $750,000 to the IRS and was pretty sure she would be more or less forced to accept his offer of $100,000 to play the lead in *The Big Show*, in spite of the fact that she felt it would be a second-rate production. And for someone who had once been a star at MGM, it was. Although her contract guaranteed her the right to make script changes, her nine pages of revisions were ignored. When she complained about it director Clark said: "So sue me."

According to the terms of her contract she was supposed to be on hand all of the time unless, of course, she was sick. She heard through the grapevine that she wouldn't be needed for a couple of days and took off for Madrid with her lover, Fernando Lamas. They were pretty much confined to their hotel room since she was supposed to be sick. Unit manager Clarence Urist came after her and threatened to withhold her salary for violating her contract.

"Fernando wadded up some Kleenex and stuffed them in my cheeks so they looked swollen," Miss Williams recalled. "Then he put some white makeup on me to give me a deathly pallor. He even made me a 'fever blister' out of library paste and a few breadcrumbs. By the time he got done with me, I was a triumph of stagecraft."[3]

A friend of Lamas posed as a doctor and told Urist the actress had a case of food poisoning, and Urist was convinced. Williams and Lamas had the weekend to play, but on the plane back to Germany that Monday, she came down with a case of amoebic dysentery.

Above: Poster art for The Big Show *(1961). Below: Esther Williams and Cliff Robertson are the stars of* The Big Show *(1961).*

Erskine Johnson interviewed Margia Dean on the set. She was in her trapeze artist costume—a pair of tights—at the time, "and on this German food they're getting tighter and tighter," she told him.

The Rank Circuit booked *The Big Show* as the top attraction in more than 100 houses, a distinction accorded to only the cream of American product. Fox ordered 375 prints, a record number for a Lippert picture.

Critics: "It is surprisingly different in its character development of a human interest story attached to the excitement and thrills of outstanding circus acts."—*Motion Picture Herald*; "...shows some nice scenery but other than that it just mopes drearily along."—*Los*

Angeles Examiner; "...very little to tackle the mind or exercise the imagination."—*Variety*; "...cannot be considered the all-time best... but it is challengingly close to the top."—*Boxoffice*; "...and unappetizing bill of goods, beautiful to look at."—*New York Times*.
Exhibitors: "A real good show that did excellent business."—Dave S. Klein, Africa; "We did only average, but will recommend it..."—B.L. Brown, GA; "This is good stuff for small towns..."—Don Stott, MD; "I'd recommend this to anyone who likes to be really entertained."—Paul Fournier, NE.

THE BLACK WHIP aka **THE MAN WITH THE BLACK WHIP** (1956) B&W/Scope 81 min. Written by Orville H. Hampton; Produced by Robert Stabler; Directed by Charles Marquis Warren. Cast: Hugh Marlowe, Coleen Gray, Paul Richards, Angie Dickenson, and Adele Mara.
Critics: "...the basic ingredients are in the script, but so are some mighty worn clichés."—*Variety*.
Exhibitors: "Good enough western...Business only fair."—D.W. Trisko, TX.

BLOOD AND STEEL aka **CONDEMNED PATROL** (1959) B&W/Scope 62 min. Written by Joseph C. Gillette; Produced by Gene Corman; Directed by Bernard Kowalski. Cast: John Lupton, Ziva Rodann, Brett Halsey, James Edwards, and John Brinkley.
Critics: "...strictly old hat..."—*Variety*; "...dull war film."—*Hollywood Reporter*; "...first rate production values and an excellent cast."—*Boxoffice*.
Exhibitors: "A good title but the customers will be disappointed."—Harold Bell, Canada; "These 60-minute Associated Releasing Corporation pictures...are the best for double bills in my opinion."—Paul Fournier, NE.

BLOOD ARROW (1958) B&W/Scope 76 min. Written by Fred Freiberger; Produced by Robert W. Stabler; Directed by Charles Marquis Warren. Cast: Scott Brady, Paul Richards, Phyllis Coates, Don Haggerty, and Rocky Shahan.
Critics: "Hazardous, at best, are efforts to substitute moods and character analyzing for...standard action ingredients..."—*Boxoffice*; "...offers little that is different or exciting..."—*Motion Picture*

Exhibitor; "...should please action-Western aficionados."—*Motion Picture Herald*; "Unreeling at a dull pace, there's little to recommend film."—*Variety*; "The value of such western entertainment has been diminished by the fact that entertainment equally good is available free on television."—*The Exhibitor*.

BREAK IN THE CIRCLE (1955) EastmanColor (released in B&W in U.S.) 69 min. Produced by Michael Carreras; Directed and Written by Val Guest based on the novel by Philip Lorraine. Cast: Forrest Tucker, Eva Bartok, Marius Goring, Reginald Beckwith, and Eric Pohlmann.
Tidbits: Filming began on August 22 with a generous six-week schedule. It was Hammer Films biggest production at the time with location work in Germany and Cornwall.
Critics: "...a rousing romp for the unsophisticated..."—*The Monthly Bulletin*; "...intriguing and exciting..."—*The Kinematograph Weekly*; "...long on action and short on logic."—*Motion Picture Herald*; "...difficult to follow because of a confused story line..."—*Variety*; "...will satisfy the adventure fans..."—*Boxoffice*.

BROKEN LAND aka **VANISHING FRONTIER** (1962) Color/Scope 60 min. Written by Edward J. Lasko; Produced by Leonard A. Schwartz; Directed by John A. Bushelman. Cast: Kent Taylor, Diana Darrin, Jody McCrea, Robert Sampson, and Jack Nicholson.
Tidbits: Shortly after this picture wrapped, Jack Nicholson was called to Lippert's office so he could pitch some story ideas. According to Jack Leewood, it was a pretty violent session. Anytime he found fault with anything, a story point or a line of dialog, Nicholson came after him physically.
Critics: "...relatively routine yarn spins its undistinguished web of circumstances."—*Boxoffice*.

THE CABINET OF CALIGARI (1962) B&W/Scope 80 min. Written by Robert Bloch; Produced by Robert L. Lippert; Directed by Roger Kay. Cast: Glynnis Johns, Dan O'Herlihy, Richard Davalos, Lawrence Dobkin, and Constance Ford.
Tidbits: A writer for the *Los Angeles Mirror* noted that while the original *Caligari* had "elements of greatness," it seemed hopelessly dated. Lippert agreed and hired television director-writer Roger

Glynnis Johns is trapped in The Cabinet of Caligari *(1962).*

Kay to fashion a modern treatment of the story. Kay had a PhD from the Sorbonne for his work in psychopathology. He told the press that his primary reason for signing on to the project was to shine a light on the fakeries perpetrated by a lot of Hollywood psychiatrists. The fact that it was a jump from the small screen to the big screen might have had something to do with it, too.

Kay's treatment changed the lead character from a man to a woman and took a more psychological approach to the story. Maury Dexter and Harry Spalding read his treatment and couldn't make heads or tails of it. They begged Lippert not to go ahead with the thing. They told him to pay Kay off and cut his losses, but Lippert dug in his heels.

"Okay, Bob," Dexter said. "It's your baby. I'll take care of the production end. You can handle Kay and everything above the line."

Harry Spalding was asked to act as a sort of unofficial liaison between Kay and Lippert. That all came to an end after he was asked to evaluate the script Kay had rewritten after Kay had had a falling out with screenwriter Robert Bloch. Spalding told Lippert he thought it wasn't commercial.

From the beginning, Kay wanted Bibi Andersson to play the lead in his picture. She was a favorite of director Ingmar Bergman. Alec Guinness was Kay's first choice for Caligari. Both Guinness and Andersson had other commitments. Kay set his sights on Janet

Leigh and Herbert Lom but had to settle for Glynis Johns and Dan O'Herlihy.

When O'Herlihy (a friend of Kay's) tried to tell the director that his script was too wordy, Kay got angry and fired him. O'Herlihy was surprised to hear from Kay the next morning, asking why he hadn't shown up for rehearsal.

"He had an enormous ego which got in his way, and in the end he had to leave Hollywood because of that," O'Herlihy said.[4]

The picture was shot at Goldwyn Studios on stage 5, a set originally built for *The Children's Hour* (1961). Dexter dropped in on the first day and found everyone standing around, eating doughnuts, and drinking coffee. Kay was sitting in his chair, smoking his cigar, looking morose. During rehearsal he had a screaming match with Glynis Johns that sent her to her dressing room in tears. She had locked herself in and refused to come out.

"You need to smooth things over," Dexter diplomatically told to Kay.

"You can't tell me what to do!" Kay snapped arrogantly.

"No," Dexter replied, "but I know someone who can."

Lippert was just stepping out of his house when he heard the phone ring. Dexter explained the situation.

"What's Kay doing about it?" Lippert asked.

"He's sitting in his chair, smoking a cigar."

"You tell him to start shooting or fire him," Lippert snarled.

"You hired him, Bob," Dexter reminded him. "*You* fire him."

Fifteen minutes later Lippert walked onto the set. Kay was still sitting in his chair, puffing on his cigar. Lippert asked him what was wrong. Kay launched into a "she said this" and "she said that" rant that concluded with: "I'm running this show and everyone is supposed to do what I say!"

Lippert, who was smoking a cigar that was much larger than Kay's, yelled: "Listen, you son of a bitch, if you don't get off your fat ass and go to her dressing room and apologize, I'll throw your ass off this set and send you back to where you came from!"

It was a shocking moment. Anyone who knew Lippert *never* heard him use that kind of language. It worked; it got the self-proclaimed genius out of his chair.

The Egyptian-born Kay returned to television and, after alienating anyone who might have hired him, fled to France where he directed one film, *La puce et le prive* (1981). He hasn't been heard from since.

Critics: "...it moves toward its climax with unnerving calmness..."—*Newsweek*; "...one of the best pictures so far this year."—*Hollywood Citizen News*; "For it is a pretty dull lot of horror they are dishing up—unimaginative and tedious—and that's all there is in the film."—*New York Times*; "...an extraordinary film shocker."—*Los Angeles Times*; "The story does not completely come to terms with itself and, under Kay's guidance, has a slight tendency to tip off its surprises."—*Variety*.

THE CANADIANS (1961) Color/Scope 85 min. Produced by Herman Webber; Written and Directed by Burt Kennedy. Cast: Robert Ryan, John Dehner, Torin Thatcher, Burt Metcalfe, and John Sutton.
Critics: "...lacks sustained action..."—*Boxoffice*; "...plodding, tepid drama..."—*Variety*; "Miserably written and directed by Burt Kennedy, this latitude horse opera is as monotonous as its frequent CinemaScope vistas of waving grass on the rolling Canadian plains."—*New York Times*.
Exhibitors: "...this will do good business any place."—W.K. Riese, Canada; "Business was about average."—B. Berglund, ND.

CATTLE EMPIRE (1958) B&W/Scope 85 min. Written by Eric Norden; Produced by Robert Stabler; Directed by Charles Marquis Warren. Cast: Joel McCrea, Gloria Talbott, Don Haggerty, Phyllis Coates, and Bing Russell.
Tidbits: Phyllis Coates was interviewed by Mike Fitzgerald and Boyd Magers in their book *Ladies of the Western*, and she had this to say about working on the film: "I admired Joel McCrea. He and his wife, Frances Dee, had a long and happy marriage. Joel was very cute. He asked me to go to dinner one night and you don't turn down the leading man. It was really very funny. He said, 'I want to apologize to you.' I said, 'For what? Whatever could you have done to offend me?' He said 'I wanted you to know I wouldn't offer to take you to bed.' Well, my jaw dropped. I didn't know what to say. He said he was very much in love with his wife, and he always made that clear to his leading ladies. I thought I'd die."
Critics: "...a big and often spectacular trail-driving saga..."—*Variety*; "All of the parts are well-played, with Gloria Talbott outstanding..."—*Hollywood Reporter*; "...most of the action is confined to breathing life into a pedestrian script..."—*Motion Picture Herald*.

Exhibitors: "Joel McCrea does as well for me as any of the other top cowboy stars. But it seems that I do about the same on westerns, regardless of what the picture is like."—Victor Webber, AK; "A fair western if you are really pressed."—Dave S. Klein, Africa.

Angie Dickinson and Gene Barry from Sam Fuller's China Gate *(1957).*

CHINA GATE (1957) B&W/Scope 97 min. Written, Produced and Directed by Sam Fuller. Cast: Gene Barry, Angie Dickinson, Nat "King" Cole, Paul Dubov, and Lee Van Cleef.

Tidbits: Lippert was the first person to make a movie about the Korean War and, again with Sam Fuller, he produced the first movie about the war in Viet Nam.

RKO Studio was in the heart of Culver City, and the police and fire departments had given their permission for Sam Fuller to blow up part of the European village that had been built on the studio's backlot. There were two conditions: the explosion had to be minimal and it had to take place in the early evening.

Fuller got behind schedule, and it was well after midnight when he set off the explosion. Ten minutes later the Culver City Police and the fire department were there to shut things down. However, Fuller wasn't done; he still had a few more scenes he needed to shoot. When he failed to change their minds, he placed a frantic call to Lippert. Lippert got there as fast as he could and somehow persuaded the officials to let Fuller continue with the promise there would be no more explosions.

The Israeli Film Censorship Board banned the film on the grounds that it indulged in excessive cruelty, which is a peculiar complaint to lodge against a war movie, to say the least.

Critics: "As a triple threat, Samuel Fuller's writing and character dissection are not on a par with his ability to keep his principals moving against an alert enemy."—*New York Times*; "Some of Fuller's dialog runs on the wordy side, and the picture seems a bit over-long."—*Los Angeles Times*; "Realistic in its action sequences, the effect frequently is dissipated through lengthy scenes of dialogue which slow movement to a walk."—*Variety*; "Vivid, suspenseful, startlingly honest and sometimes shockingly realistic..."—*Los Angeles Examiner*; "Often the dialog shifts from high quality to stilted propaganda."—*Boxoffice*; "...raised above the routine by the director's gift for bizarre incident and dramatic counter point."—*Motion Picture Herald*.

Exhibitors: "I had a hunch this would do okay, and it did just that, okay."—Jim Fraser, MN; "Below average business..."—Mel Danner, OK; "We prefer more fun---which we don't get—so no business."—Mayne P. Musselman, KS.

COPPER SKY aka **THE FAR WEST** (1957) B&W/Scope 77 min. Written by Eric Norden and Robert S. Stabler; Produced by Robert S. Stabler and Charles Marquis Warren; Directed by Charles Marquis Warren. Cast: Jeff Morrow, Coleen Gray, Strother Martin, Paul Brinegar, and John Pickard.

Tidbits: "It was another Charles Marquis Warren picture—sort of a western remake of *African Queen* [1951]," Coleen Gray remarked. "I acted all over the place. You have to know with me, most directors who have any sense at all will say, 'Coleen, on a scale of 10, will you take it down to 3.' Then I behave."[5]

Critics: "...plodding pace maintained between action sequences."—*Motion Picture Herald*; "...probably sets a record high for lack of action and overage of dialog...:--*Variety*; "...a tedious western."—*Hollywood Reporter*.

CURSE OF THE FLY (1965) B&W/Scope 86 min. Written by Harry Spalding based on characters created by George Langelaan;

Produced by Robert L. Lippert and Jack Parsons; Directed by Don Sharp. Cast: Brian Donlevy, George Baker, Carole Gray, Yvette Rees, and Burt Kwouk.

Tidbits: *The Fly* had been one of Lippert's biggest hits and, since he still owned the rights to the story, he thought he should take advantage of it. His right hand man, Harry Spalding, thought they should leave well enough alone. They had already made one sequel to *The Fly*. There was no reason to press their luck.

"Actually, considering the basic problem, it was not all that bad a script," Spalding told Tom Weaver. "As a matter of fact, Don Sharp said that the opening ten pages, where the girl [Carole Gray] is coming out of the insane asylum, was the best opening he had ever had on a film."

The film was packaged with *Devils of Darkness* (1965).

THE DAY MARS INVADED EARTH (1963) B&W/Scope 70 min. Written by Harry Spalding; Produced and Directed by Maury Dexter. Cast: Kent Taylor, Marie Windsor, William Mims, Betty Beall, and Lowell Brown.

Tidbits: Lippert paid $2,000 a day for the use of Greystone; a fifty-five room mansion built in 1928 by the oil rich Edward Doheny for his son Ned, his wife Lucy, and their five-children. It had a pool, greenhouse, stables, movie theatre and a bowling alley. Harry Spalding wrote his script to take full advantage of the location. Except for the opening sequence, shot in one of Lippert's offices, the entire movie was shot at Greystone.

The history of the estate is far more interesting than the movie. Five months after the young Doheny and his family moved into the mansion, the night watchman found Hugh Plunkett, a loyal employee for fifteen years, dead in the hallway to the guest room. There was blood streaming from his head and a gun tucked beneath his body. Ned was still alive on the floor of the bedroom, bleeding from both sides of his head. Thirty minutes later he was dead, too. Officially it was called a murder/suicide, but because there were no fingerprints on the gun, everyone wondered who killed whom, and why. There were those who suggested it may have been a professional hit, a way to silence the people who knew too much about what came to be known as the Teapot Scandal.

Others suspected that Ned and Hugh were lovers who had been caught in the act by Ned's wife.

For the record, Richard La Salle's score for *The Day Mars Invaded the Earth* is a shameless rip-off of Bernard Herrmann's score for Alfred Hitchcock's *Vertigo* (1958). La Salle wasn't satisfied with simply stealing Herrmann's main title, he hi-jacked three or four other themes as well, changing however many notes were needed to keep him out of court.

Critics: "...does not provide the conventional happy ending..."—*Product Digest*; "...science fiction fans...may well be disappointed."—*Boxoffice*.

THE DEERSLAYER (1957) DeLuxe Color/Scope 78 min. Written by Carroll Young based on the novel by James Fenimore Cooper; Produced and Directed by Kurt Neumann. Cast: Lex Barker, Rita Moreno, Forrest Tucker, Cathy O'Donnell, and J.C. Flippen.

Tidbits: Much of this movie was filmed on location at Bass Lake in the Sierra Nevada Mountains in Northern California. "We all had a lot of fun filming on all those beautiful locations," actor Carlos Rivas told Reiner Boller. "There was more fun than work."

Critics: "...a well-turned-out derring-do actioner..."—*Variety*.

Exhibitors: "...did real well with it on one of my off nights."—I. Roche, FL; "We did very good on this..."—B. Berglund, ND; "Lots of laughs in the wrong places..."—Jim Fraser, MN; "Indians are beginning to bite the dust here, but this did okay."—Victor Webber, AK.

DESERT HELL (1958) B&W/Scope 82 min. Written by Endre Bohem; Produced by Robert Stabler; Directed by Charles Marquis Warren. Cast: Brian Keith, Barbara Hale, Richard Denning, Johnny Desmond, and Phillip Pine.

Critics: "Good direction and a good musical back by Raoul Kraushaar give the film a lift."—*Motion Picture Herald*; "...the picture is too long for its routine plot..."—*Boxoffice*; "The production is handicapped by a situation that appears overly familiar, but this is overcome to some extent by authentic desert locations..."

Exhibitors: "Brian Keith and Barbara Hale played good roles but don't have too much drawing power."—A.P. Quensel, Canada.

Poster for Desert Hell *(1958).*

DESIRE IN THE DUST (1960) B&W/Scope 102 min. Written by Charles Lang based on the novel by Harry Whittington; Produced and Directed by William F. Claxton. Cast: Raymond Burr, Martha Hyer, Joan Bennett, Brett Halsey, and Anne Helm (debut).

Tidbits: For this one, Lippert went on location to a small town outside of Baton Rouge, Louisiana. "We worked inside big old mansions and sharecropper cabins and I challenge you to tell me that they aren't as good as anything made on a sound stage," he bragged to Dick Williams from the *Los Angeles Mirror*.

Leading lady Martha Hyer said it was the best picture she ever made. (Can that be possible?)

The movie had its premier on September 15, 1960 at the Paramount Theatre in Baton Rouge, Louisiana. The stars were on hand, along with Mayor John Christian and other social leaders of the city.

Critics: "...stark, gripping drama..."—*Boxoffice*; "...cannot be taken seriously..."—*Hollywood Reporter*; "...the hero declares, 'I'm the biggest damn fool who ever lived.' He then spends the remaining 90 minutes or so conscientiously proving his point."—*Hollywood Citizen News*; "...a synthetic, essentially pointless tale of greed and lust in the backwaters of the present-day South."—*Variety*. "...

shifts from the beguiling to the ridiculous."—*New York Times*; "...this slice of raw life, scented with corn likker and bittersweet magnolia blossoms takes the honors in presenting the finest batch of performances seen in one film in some time."—*Limelight*.
Exhibitors: "...the few who came liked it."—Jim Fraser, MN; "We starved on this one."—Albert Agular, CA.

THE DESPERADOS ARE IN TOWN (1956) B&W/Scope 73 min. Written by Kurt Neumann and Earle Snell, based on Bennett Foster's story *The Outlaws are in Town*; Produced and Directed by Kurt Neumann. Cast: Robert Arthur, Kathleen Nolan (debut), Rhys Williams, Dave O'Brien, and Rhodes Reason.
Critics: "...while the doings cover familiar ground, there are moments of suspense..."—*Motion Picture Herald*; "...not as much action as there should be..."—*Variety*; "The characters are stock and the situations never generate much excitement..."—*Hollywood Reporter*.
Exhibitors: "They must have been in town and forbidden everyone to go to the show."—Sam Holmberg, Canada; "Because this film is in RegalScope, it definitely makes it twice as bad."—Dave S. Klein, Africa.

*DIAMOND SAFARI (1958) Color (released in B&W) 67 min. Written by Larry Marcos; Produced and Directed by Gerald Meyer. Cast: Kevin McCarthy, Robert Bice, Tommy Buson, John Clifford, and Joanna Douglas.
Tidbits: This was comprised of two, unsold 1955 television pilots for a show shot in South Africa called *African Drumbeat*. New footage was shot to meld the episodes together.
Critics: "...high adventure action drama..."—*Boxoffice*; "...an appealing package..."—*Motion Picture Herald*.
Exhibitors: "If I had a lick of sense I wouldn't have bought it."—Frank E. Sabin, MT.

DOG OF FLANDERS (1959) DeLuxe Color/Scope 97 min. Written by Ted Sherdeman, based on the novel by Ouida; Produced by Robert B. Radnitz; Directed by James B. Clark. Cast: David Ladd, Donald Crisp, Theodore Bikel, Max Croiset, and Monique Ahrens.

Tidbits: Lippert called Belgium and Holland "the last bastion of motion picture production freedom." He told the *Los Angeles Examiner* that they were determined to give the simple tale of a boy, his dog, his grandfather, and a little girl the finest productions possible. "From the time the company arrived," he said, "until the last shot was made, the harmonious relationships with the people, the officials, and the clergy of the Low Countries assured a smooth, relaxed and confident production."

The studio got behind the picture with a large scale campaign to bolster its Easter engagement at the RKO Proctor's theatre in Newark.

Critics: "It is told quietly, rather slowly, and with admirable restraint..."—*Saturday Review*; "...delightful and touching..."—*Los Angeles Times*; "Here, thank God, is a picture about people and creatures you are bound to like."—*Hollywood Reporter*; "Couldn't be more lovable."—*New York Times*.

Exhibitors: "This is truly a family picture but where are our families?"—Bruce Wendorff, MT; "Play it by all means, but try to get the parents too, instead of being a baby sitter."—Arlen S. Peahl, OR; "They want family pictures and this is what happens. Business below average."—Bob Smith, OK; "Good family show, but where are the families?—Mel Kruse, NE; "Public veils for family pictures, but they won't come to see them..."—Terry Ashley, AK.

DOUBLE TROUBLE aka **SWINGIN' ALONG** (1961) B&W 74 min. Written by Jameson Brewer; Produced by Jack Leewood; Directed by Charles Barton. Cast: Tommy Noonan, Peter Marshall, Barbara Eden, Ray Charles, and Roger Williams.
Critics: "Bantamweight comedy with songs."—*Variety*.

THE EARTH DIES SCREAMING (1964) B&W 64 min. Written by Henry Cross (Harry Spalding); Produced by Robert L. Lippert and Jack Parsons; Directed by Terence Fisher. Cast: Willard Parker, Virginia Field, Dennis Price, Thorley Walters, and David Spenser.
Tidbits: This movie lifted footage from MGM's *Village of the Damned* to supply what little production value it had.
Critics: "...a credible piece of entertainment."—*Boxoffice*.

Poster for The Earth Dies Screaming *(1964).*

ESCAPE FROM RED ROCK (1957) B&W/Scope 75 min. Produced by Bernard Glasser; Written and Directed by Edward Bernds. Cast: Brian Donlevy, Eilene Janssen, Jay C. Flippen, Gary Murray, and William Phipps.
Critics: "One of the lesser Regalscope pictures..."—*Boxoffice*; "...original and tightly-conceived..."—*Hollywood Reporter*; "...sufficiently different to warrant good suspense..."—*Variety*.
Exhibitors: "...these shows have more original stories than the big pictures. Drew a good crowd and satisfied all."—B. Berglund, ND.

FELICIA (1964) Color. Directed and Written by David E. Durston, based on a screenplay by Belmon Brooks. Cast: Louise Allbritton, Chet Sommers, Mark Daniel, Mona Marti, and Fran Michaels.
Tidbits: This was Puerto Rico's first wide-screen color feature and, according to the International Movie Database, it was never released in this country.

THE FIREBRAND (1962) B&W/Scope 63 min. Written by Harry Spalding; Produced and Directed by Maury Dexter. Cast: Kent Taylor, Lisa Montell, Valentin De Vargas, Joe Raciti, and Chubby Johnson.

Five Gates to Hell (1959).

FIVE GATES TO HELL (1959) B&W/Scope 98 min. Written, Produced and Directed by James Clavell. Cast: Dolores Michaels, Patricia Owens, Neville Brand, Nobu McCarthy, and Irish McCalla. **Critics**: "...an absorbing story of sex, suspense and violence..."—*Hollywood Reporter*; "The action is ruthless, fear-laden and almost beyond comprehension..."—*Los Angeles Examiner*; "...hard-to-take dialogue..."—*Citizen News*; "...first rate story telling..."—*Variety*; "...stark, sanguinary, suspenseful saga..."—*Boxoffice*; "...steadily suspenseful, generally convincing and, now and then, even moving. And definitely not for children."—*New York Times*.
Exhibitors: "A good picture that did good business. One thing wrong—no color."—Harold L. Rackley, AR; "Another good picture that deserves color..."—Harold Bell, Canada; "Entire cast dead at finish including boxoffice."—George Jenner, Canada.

FLAMING FRONTIER (1958) B&W 70 min. Written by Louis Stevens; Produced and Directed by Sam Newfield. Cast: Bruce Bennett, Jim Davis, Don Girrard, Paisley Maxwell, and Cecil Linder. **Critics**: "There is some action, some intrigue, and considerable conversation..."—*Motion Picture Exhibitor*; "Repetition never helped anything in drama, let alone ostensible action."—*Motion Picture Herald*; "Run-of-the-mill..."—*Boxoffice*.

FLIGHT TO FURY (1964) B&W 80 min. Written by Jack Nicholson; Produced by Eddie Romero and Fred Roos; Directed by Monte Hellman. Cast: Jack Nicholson, Dewey Martin, Fay Spain, Vic Diaz, and Joseph Estrada.

Tidbits: Bob Lippert liked Jack Nicholson's work in *Thunder Island* so he gave Nicholson and his buddy, Monte Hellman, who had become friends while working for producer-director Roger Corman, $160,000 to make two pictures back to back in the Philippines. Nicholson wrote the script during the 28 days it took them to travel by ship. They either could not afford a camera dolly, or it was not something readily available, so Hellman improvised and used bicycles and wheelchairs to move the camera. They were between pictures, and Hellman was getting ready to scout locations for the next one, when he came down with a mysterious illness that put him in the hospital for three weeks. Nicholson showed up one day, put his hands on the side of Hellman's head and said: "You will be well." The next day Hellman jumped out of bed, got in the jeep and went looking for locations.

THE FLY (1958) Color/Scope 94 min. Written by James Clavell, from the short story by George Langelaan; Produced and Directed by Kurt Neumann. Cast: Al (David) Hedison, Patricia Owens, Vincent Price, Herbert Marshall, and Charles Herbert.

Critics: "...a memorable experience for the horror movie-goer..."—*Film Daily*; "...it should be a gold mine..."—"*Hollywood Reporter*; "A quiet, uncluttered and even unpretentious picture, building up almost unbearable tension by simple suggestion."—*New York Times*; "There is an appealing and poignant romance between Miss Owens and Hedison, which adds to the reality of the story."—*Variety*.

Exhibitors: "I have never worked so hard in publicizing any one film, and it paid off quite handsomely."—Dave S. Klein, Africa; "Business was not so much so maybe horror pictures are dying. Sure hope not."—Victor Weber, AR; "Barely hit average. Would be appropriate for a midnight show."—Leonard J. Leise, NE; "This had the girls on the edge of their seats...Business good on this."—Harold Smith, IA.

Barbara Stanwyck in the clutches of John Ericson in Forty Guns *(1957).*

FORTY GUNS aka **WOMAN WITH A WHIP** (1957) B&W/Scope 79 min. Written, Produced and Directed by Sam Fuller. Cast: Barbara Stanwyck, Barry Sullivan, Dean Jagger, John Ericson, and Gene Barry.

Tidbits: William K. Everson called this surprising and sometimes shocking western Fuller's most violent and extreme film, "a western that takes place not in the familiar landscape, but in a strange, grotesquely distorted world located in the lower depths of the director's mind." Everson would have found Fuller's original ending even more so. The hero shoots and kills the Barbara Stanwyck character when her murderous brother uses her as a shield. Once Stanwyck falls, the hero kills her brother. Fuller said Darryl Zanuck loved his ending but couldn't sell it to his marketing people. Most of the picture was shot on Fox's backlot. When the opening scene of Stanwyck and her forty gunmen riding into town was finished,

Fuller cleared the set and shot out most of the windows in the buildings. No one knew he was going to do it. When the studio production office found out they raised hell with Bill Magginetti. By that time Fuller was long gone.

Critics: "...sustains an unusually high level of audience interest and participation..."—*Hollywood Reporter*; "...sexy action-packed and splendidly played..."—*Citizen News*; "...notably undistinguished..."—*Los Angeles Times*.

Exhibitors: "...entertaining western that did not pull too well."—Dave S. Klein, Africa; "This is one of the best westerns we've played here."—Val Dage, NV.

FRECKLES (1960) Deluxe Color/Scope 84 min. Written and Produced by Harry Spalding; Directed by Andrew V. McLaglen. Cast: Martin West, Carol Christensen, Jack Lambert, Steven Peck, and Roy Barcroft.

Critics: "Stirring drama..."—*Boxoffice*; "...plenty of excitement..."—*Motion Picture Herald*; "...produced and written with care and love..."—*Hollywood Reporter*; "...charming and appealing..."—*Variety*.

Exhibitors: "...too much like TV..."—Chuck Garard, IL; "The first family picture of late that 'hit' average business here."—Ken Christianson, ND.

FRONTIER GAMBLER aka **FRONTIER QUEEN** (1956) B&W 70 min. Written by Orville Hampton; Produced by Sigmund Neufeld; Directed by Sam Newfield. Cast: John Bromfield, Coleen Gray, Kent Taylor, Jim Davis, and Margia Dean.

Critics: "...opens with a promisingly dramatic premise, dawdles along at mid-point, and then races for the windup in an atmosphere of tautness and surprise."—*Motion Picture Herald*.

FRONTIER GUN (1958) B&W 70 min. Written by Stephen Kandel; Produced by Richard E. Lyons; Directed by Paul Landres. Cast: John Agar, Joyce Meadows, Barton MacLane, Robert Strauss, and Morris Ankrum.

Critics: "...moves along with a fast pace..."—*Motion Picture Herald*; "...well-paced action..."—*Hollywood Reporter*; "...a dull item..."—*Variety*; "...an above average western."—*Boxoffice*.

GANG WAR (1958) B&W/Scope 74 min. Written by Louis Vittes based on the novel *The Hoods Take Over* by Ovid Demaris; Produced by Harold E. Knox; Directed by Gene Fowler, Jr. Cast: Charles Bronson, Kent Taylor, Jennifer Holden, John Doucette, and Gloria Henry.
Critics: "...holds up as a bang-bang opus..."—*Variety*; "...shows that good pictures can be made on a low budget..."—*Hollywood Reporter*; "...Bronson gives a quietly effective performance."—*Motion Picture Exhibitor*.
Exhibitors: "...should be left in the can."—W.G. Hall, NE.

GHOST DIVER (1957) B&W 76 min. Produced by Richard Einfield; Written and Directed by Richard Einfield and Merrill G. White. Cast: James Craig, Audrey Totter, Nick Minardos, Lowell Brown, and Rudolfo Hoyos, Jr.
Critics: "...a neat programmer..."—*Motion Picture Exhibitor*; "...well-handled programmer..."—*Variety*; "It is routine in conception, structure and execution..."—*Motion Picture Herald*.

GOD IS MY PARTNER (1957) B&W/Scope 82 min. Written by Charles F. Royal; Produced by Sam Heish; Directed by William F. Claxton. Cast: Walter Brennan, Marion Ross, John Hoyt, Jesse White, and Nelson Leigh.
Tidbits: Lou Tarasluk, the manager of the Roxy theatre in Ontario, took out a half page, co-op advertisement in the local paper, sent 1,300 heralds to the farm folks, and 700 more around the city. He invited all of the religious leaders, school principals, members of the City Council, YMCA, and YWCA to be his guest at a special screening. Alas, God wasn't *his* partner. A flu epidemic swept through the area and he played to an empty house.
Critics: "...Claxton's over-leisurely direction keeps film at a sometimes tedious tempo and script doesn't allow for much realism..."—*Variety*; "...a heart-warming theme but no plot."—*Hollywood Reporter*; "...will bring the family audience to the movies..."—*Motion Picture Herald*.
Exhibitors: "Just another black and white picture that did nothing and no one got very excited about it."—Jim Fraser, MN; "Many patrons said this was the best film we have played in months... We did good business with it."—Stan Farnsworth, NS; "A very

Poster for Ghost Diver *(1957).*

good Regalscope picture"—B. Berglund, ND; "It outgrossed the last 21 pictures from 20th-Fox in a row...and best of all it pleased everyone."—Ken Christianson, ND; "Wish it had been in Technicolor—then it could have been the biggest small town hit of the season."—C.J. Otts, TX.

John Agar has a lethal touch in Hand of Death *(1962)*.

HAND OF DEATH aka **FIVE FINGERS OF DEATH** (1962) B&W/
Scope 60 min. Written and Produced by Eugene Ling; Directed by
Gene Nelson. Cast: John Agar, Paula Raymond, Steve Dunn, Roy
Gordon, and John Alonzo.

Tidbits: Eugene Ling came to Lippert with a pretty bad science
fiction script that he wanted to produce. Because Lippert owed
him a favor, he gave the script to Harry Spalding to fix. Spalding
told Lippert the only way to fix it was to start from scratch, and he
was not willing to tackle it; so, Lippert gave it to Maury Dexter who
gave it to Gene Nelson.

Gene Nelson was an actor-dancer, who had been in one of
Lippert's pictures and had expressed a desire to become a director.
Dexter told him if he could figure out a way to make the script work,
he could direct it. It was the chance Nelson had been waiting for.

Sci-fi veteran John Agar was cast as the well-meaning scientist
who becomes a monster half way through the movie. Normally, a
stunt man would have replaced Agar in the monster scenes, but
Agar said he did it himself. "They put me in a pair of padded long
johns," the actor recalled. "I wore a mask and a pair of rubber
hands. Loretta brought our oldest son to the set. He was two or

three at the time and when he heard my voice coming out of this monster get-up it scared him half to death."

During the second half of the movie Agar stumbles around the city, hell-bent on going somewhere, but we never find out where or why he wants to go there. It doesn't matter because he never gets there, wherever it was; the cops gun him down at the beach. **Critics**: "Mr. Nelson's directing, unlike his dancing, is lethargic, and the camera work is static."—*New York Herald-Tribune*; "...completely routine and unenterprising."—*Monthly Film Bulletin*; "...has little to recommend it..."—*Boxoffice*.

HARBOR LIGHTS (1963) B&W/Scope 68 min. Written by Henry Cross (Harry Spalding); Produced and Directed by Maury Dexter. Cast: Jeff Morrow, Miriam Colon, Kent Taylor, Antonio Torres Martino, and Art Bedlard.
Critics: "A small budget film, in every sense of the term..."—*Motion Picture Herald*; "...not a film that attempted to do very much, and it succeeded in this."—*The Film Daily*; "...has too little to hold attention of moviegoers who are accustomed to seeing similar fare on their TV screen..."—*Boxoffice*.

HELL ON DEVIL'S ISLAND (1957) B&W/Scope 73 min. Written by Steven Ritch; Produced by Leon Chooluck; Directed by Christian Nyby. Cast: Helmut Dantine, William Talman, Donna Martel, Jean Willes, and Rex Ingram.
Critics: "...the screenplay tends to hang interminably on scenes that have no intrinsic value."—*Hollywood Reporter*; "...long on brutality and short on entertainment."—*Variety*; "...average entertainment..."—*Citizen News*; "Direction by Christian Nyby is deliberate, firm and uncompromising."—*Motion Picture Herald*.

HERE COME THE JETS (1959) B&W/Scope 72 min. Written by Louis Vittes; Produced by Robert Einfield; Directed by Gene Fowler, Jr. Cast: Steve Brodie, Lyn Thomas, Mark Dana, John Doucette, and Jean Carson.
Critics: "...better than average action programmer..."—*Boxoffice*; "...manages to turn up an adequate amount of interest."—*Film Daily*; "...has its best moments when the action is up in the sky."—*Motion Picture Herald*; "...a competent and interesting

melodrama..."—*Variety*; "Much technical information on the build-ing and testing of jet planes is a by-product in the story of the regeneration of a derelict combat pilot."—*The Green Sheet*.

HIGH POWERED RIFLE (Shooting title: **DUEL IN THE CITY**
1960) B&W/Scope 60 min. Written by Joseph Fritz; Produced and Directed by Maury Dexter. Cast: Willard Parker, Allison Hayes, Dan Simmons, Shirley O'Hara, and John Holland.
Tidbits: This was the first feature under Lippert's new Associated Producers, Inc. banner, and it was an experiment to see how cheaply one could make a saleable film. Maury Dexter tried to talk Lippert out of it but finally agreed to produce it if Lippert would let him direct it. Lippert came up with the title, and Harry Spalding wrote a script around it. It cost around $50,000.
Critics: "...no better than the dozens of hour-long TV gangster films..."—*Boxoffice*; "...swift, efficient, but uninspired..."—*Variety*; "...low-caliber..."—*Hollywood Reporter*; "...has a satisfactory amount of action and excitement."—*The Film Daily*.
Exhibitors: "Leave it in the can if you want customers again."—Paul Fournier, NE.

THE HORROR OF IT ALL (1964) B&W 75 min. Written by Ray Russell; Produced by Margia Dean; Directed by Terence Fisher. Cast: Pat Boone, Dennis Price, Valentine Duall, Andre Melly, and Archie Duncan.
Tidbits: This was Pat Boone's last (and cheapest) picture for 20th Century-Fox. It was made in England in 10 days. Boone thought it was "schlocky" but admitted he had fun making it. It played as a bottom-of-the-bill second feature to another Lippert movie, *Witchcraft*.
Critics: "...pleasant and harmless..."—*Boxoffice*; "...a weak mixture of unfunny gags and standard horror situations that gets laughs when they're not supposed to."—*Variety*; "...snail's pace spoils the show."—*Los Angeles Times*; "Clean living, open faced Pat Boone is scarcely the kind of young man apt to be found in the currently popular monster pictures..."—*Boston Globe*; "The sad note is in the apparent defect of Pat Boone in his efforts to remain a 'good guy' in his entertainment career."—*Desert News*.

HOUSE OF THE DAMNED (1963) B&W 72 min. Written by Harry Spalding; Produced and Directed by Maury Dexter. Cast: Ron Foster, Merry Anders, Richard Crane, Erika Peters, and Dal McKennon.

Tidbits: The movie was shot in a house in the Hollywood Hills, which had once been a speakeasy.

Critics: "...a relatively shockless conglomeration..."—*Boxoffice*; "...a conventional puzzle-thriller with a syrupy ending."—*Films and Filming*.

Jayne Mansfield is the star of It Happened in Athens *(1962).*

IT HAPPENED IN ATHENS aka **WINGED VICTORY** aka **WINGED VICTORY IN ATHENS** (1962) Color/Scope 100 min. Written by Laslo Vadnay; Produced by James S. Elliott; Directed by Andrew Martin. Cast: Jayne Mansfield, Trax Colton, Nico Minardos, Bob Mathias, and Maria Xenia.

Tidbits: Spyros Skouras brought producer James Elliott to Hollywood after seeing one of his New York plays. He told Elliot to find some property he would like to make. When Elliott read a script by Laslo Vadnay, which was based on a true incident about a shepherd boy in Greece who won the Marathon race at the first revival of the Olympic Games in 1896, he was hooked. He told Skouras he had found his movie. Unfortunately, the script had already been sold to MGM nine years earlier. Skouras used his considerable influence to buy it and offered Suzi Parker, a Fox contract player, the lead role which, without hesitation, she turned down. It was then offered to another studio contract player, Jayne Mansfield, and she took it.

Mansfield made a splash on Broadway in a play called *Will Success Spoil Rock Hunter* in which she played a breathy, Marilyn Monroe-like sexpot. Fox signed her to a contract with the expectation that she might be a replacement for Monroe, who was the studio's biggest money-maker, as well as being its biggest pain-in-the-ass. Unlike Monroe, however, the studio did little to develop Mansfield's talents as a dramatic actress. Although she received a Golden Globe award for her dramatic performance in *The Wayward Bus* (1957), it was her resemblance to Monroe as a sexpot that the studio wanted to promote. After *It Happened in Athens*, they let her go, and the film sat on the shelf for two years.

One scene called for a soup-tossing baby. Mansfield volunteered her 22-month old son, Miklos Hargitay. It took about eight or ten takes, but the kid finally threw the soup the way the director wanted him to.

Filmed in 1960, *It Happened in Athens* was released in 1962 and was a resounding boxoffice dud.

Critics: "...simple-minded tribute to sportsmanship, Greek hospitality and Miss Mansfield's chasses..."—*New York Times*; "The wonder of It *Happened in Athens* is how it ever got beyond the drawing board."—*Variety*; "...builds to a sizzling climax..."—*Film Daily*.

KRONOS (1957) B&W/Scope 78 min. Written by Lawrence Louis Goldman; Produced and Directed by Kurt Neumann. Cast: Jeff Morrow, Barbara Lawrence, John Emery, George O'Hanlon, and Morris Ankrum.

Tidbits: It had been six years since Fox had made a sci-fi movie. Their last effort, *The Day the Earth Stood Still* (1951), a serious and dramatic film, had not performed the way they had hoped. What Jack Rabin and Irving Block had in mind, when they approached Lippert, was more of an action picture; something they could really exploit. Lippert took it to Spyros Skouras who tripled the budget of the usual Regal picture. Then, at the last minute, Skouras got cold feet and slashed the budget, or so the story goes. According to Rabin, the cost of the film was $160,000, which is still more than usual. The special effects that he and Block created are impressive, especially for a low budget feature. The critics thought so, too, and so did Lippert. He submitted the film for consideration for the 30th Annual Awards of the Academy of Motion Picture Arts and Sciences in the following Special Effects categories: Full-sized mechanical effects; Matte paintings; Miniatures; Optical Effects; Transparency projection; Sound effects. As one could have predicted, the film wasn't even nominated. This was an era where science fiction films were frowned upon. One needs only to remember that Ray Harryhausen, an acknowledged master of special effects, was never even nominated for an Oscar. He had to retire before the Academy saw fit to give him the award for his body of work and then only after they were heavily lobbied. For the record, the Oscar went to another Fox film that year, *The Enemy Below*.

Critics: "...effects which rate high consideration for Academy technological award for 1957."–*Motion Picture Herald*; "...quality special effects that would do credit to a much costlier film..."–*Variety*; "... an extremely good picture of its kind..."–*Hollywood Reporter*; "... outstanding special effects, the best seen in a long time..."–*Los Angeles Times*.

THE LAST SHOT YOU HEAR (1969) B&W 90 min. Written by Tim Shields, based on the play by William Fairchild; Produced by Jack Parsons; Directed by Gordon Hessler. Cast: Hugh Marlowe, Patricia Haines, Julian Holloway, John Nettleton, and Thorley Walters.

Tidbits: This four-character, one-set story was based on a play that ran for six months in London with Peter Cushing and Elizabeth Sellers called *The Sound of Murder*. Since Fox was still making money from their big budget musical, *The Sound of Music* (1965), they thought a movie with a similar title might not be such a good idea so they changed it to *The Last Shot You Hear*.

Lippert didn't want to spend more than $100,000. The unions bent over backwards to meet that goal but "if somebody coughed I would have blown my limit," director Gordon Hessler told *Variety* and, for that reason, they went overseas.

The movie was given an R-rating when it was first submitted. Four bedroom scenes were cut, and it was re-classified with an M-rating. Director Hessler had high praise for Lippert, who didn't give him the budget he would have liked, but backed him to the limit in every other way.

Critics: "...tedious staginess."—*Hollywood Reporter*; "...a dull, lower-case suspensor."—*Variety*.

THE LITTLE SAVAGE (1969) B&W/Scope 73 min. Written by Eric Norden, Produced by Jack Leewood; Directed by Byron Haskin. Cast: Pedro Armendariz, Rudolfo Hayes, Terry Rangne, Christiane Martel, and Robert Palmer.

Critics: "...strictly for the juve trade, there being little or no appeal for the adult patron."—*Variety*; "...a bit on the amateurish side..."—*Boxoffice*; "When it isn't as dull as a stale salad it's laughable."—*Los Angeles Times*; "Few adults will find it worth their time."—*Hollywood Citizen News*.

Exhibitors: "Very poor picture..."—Murray Johnston, Canada; "This is half of combo with *The Sad Horse*, both of which you'll be smart to leave alone."—Paul Camoche, VT.

THE LITTLE SHEPHERD OF KINGDOM COME (1960) Written by Barré Lyndon from the novel by John Fox, Jr.; Produced by Maury Dexter; Directed by Andrew McLaglen. Cast: Jimmie Rodgers, Luana Patten, Chill Wills, Linda Hutchings, and Robert Dix.

Tidbits: In the summer of 1957, Jimmie Rodgers arrived on the scene with a huge hit record called "Honeycomb" and several more hits followed. Lippert signed him for two pictures, this one and *Back Door to Hell*. Rodgers wasn't a very good actor and returned to the music world. In 1967 he suffered a severe skull fracture at the hands of an off-duty policeman named Richard Duffy, who had pulled Rodgers over for "erratic driving." Later, a friend found Rodgers unconscious on the side of the road and took him to the hospital. The singer couldn't remember what happened. Duffy claimed that Rodgers fell and hit his head on the pavement, but the injuries didn't support his statement. Although Rodgers sued, the police department denied that there was any wrong-doing but settled the case for $200,000. Nobody knew for sure what happened that night, but one thing was clear: Duffy left an unconscious and severely injured man to fend for himself.

Critics: "...an engaging yarn of particular appeal to the teen-agers..."—*Motion Picture Herald*; "It holds up the mirror to a phase

of American life at a critical period of our history."—*Moving Picture World.*
Exhibitors: "Play it by all means."—James Hardy, IN.

THE LONE TEXAN (1959) B&W 71 min. Written by James Landis and Jack W. Thomas; Produced by Jack Leewood; Directed by Paul Landres. Cast: Willard Parker, Audrey Dalton, Grant Williams, Douglas Kennedy, and Dabbs Greer.
Critics: "...this is first rate."—*Boxoffice*; "...a strikingly good film..."—*Variety*; "...direction by Paul Landres fails to get any emotional dimension into the proceedings."—*Hollywood Reporter.*
Exhibitors: "...better than average and was well liked here."—Paul Fournier, NE.

THE LONG ROPE (1961) B&W/Scope 61 min. Written by Robert Hammer; Produced by Margia Dean; Directed by William Witney.

Cast: Hugh Marlowe, Alan Hale, Robert Wilkie, John Alonzo, and Lisa Montell.
Tidbits: Before she became a producer, actress Margia Dean believed that producers should take a chance and hire unknown actors and actresses. "Now I have to be practical," she said to explain her about face. "I'm not keen on having an artistic success." Asked if men resented taking orders from a woman she replied: "Some do, but I'm the nicest, kindest producer in the business."[6] She produced a TV pilot that was similar to *The Long Rope*, but it didn't sell.

Hugh Marlowe stars in The Long Rope *(1961).*

Critics: "Margia Dean...makes good in her first try as a producer."—*Boxoffice*; "...moderately entertaining..."—*Motion Picture Herald*;

"...a routine, unpretentious western..."—*Variety*; "...more original and novel than is generally the case..."—*Hollywood Reporter*; "*The Long Rope* will not be needed to hold the crowds back..."—*Limelight*.
Exhibitors: "I hope they decide to put the producer at the end of it!"—Dave S. Klein, Africa.

THE LURE OF THE SWAMP (1957) B&W/Scope 75 min. Written by William George; Produced by Sam Hersh; Directed by Hubert Cornfield. Cast: Marshall Thompson, Joan Vohs, Willard Parker, and Jack Elam.
Critics: "...powerful in its creation of suspenseful situations..."—*Motion Picture Herald*; "...slow moving and unexciting..."—*Variety*; "...more swamp than lure..."—*Hollywood Reporter*.

MASSACRE (1956) Color 76 min. Written by D. D. Beauchamp; Produced by Robert L. Lippert, Jr. and Olallo Rubio Candara; Directed by Louis King. Cast: Dane Clark, James Craig, Martha Roth, Jaime Fernández, and José Muñoz.
Critics: "Dialog is trite and the direction formula, with [acting] on the same level."—*Variety*; "...the story never gets off the ground, although it covers plenty of it."—*Hollywood Reporter*; "...the screenplay and direction are only fair."—*Motion Picture Herald*.

MIRACLE OF THE HILLS (1959) B&W 73 min. Written by Charles Hoffman; Produced by Richard E. Lyons; Directed by Paul Landres. Cast: Rex Reason, Nan Leslie, Betty Lou Gerson, Jay North, and June Vincent.
Critics: "...a budget inspirational western made with the 'Bible Belt' primarily in mind. However, it's good enough not only to do well in that market but also to fill programs in more sophisticated situations."—*Variety*.
Exhibitors: "...it takes color to bring them in. If they keep neglecting that...there won't be enough of us left to keep the industry going."—B. Berglund, ND; "Fine film all around. Should have been in color."—Paul Fournier, NE.

MORO WITCH DOCTOR (1964) B&W 61 min. Written, Produced and Directed by Eddie Romero. Cast: Jock Mahoney, Margia Dean, Pancho Magalona, Reed Hadley, and Paraluman.

Tidbits: "It was a dangerous film to do," Margia Dean told Mike Fitzgerald. "That was really roughing it. We had machine-gunned guards all along." Margia didn't care for leading man Jock Mahoney whom she called a "pompous ass." She didn't find him gracious or warm. "Jock and I were the only whites, and I wore a blonde wig that, due to the humidity and filth, began to look like Harpo Marx's hair!"

Critics: "...a modest item with considerable action..."—*The Film Daily*; "...will satisfy undemanding patrons..."—*Boxoffice*; "...suitable only for the least discriminating trade."—*Variety*.

THE MURDER GAME (1965) B&W 76 min. Written by Harry Spalding, Produced by Robert L. Lippert; Directed by Sidney Salkow. Cast: Ken Scott, Marla Landi, Trader Faulkner, Dyan Cannon, and John Dunbar.

Critics: "...has a modest complement of thrills and excitement..."—*Film Daily*; "...too wordy and lacking in punch."—*Variety*; "More attention should have been paid to making the story airtight."—*Hollywood Reporter*.

MURDER INC. aka **SHADOW OF FEAR** (1960) B&W/Scope 103 min. Written by Mel Barr and Irve Tunick based on the novel by Burton Turkus; Produced by Burt Balaban; Directed by Stuart Rosenberg and Burt Balaban. Cast: Stuart Whitman, May Britt, Henry Morgan, Peter Falk, and David J. Stewart.

Tidbits: *Murder, Inc.* (1960) was the title of a book written by Burton Turkus, one of the prosecutors who helped expose the murder-for-hire organization. Lippert knew they had to shoot the picture in New York to give it the right look, which meant a bigger budget. "The brutal viciousness of criminals fighting criminals will be depicted as it actually happened," producer Burt Balaban promised the press.[7] The director, Stuart Rosenberg, had come out of television, which was a good training ground for directors. As far as Lippert was concerned, there wasn't any foot-dragging in television. A guy had to think on his feet, which is why Lippert gave Rosenberg the job.

Fox had Stuart Whitman under contract, so they sent him to New York with a copy of the script. "So on the plane I'm reading the script," he recalled, "and I'm thinking, 'Wow! What a role here...

Abe Reies..."[8] However, when he got to New York he was told he would be playing the romantic lead; Peter Falk was going to play the sociopathic Reies.

Three days into production Bob Lippert and Maury Dexter were sitting in the screening room watching the dailies, when the door flew open and in came Spyros Skouras, madder than a hornet. "Whose bright idea was it to hire that cockeyed actor?" he raged, talking about Falk. "How the hell much would it cost to replace him?"

"You're talking about scrapping three days worth of film," Lippert said blandly and turned to Dexter. "You have any idea what that would cost, kid?"

"Not off the top of my head," Dexter replied. "But I can tell you this: it won't be pretty."

"Christ!" Skouras fumed. "Maybe no one will notice."

An impending actor's strike was the reason given to explain why director Rosenberg walked away from the project, but according to Whitman, the studio thought he was taking too long. Balaban replaced Joe Brun with cameraman Gayne Rescher and stepped in to direct the last five days of the picture. Working around the clock, Balaban finished one hour ahead of the strike. Balaban praised his New York crew who he called more eager and ambitious than their Hollywood counterparts.

Peter Falk got a best supporting actor nomination. Commenting on his performance in the *New York Times*, Bosley Crowther wrote: "Mr. Falk, moving as if weary, looking at people out of the corners of his eyes and talking as if he had borrowed Marlon Brando's chewing gum, seems a travesty of a killer, until the water suddenly freezes in his eyes and he whips an icepick from his pocket and starts punching holes in someone's ribs. Then viciousness pours out of him and you get a sense of a felon who is hopelessly cracked and corrupt."

Critics: "...an average gangster film that slacks off too much for proper tension and runs a great deal too long."—*New York Times*; "...breathtaking..."—*Boxoffice*; "...good, solid cops-and-robbers melodrama..."—*Motion Picture Daily*; "...slashingly realistic..."—*Cue*; "...extremely well-done..."—*Film Daily*; "...sordid story is well told in this superior, modestly-budgeted...programmer."—*Films in Review*;

"Although a bit overlong, the film is a far cut above the average crime melodrama..."—*Limelight*.

Exhibitors: "...grossed miserably."—Leonard J. Leise, NE; "Your patrons will be terribly mad at you if you serve them this one."— Paul Fournier, NE; "...do let up making these for a while."—Dave S. Klein, Africa.

THE NAKED GUN (1956) B&W 69 min. Written by Ron Ormond and Jack Lewis; Produced by Ron Ormond; Directed by Edward Dew. Cast: Willard Parker, Mara Corday, Barton MacLane, Billy House, and Veda Ann Borg.

Tidbits: By necessity, television directors knew how to move fast, which is why Lippert told Ron Ormond to hire one to make this movie. Ormond chose Edward Dew who had directed some episodes of the *Sergeant Preston of the Yukon* series. Ormond's writer, Jack Lewis, had seen Dew in action and warned Ormond that Dew didn't know what he was doing.

"I spent one afternoon on a set at what was then Carthey Sound Stages near the intersection of Pico and Fairfax," Lewis recalled. "Most of the interiors for the *Lone Ranger* TV series were shot there. Dew was screwing things up royally, when I departed. Ormond was sitting on the sidelines, looking properly pained. It was supposed to be a five-day show. The following week, some of the actors and a respected TV director named Paul Landres were back in the studio, putting together the missing pieces."[9]

When they started shooting the movie, it was called *Sarazin Curse*. Two days later they changed the focus of the film to revolve around the judge in the story and changed the title to *The Hanging Judge*. The very next day they were calling the picture *The Naked Gun*. Leading lady Mara Corday knew they were in trouble from the get-go when they asked her if she wanted to be the heavy or the ingénue.

NIGHT TRAIN TO PARIS (1964) B&W 65 min. Written by Henry Cross (Harry Spalding); Produced by Robert L. Lippert; Directed by Robert Douglas. Cast: Leslie Nielsen, Aliza Gur, Dorinda Stevens, Eric Pohlman, and Edina Ronay.

Critics: "There's enough here to please the adventure fans."—
Motion Picture Herald; "...a neat little suspense film..."—*Film Daily*;
"...thumpingly mediocre..."—*New York Times*.

Gloria Talbott, Fred MacMurray and John Dierkes from The Oregon Trail *(1959).*

THE OREGON TRAIL (1959) DeLuxe Color/Scope 86 min. Written
by Gene Fowler, Jr. and Louis Vittes; Produced by Richard Einfield;
Directed by Gene Fowler, Jr. Cast: Fred MacMurray, William
Bishop, Nina Shipman, Gloria Talbott, and Henry Hull.
Tidbits: *"The Oregon Trail*, that was a son of a bitch—Lippert really
screwed that one up," Gene Fowler grumbled. "He made a bet with
Spyros Skouras that he could make a big outdoor Western without
ever leaving the Fox lot, and like an idiot I agreed to direct it!"[10]

     Even with triple the usual Lippert budget, the Louis Vittes
screenplay proved to be a bit too ambitious for this on the lot production, and it had to be heavily revised. On a Sunday morning, the
day before the start of production, the new pages were rushed to
the home of the film's star, Fred MacMurray. Maury Dexter called
MacMurray to apologize for the inconvenience. "Don't worry about
it," the actor told him. "For the amount of money you people are
paying me I'd ride a bicycle down Hollywood Boulevard in the nude!"

Fox wanted the fabulous Mara Corday to co-star with MacMurray in this pseudo-epic but her husband, Richard Long, told Lippert she wasn't interested. Had she not been within an earshot of the conversation in the other room, she wouldn't have known anything about it. The problem continued throughout their 17-year marriage. Long didn't want his wife to have a career.

"One thing I always wanted to do," Gene Fowler said, "particularly in these low-budget pictures, was have one day with a crane. Well, the crane cost maybe $250 a day and $250 for the operator." To get the crane, Fowler made a deal with Lippert: he traded 25 Indian salaries for one day with the crane. "It sounds stupid, but that's the way you had to work."[11]

Critics: "...manages to include most of the standard wagon-train clichés of the past twenty-five years...production is as wholesome as it is dull."—*New York Times*; "...confused and meandering..."—*Monthly Film Bulletin*; "The single most important element in the film is Fred MacMurray's portrayal of a New York reporter..."—*Variety*. "...fails to achieve either pace or audience identification."—*Hollywood Reporter*; "...vibrates with action and excitement."—*Film Daily*; "...seldom drags under the crisp direction of Gene Fowler, Jr."—*Motion Picture Herald*; "...handsomely mounted...filled with action."—*Boxoffice*.

Exhibitors: "A waste of money."—Dave S. Klein, Africa; "One of the good westerns in color really adds up at our boxoffice."—R. Berglund, ND; "I thought this would do business but what happened I don't know."—Joe Machetto, CO.

PLUNDER ROAD aka **THE VIOLENT ROAD** (1957) B&W/Scope 71 min. Written by Steven Ritch; Produced by Leon Chooluck and Laurence Stewart; Directed by Hubert Cornfield. Cast: Gene Raymond, Jeanne Cooper, Wayne Morris, Elisha Cook, and Staffos Repp.

Critics: "...shows once again that it is possible to make a first-rate picture on a second-rate budget."—*Hollywood Reporter*; "...engrossing..."—*Motion Picture Herald*; "A well-made little crime melodrama..."—*Variety*.

POLICE NURSE (1963) B&W/Scope 64 min. Written by Harry Spalding; Produced and Directed by Maury Dexter. Cast: Ken Scott, Merry Anders, Oscar Beregi, Barbara Mansell, and John Holland.

Tidbits: This picture was written around Lippert's title. "The only problem was," said director Maury Dexter, "there was never a capacity for a nurse in the police department. We shot the film anyway."

Critics: "...seen and quickly forgotten."—*Boxoffice*; "...manages at time to generate a measure of suspense and excitement."—*Motion Picture Herald*.

THE PURPLE HILLS (1961) Color/Scope 60 min. Written by Russ Bender and Edith Cash Pearl; Produced and Directed by Maury Dexter. Cast: Gene Nelson, Joanna Barnes, Kent Taylor, Danny Zapien, and Medford Salway.

Critics: "...fast-paced and absorbing..."—*Boxoffice*; "Customers looking for surprises or story subtlety won't find them..."—*Variety*; "...briskly paced and continuously absorbing."—*Hollywood Reporter*; "The Grade 'B' western was shot in six days but, while you're looking at it, it seems twice that long."—*Limelight*.

THE QUIET GUN aka **FURY AT ROCK RIVER** (1957) B&W/Scope 77 min. Written by Earle Lyon and Eric Norden; Produced by Earle Lyon; Directed by William F. Claxton. Cast: Forrest Tucker, Mara Corday, Jim Davis, Kathleen Crowley, and Lee Van Cleef.

Critics: "...a little too quiet for a good western."—*Variety*; "...a good picture..."—*Hollywood Reporter*; "...in its use of the [love] triangle formula as a major plot factor it makes of itself a subject for special consideration as to handling."—*Motion Picture Herald*.

RAIDERS FROM BENEATH THE SEA (1964) B&W 73 min. Written by Harry Spalding; Produced and Directed by Maury Dexter. Cast: Merry Anders, Russ Bender, Booth Colman, Garth Benton, and Bruce Anson.

Critics: "...discriminating viewers will poke logical holes through the Spalding script..."—*Boxoffice*; "...fan-pleasing touches."—*Film Daily*.

RISING FROM THE SEA—
TO COMMIT A DARING
CRIME ON LAND!

Raiders FROM Beneath THE Sea

STARRING
KEN SCOTT
MERRY ANDERS
Co starring RUSS BENDER · BOOTH COLMAN · GARTH BENTON
Produced and Directed by MAURY DEXTER · Screenplay by HARRY SPALDING
A Lippert Inc. Production · Released by 20th Century-Fox

Poster for Raiders from Beneath the Sea
(1964).in Athens (1962).

THE RETURN OF MR. MOTO

(1965) B&W 71 min. Written by Fred Eggers based on characters created by John P. Marquand; Produced by Robert L. Lippert and Jack Parsons; Directed by Ernest Morris. Cast: Henry Silva, Terence Longdon, Suzanne Lloyd, Marne Maitland, and Martin Wyldeck.

Critics: "The casting is thoroughly inept all around. The only thing more inept is the plot."—Cue.

RETURN OF THE FLY

(1959) B&W/Scope 80 min. Produced by Bernard Glasser; Written and Directed by Edward Bernds. Cast: Vincent Price, Brett Halsey, David Frankham, Danielle De Metz, and Dan Seymour.

Tidbits: After working for peanuts for years, Brett Halsey told his agent that he wanted a thousand dollars to be in this picture. His agent passed the word along to Lippert who asked Halsey to come to his office. "I really want you for this movie," Lippert told him. "Understand, half of the time you're part is going to be played by a stunt man. You won't have to show up for the full two weeks, which is why I'm not going to pay you a thousand dollars. But I want you in this picture and I think it'll be good for your career." Nobody was more surprised than Halsey when, as a result of his appearance in this film, Fox put him under contract. His next movie was *The Best of Everything* (1959), a major Fox production.

"Doing *Return of the Fly* I thought it'd be wise to look at the original; find out what the dickens I was doin'," said John Mansbridge who was the art director on the film. "It was shot at Fox. And all of the stuff that was used in the original *Fly*, they had still kept all of the units, so I was able to set that back up like it was. And the house was a standing set on the stage."

"I'd made a couple of pictures for Lippert and this was the first time we were asked to shoot on the lot," director Edward Bernds told me. "Fox was going through a tough time and I think they wanted us to absorb some of their overhead. Knowing Lippert I'm sure he had some kind of a special deal. We had more production value than we would have had if we'd done it off the lot."

Critics: "...lacks its predecessor's carefully and logically built up suspense and philosophical undertones..."—*Film Daily*; "...upholding the impact and suspense created by the original..."—*Motion Picture Herald*; "...without the reputation of *The Fly* to trade on, this one would be a dud."—*Variety*; "There are plenty of thrills and chills."—*Citizen News*; "Though not a classic, it is considerably better than the run-of-the-mine 'B' horror picture."—*Hollywood Reporter*; "...gimmicky, implausible and only intermittently suspenseful."—*Los Angeles Examiner*; "[Price] becomes less convincing and more mannered with every low budgeter he appears in."—*Los Angeles Times*.

Exhibitors: "Played to average business."—Simon M. Cherivtch, NJ; "...got by, doubled with *The Alligator People*."—E. A. Reynolds, MN.

RIDE A VIOLENT MILE (1957) B&W 80 min. Written by Eric Norden; Produced by Robert W. Sabler; Directed by Charles Marquis Warren. Cast: John Agar, Penny Edwards, John Pickard, Bing Russell, and Richard Shannon.

Critics: "This celluloid could have been put to better use as banjo picks."—*Variety*; "...action-packed western keeps moving fast... hardly giving one time to notice its plot deficiencies."—*Motion Picture Herald*; "After a while, the meandering plot becomes so thick, it doesn't make much difference..."—*Film Daily*.

Exhibitors: "Very good picture with good draw."—D.W. Trisko, TX.

John Agar and Penny Edwards from Ride a Violent Mile *(1957).*

ROCKABILLY BABY Shooting title: **MOTHER WAS A STRIPPER**
(1957) B&W/Scope 81 min. Written by Will George and William
Driskill; Produced and Directed by William F. Claxton. Cast:
Virginia Field, Douglas Kennedy, Les Brown, Irene Ryan, and Ellen
Corby.
Critics: "Bright and breezy..."—*Variety*; "...tastefully done but
without much excitement."—*Hollywood Reporter*; "...wholesome,
enjoyable teenage musical..."—*Motion Picture Herald*.
Exhibitors: "These Regalscope pictures are real good."—B.
Berglund, ND; "...this program did better than we anticipated. No
complaints."—Velva Otts, TX; "Played with *Young and Dangerous*...
Everyone like the combination and it did average business."—Jim
Fraser, MN; "...the quality is very thin."—Harold Bell, Canada.

Rockabilly Baby *(1957.)*

THE ROOKIE (1959) B&W/Scope 84 min. Written by Tommy Noonan and George O'Hanlon; Produced by Tommy Noonan; Directed by George O'Hanlon. Cast: Tommy Noonan, Peter Marshall, Julie Newmar, Jerry Lester, and Claude Stroud.

Tidbits: Thirty-four exhibitors and newspaper reporters were invited to lunch at the Beverly Hills Hotel to see Lippert's new comedy find—Tommy Noonan and Peter Marshall. Among those in attendance were: Edwin F. Zabel, managing director of Electrovision Theaters; Bert Pirosh, chief film buyer for Pacific Drive-ins; M. A. Lundgren, head film buyer for National Theatres; Everett Sharp and Gordon Hewitt, film buyers for National Theatres; Bob Benton, General Manager of Serro Drive-Ins; George Smith, advertising manager for Pacific Drive-ins and Consolidated Theatres of Hawaii; and Fay Reeder, advertising and publicity director for National Theatres. These people were told that Fox was prepared to spend $240,000 to promote *The Rookie* which starred this remarkable new comedy team, and if things went according to plan, there would be five more, bigger-budgeted films to follow. Two of the titles being bandied about were *Coffee House* and *3 Nuts in Search of a Bolt*. (Noonan independently made the latter title a few years later with Mamie Van Doren but not with Fox.)

Once the comedians took the stage, they asked the exhibitors for their cooperation in launching their picture. They took it to Pittsburg, Cincinnati, Columbus, Kansas City, Dallas, New Orleans,

Atlanta, Philadelphia, Washington, New York, Boston, Toronto, Montreal, Chicago, San Francisco and Los Angeles, an 18-day junket paid for by the studio. A luncheon for the exhibitors was held at each city, after which the film was shown in one of the major theaters. According to Fox, the turn-out was good, the showmen endorsed the team, and audiences reacted enthusiastically.

Riding high on what was beginning to look like a bonanza, the team was booked for five segments of *The Jack Paar Show*, a popular late night show that set the stage for Johnny Carson's program a few years later. In another piece of cross-promotion, Capital Records was releasing a soundtrack album of *The Rookie*. In addition, Fox produced a theatrical short called *Introducing Noonan and Marshall* and a shorter version for TV. But all of this effort was for not. The film failed to perform at the boxoffice. **Critics**: "...old hat and unimaginative...Noonan and Marshall over-play throughout..."—*Variety*; "...when previewed before a house of college students, there was a high percentage of walkouts and a low percentage of belly lights."—*Los Angeles Examiner*. **Exhibitors**: "It didn't go over here..."—Arlen W. Peohl, OR; "A waste of time and money."—Paul Fournier, NE; "...it missed being a comedy that will build trade when word-of-mouth gets out."—Ken Christianson, ND.

Alan Ladd visits his son on the set of The Sad Horse *(1959).*

David Ladd and Chill Wills are the stars of The Sad Horse *(1959).*

THE SAD HORSE (1959) B&W/Scope 79 min. Written by Charles Hoffman; Produced by Richard E. Lyons; Directed by James B. Clark. Cast: David Ladd, Chill Wills, Rex Reason, Patricia Wymore, and Gregg Palmer.

Tidbits: In exchange for free air time to run TV spots for this movie, Lippert gave 26 television stations ten percent of the gross on this movie.

Critics: "...a believable, heartwarming, wholesome entity..."– *Boxoffice*; "...highly recommended..."–*Citizen News*; "...a pleasant family picture..."–*Motion Picture Herald*; "...

heartwarming..."–*Variety*; "...a warm yarn..."–*Los Angeles Times*; "...
refreshing and wholesome..."–*Los Angeles Examiner*.
Exhibitors: "It did below average business but I honestly think we
need this sort of film."–Paul Fournier, NB; "This is a good family
picture that was a flop here."–Ken Christianson, ND; "We pro-
grammed it with *The Little Savage* to poor results."–Simon M.
Cherivtch, NJ; "Not worth buying."–William Duncan, OH; "The kids
came in droves. They don't add up to much, but after all they are
tomorrow's movie fans."–Carl P. Anderka, TX; "Biggest weekend in
months! Enjoyed by everyone."–Murray Johnston, Canada.

SECRET OF THE PURPLE REEF (1960) DeLuxe Color/Scope
80 min. Written and Produced by Gene Corman based on the
Saturday Evening Post serial by Dorothy Cottrail; Directed by
William N. Witney. Cast: Jeff Richards, Margia Dean, Peter Falk,
Richard Chamberlain (debut), and Robert Earl.
Critics: "...okay despite some illogical sequences..."–*Boxoffice*;
"...would have been more satisfactory if it had been given more
story to deal with."–*Hollywood Reporter*; "...simple, predictable
sequences of chase and gunplay..."–*Los Angeles Times*; "Watered-
down mystery meller..."–*Variety*.
Exhibitors: "I hope Fox doesn't handle many more of these...too
draggy. Did way below average."–Mel Cruse, NE; "Book it only if
you're hard up."–Paul Gamache, W

SEVEN WOMEN FROM HELL (1961) Color/Scope 88 min. Written
by Jesse Lasky, Jr. and Pat Silver-Lasky; Produced by Harry
Spalding; Directed by Robert D. Webb. Cast: Patricia Owens,
Denise Darcel, John Kerr, Yvonne Craig, and Cesar Romero.
Tidbits: Lippert had a lot of trouble deciding on a title for this
one. It started as *Womanhunt*, then *Escape from Danger*, changed
again to *Five Women in Danger*, and yet again to *Escape from Hell*.
Somehow, in all that confusion, Lippert managed to add two more
women to the title.
Critics: "A grim and often exciting..."–*Boxoffice*; "...fast and furious..."–*Los Angeles Examiner*; "Some of the funniest dialog
of the year..."–*Variety*; "...a contrived bushel of hokum..."–
Hollywood Citizen News; "...a fairly good melodramatic chase
picture..."–*Limelight*.

*Patricia Owens, Cesar Romero, Pilart Seurat, and Yvonne Craig are featured
in this scene from* Seven Women from Hell *(1961).*

Exhibitors: "Title and locale brought all of the men in to see this
one which they all seemed to enjoy."—Dave S. Klein, Africa.

SHE DEVIL (1957) B&W/Scope 77 min. Written by Carroll Young
and Kurt Neumann based on "The Adaptive Ultimate" by John
Jessell (Stanley G. Weinbaum); Produced and Directed by Kurt
Neumann. Cast: Mari Blanchard, Jack Kelly, Albert Dekker, John
Archer, and Fay Baker.
Tidbits: John Jessell's short story, "The Adaptive Ultimate," was
published in the November 1935 edition of *Astounding* magazine.
It was adapted by radio's *Escape* in 1949 and by television's *Tales of
Tomorrow* under the title "The Miraculous Serum" and, as "Beyond
Return" on *Science Fiction Theatre* in 1955. Jessell's story con-
cerned a woman who, having been subjected to a new scientific
breakthrough, was able to change her features to suit her needs.
Writers Carroll Young and Kurt Neumann threw out everything
but the woman's ability to change the color of her hair, which any
woman could do with a wig or a bottle of hair dye. The best thing
about this sophomoric and dull movie is Paul Sawtell's terrific
score. His sleazy main title is a standout.

Jack Kelly, Mari Blanchard and Albert Dekker from She Devil *(1957).*

Critics: "Stripped of its supernatural hocus-pocus, this is just another melodrama about one of these scheming women who lie and cheat to get what they want and then come to no good end. Miss Blanchard is not quite up to the task."–*Motion Picture Herald*; "The entire cast suffers from an overdose of clichés and poor dialog."–*Los Angeles Times*; "...fails to generate much of a chiller atmosphere for the melodramatics and the screenplay is rather talky."–*Variety*; "...a little thin on invention..."–*Hollywood Reporter*. **Exhibitors**: "As one customer said, 'Wonder what the fellow was drinking who wrote that one?'"–Elaine S. George, OR.

SHOWDOWN AT BOOT HILL aka **SHADOW OF BOOT HILL** aka **THE LONE TEXAN** (1958) B&W 71 min. Written by Louis Vittes; Produced by Harold E. Knox; Directed by Gene Fowler, Jr. Cast: Charles Bronson, Robert Hutton, Carole Mathews, John Carradine, and Paul Maxey.
Critics: "...charged with suspense and excellent camera movement..."–*Motion Picture Herald*; "...better than most films of its ilk..."–*Boxoffice*; "...well directed and well acted..."–*Variety*; "There's enough gunplay for the action fans and enough story for the thinkers."–*Hollywood Reporter*; "...charged with suspense."–*Motion Picture Herald*.

SIERRA BARON (1958) Color/Scope 80 min. Written by Houston Branch; Produced by Plato A. Skouras; Directed by James B. Clark. Cast: Brian Keith, Rita Gam, Mala Powers, Allan Lewis, and Steve Brodie.

Tidbits: "I was supposed to be running around the desert," Mala Powers told Mike Fitzgerald, "and the *man* they used [to double me] was awkward—he ran through the desert in a dress like mine. I saw the rushes and was quite upset over the results. I didn't even know they were filming that sequence—they just *did* it with this guy."

Critics: "...superior acting right down the line..."—*Variety*; "Definitely an 'A' western..."—*Hollywood Reporter*; "Its major distinction is some handsome scenery..."—*Motion Picture Herald*; "...will linger in the memory for a long time."—*Citizen News*.

Exhibitors: "They still like westerns and this one brought in the bacon."—Harold Smith, IA; "A very well-made picture, but nothing big at the boxoffice."—James Hardy, IN.

SILENT CALL (1961) B&W/Scope 63 min. Written by Tom Maruzzi; Produced by Leonard A. Schwartz; Directed by John Bushelman. Cast: Gail Russell (final film), David McLean, Roger Mobley, Roscoe Ates, and Milton Parsons.

Critics: "...hobbled direction...performances leave much to be desired."—*Boxoffice*; "...there must be a story in this story someplace."—*Limelight*; "...affectionate and easy to take."—*Variety*; "All the clichés of a boy and his dog are on hand."—*Film Daily*; "...essentially a youngster's picture..."—*Motion Picture Herald*.

SNIPER'S RIDGE (1961) B/W/Scope 61 min. Written by Tom Maruzzi; Produced and Directed by John Bushelman. Cast: Jack Ging, Stanley Clements, John Goddard, Doug Henderson, and Gabe Castle.

Critics: "...neither better nor worse than the run-of-the-mill TV dramas..."—*Boxoffice*; "The enemy...receives no attention from this self-centered crew and patriotic sentiments are the furthest thing from their minds...the whole thing would have flabbergasted Errol Flynn."—*New York Times*.

SON OF ROBIN HOOD (1959) DeLuxe Color/Scope 81 min.
Written by George W. George and George Slavin; Produced and
Directed by George Sherman. Cast: Al (David) Hedison, June
Laverick, David Garrar, Marius Goring, and Philip Friend.
Tidbits: Producer Clifford Sanforth sued 20th Century-Fox, Argo
Productions, Fox West Coast Theaters, and Pacific Drive-In
Theaters claiming that he was the owner of all motion picture and
TV rights to the son of Robin Hood character, which he bought
from Paul A. Castle. Sanforth had given Columbia permission
to use the character in two of their movies—*Bandit of Sherwood
Forest* (1946) and *Rouges of Sherwood Forest* (1950). Now he
expected Fox to pony up. He wanted $300,000 in damages, which
happened to be the budget of the film. Outcome: unknown.
Critics: "...should delight the young fry and interest a large
number of their more elderly companions."—*Motion Picture
Herald*; "...it's fast enough to hold the juvenile trade..."—*Variety*; "...
vigorously directed..."—*Hollywood Reporter*.
Exhibitors: "No business on this kind of show."—Paul Fournier, NE.

SPACE FLIGHT IC-1: AN ADVENTURE IN SPACE (1965) B&W 65
min. Written by Harry Spalding; Produced by Robert L. Lippert and
Jack Parsons; Directed by Bernard Knowles. Cast: Bill Williams,
Kathleen Breck, John Cairney, Donald Churchill, and Norma West.
Critics: "...production is thin in story, acting, directing and produc-
tion value departments..."—*Variety*.

SPACE MASTER X-7 aka **MISSILE INTO SPACE** (1958) B&W/
Scope 71 min. Written by Daniel Mainwaring and George Worthing
Yates; Produced by Bernard Glasser; Directed by Edward Bernds.
Cast: Bill Williams, Robert Ellis, Lyn Thomas, Paul Frees, and Moe
Howard.
Tidbits: Daniel Mainwaring and George Worthing Yates had written a spec sci-fi script for what they hoped would be a multi-million
dollar movie. They had shopped it around but couldn't sell it
because, unlike now, no studio was interested in investing that kind
of money in a science fiction picture. Fox needed a sci-fi second
feature to package with *The Fly*, so Bernard Glasser bought their
script for $25,000, $10,000 more than he usually spent for a script.

Paul Frees and Lyn Thomas from Space Master X-7 (1958).

"I rewrote the script to fit our budget," Edward Bernds recalled, "which was something like $100,000, only now it was more like $90,000 because we'd spent the extra money for the script. We were given the freedom to make the picture pretty much the way we wanted as long as we stayed on budget. Bob Lippert and Harry Spalding might look at the rushes and make some suggestions but we were left alone for the most part because they trusted us. They knew we'd do a good job. That's why we were hired in the first place. Lippert hired people he wouldn't have to worry about. Bill Magginetti was the only one who was worried."

Critics: "...is better than most films of this caliber."—*Hollywood Reporter*; "...it wears thin toward the end..."—*Variety*; "...direction manages to sustain interest."—*Motion Picture Exhibitor*; "The climax is filled with terror..."—*Boxoffice*.

SQUAD CAR (1960) B&W 60 min. Written by E.M. Parsons and Scott Flohr; Produced and Directed by Ed Leftwich. Cast: Vici Raff, Paul Bryar, Don Marlowe, Lyn Moore, and Jack Harris.

STAGECOACH TO FURY (1956) B&W/Scope 75 min. Written by Eric Norden; Produced by Earle Lyon; Directed by William F. Claxton. Cast: Forrest Tucker, Mari Blanchard, Wallace Ford, Margia Dean, and Rodolfo Hoyos, Jr.

Tidbits: Walter Strenge was nominated by the Academy for his black and white cinematography for this picture.

Critics: "...proves once again that imagination is sometimes a very good substitute for money."—*Hollywood Reporter*; "...suspense is so steadily maintained and the story is so smoothly told..."—*Motion Picture Herald*; "While the budget was small and tight, good effects have been achieved..."—*Variety*.

Exhibitors: "Sooner or later some of these producers will realize that westerns in black and white aren't worth a damn."—Jim Fraser, MN; "Good for its share of holding up the Friday-Saturday double bill."—I Roche, FL; "Fairly good western in black and white."—B. Berglund, ND.

THE STORM RIDER (1957) B&W/Scope 72 min. Produced by Bernard Glasser; Written and Directed by Edward Bernds. Cast: Scott Brady, Mala Powers, Bill Williams, John Goddard, and William Fawcett.

Critics: "...top drawer..."—*Motion Picture Herald*; "...credit is due Edward Bernds for his sure-footed direction."—*Boxoffice*; "The screenplay has nothing new to contribute..."—*Hollywood Reporter*; "...both characters and story are convincing enough to rate as okay entertainment."—*Variety*.

Exhibitors: "...they should have raised more dust in this storm... thereby obliterating the entire production."—Dave S. Klein, Africa.

SURF PARTY (1964) B&W 68 min. Written by Harry Spalding; Produced and Directed by Maury Dexter. Cast: Bobby Vinton, Jackie DeShannon, Miki Dora, Martha Stewart, and Patricia Morrow.

Tidbits: Singer Bobby Vinton was performing at the Twin Coaches in Pittsburgh when he was told he would have to pay $1,000 in back rental fees for the print of *Surf Party*, which he had for six months. He didn't think the charge was fair since it was more than he had been paid to be in the picture.

Critics: "...at its best when it's singing and dancing..."—*Motion Picture Herald*; "...it's rather insipid..."—*Films and Filming*; "Mislabeled a comedy..."—*Boxoffice*.
Exhibitors: "...this was a miserable flop for me."—Jim Fraser, MN.

TESS OF THE STORM COUNTRY (1960) DeLuxe Color/Scope 84 min. Written by Charles Lang based on the novel by Gloria Miller White; Produced by Everett Chambers; Directed by Paul Guilfoyle. Cast: Diane Baker, Jack Ging, Lee Phillips, Wallace Ford, and Robert F. Simon.
Tidbits: Lippert talked Fox into doubling the budget on this one, which added six additional days to the shooting schedule. Millie Perkins, who hadn't made a picture since *The Diary of Anne Frank* (1959), was offered the title role, but she turned it down. Lippert thought she made a mistake.
Critics: "The picture shines best through the distinguished efforts of character actors..."—*Motion Picture Herald*; "...the more discriminating movie-goer will not find much subtlety or freshness of approach here."—*Film Daily*; "...is not much of an attraction for the busy, sophisticated urbanite..."—*Variety*; "Considering the speed at which these medium budget pictures are filmed...Guilfoyle gets quite a lot of action and camera movement into his story."—*Hollywood Reporter*.

THAT TENNESSEE BEAT (1966) B&W 84 min. Written by Paul Schneider; Produced by Richard Brill; Directed by Richard Bell. Cast: Sharon De Bord, Earl Richards, Dolores Faith, Minnie Pearl, and Merle Travis.
Critics: "...a cornball picture with a less than notable screenplay..."—*Motion Picture Herald*; "...lively entertainment..."—*Film Daily*.

THE 3rd VOICE (1958) B&W 80 min. Produced by Maury Dexter; Directed and Written by Herbert Cornfield based on the novel *All the Way* by Charles Williams. Cast: Edmond O'Brien, Julie London, Larraine Day, Olga San Juan, and George Eldredge.
Tidbits: Hubert Cornfield, son of Albert Cornfield, the head of Fox's distributions in Europe wanted to make a film from the novel *All the Way Home* by Charles Williams. Cornfield had two Lippert movies under his belt, *Lure of the Swamp* and *Plunder Road* (both 1957), but Lippert still didn't trust him. He bought the rights to the

book, talked Skouras into moving the project into the nervous "A" category, and told Maury Dexter to keep an eye on things to make sure Cornfield didn't go over budget.

Edmond O'Brien, Julie London and Laraine Day (replacing Anne Baxter) were cast in the lead roles and the movie was shot in and around Los Angeles. Malibu and the hills above it stood in for Mexico where a third of the story takes place.

For the first three days everything went smoothly, much to Dexter's relief. On the fourth day they had what one might call a bit of trouble.

They were shooting a scene with Edmond O'Brien, sitting on a barstool, talking into a tape recorder. His monologue, which ran four pages, set up the plot. Cornfield wanted to get it in one take. O'Brien was letter perfect until he reached the last couple of lines and then he blew it. After he apologized to everyone he heard Cornfield mumble something. "What did you say?" he asked. Cornfield replied: "I said if you knew your lines, you wouldn't have to apologize."

O'Brien flew off the barstool, grabbed Cornfield by the neck and slammed his head against the wall. It wasn't easy but Dexter and a couple of the grips managed to restrain him. The actor threatened to walk off the show but Dexter knew he was too much of a pro to ever do that. He just needed to calm down.

As they were getting ready to start up again, O'Brien got nose-to-nose with Cornfield and said: "I'm going to finish this show, but the day we wrap, I'm going to beat your head into a pulp."

The camera rolled again and this time O'Brien got through his monologue without a flub and gave a terrific performance. Everyone but Cornfield applauded; he was still worried about what was going to happen when they finished the film.

The final day of shooting took place on one of the back roads above Malibu. When Cornfield called "Cut" on the last scene, he made a beeline for his car, but before he could start the motor, O'Brien was tapping on his window. Expecting the worst, Cornfield lowered the window, and O'Brien shook his hand.

Critics: "...properly taut complex and eerily fascinating for only about three-quarters of the way."—*New York Times*; "...is about three-quarters of an excellent suspense film."—*Variety*; "...a superior crime melodrama."—*Saturday Review*; "...well-paced, artful

direction..."—*Motion Picture Herald*; "...ingenious and generally absorbing..."—*Cue*; "...a well-conceived, clear-cut murder
story..."—*Los Angeles Examiner*; "...put together with tingling
excitement."—*Film Daily*; "O'Brien makes most of this tricky
role..."—*Mirror-News*.

13 FIGHTING MEN (1960) B&W 70 min. Written by Robert
Hammer and Jack W. Thomas; Produced by Jack Leewood;
Directed by Harry Gerstad. Cast: Grant Williams, Brad Dexter,
Carole Mathews, Robert Dix, and Richard Garland.
Critics: "Satisfactory, if machine-made, supporting fare..."—
Boxoffice; "...a routine programmer..."—*Variety*.
Exhibitors: "...I have a complaint to make about these RegalScope
pictures...When I have one of these half of my crowd will get up and
leave."—L.R. McIntosh, MS; "TV can have this."—James Hardy, IN.

THUNDER ISLAND (1963) Color/Scope 65 min. Written by
Jack Nicholson and Don Devlin; Produced and Directed by Jack
Leewood. Cast: Gene Nelson, Fay Spain, Brian Kelly, Miriam Colon,
Art Bedard, and Antonio Torres.
Tidbits: The film was shot back to back with *Harbor Lights* in
Puerto Rico. One of the settings of the story was the zoo at
Mayaguez where the film's star, Brian Kelly, took delight in throw-
ing small pebbles at one of the lions. Later that day, the lion got his
revenge. While the actor was filming a scene with his back to the
cage, the lion lifted his rear leg and gave Kelly his best.
Critics: "An entertaining, well-paced adventure story."—*Boxoffice*;
"...swift-paced little picture..."—*Motion Picture Herald*; "...pound-
for- pound, dollar-for-dollar a cut above average for its diminutive
size."—*Variety*; "...gets every nickel of its limited budget on
screen..."—*Hollywood Reporter*; "...an adroitly made film..."—*Film
Daily*.

THUNDERING JETS aka **JET COMMANDOES** (1958) 73 min.
Written by James Landis; Produced by Jack Leewood; Directed
by Helmut Dantine. Cast: Rex Reason, Audrey Dalton, Dick Foran,
Barry Coe, and Buck Glass.
Critics: "...transcends it budgetary limitations in both enter-
tainment values and financial possibilities..."—*Boxoffice*; "...an

interesting and sometimes absorbing programmer..."—*Film Daily*;
"...a respectable little picture..."—*Variety*; "...fascinating footage
once the attraction get airborne and stays there."—*Motion Picture
Herald*; "...has lower thrill calories than most outdoor yarns."—
Hollywood Reporter.
Exhibitors: "Previews of this picture are not good. Picture itself...is
very good."—W.E. Seaver, TN.

TWELVE HOURS TO KILL (1960) B&W/Scope 83 min. Written
by Jerry Sohl; Produced by John Healey; Directed by Edward L.
Cahn. Cast: Nino Minardos, Barbara Eden, Grant Richards, Russ
Conway, and Art Baker.
Critics: "Like a magazine story, read during an idle hour on a train or
bus and immediately forgotten..."—*Boxoffice*; "...the story seems on
the verge of lapsing, unintentionally, into a parody of itself."—*Variety*;
"...has good action elements as its contrived story spins along."—*Film
Daily*; "afflicted with an incredible story..."—*Limelight*; "...sags in the
middle and baffles throughout..."—*Monthly Film Bulletin*.
Exhibitors: "It's in CinemaScope, but back and white, which
doesn't mean much to us."—Harold Bell, Canada.

20,000 EYES (1961) B&W/Scope 60 min. Written by Jack W.
Thomas; Produced and Directed by Jack Leewood. Cast: Gene
Nelson, Merry Anders, James Brown, John Banner, and Barbara
Parkins (debut).
Critics: "...lightning paced, suspenseful film..."—*Boxoffice*.

TWO LITTLE BEARS (1961) B&W/Scope 81 min. Written and
Produced by George W. George; Directed by Randall Hood. Cast:
Eddie Albert, Jane Wyatt, Brenda Lee, Soupy Sales, and Butch Patrick.
Critics: "...average programmer with skimpy boxoffice appeal."—
Boxoffice; "...will delight the youngsters..."—*Motion Picture Herald*;
"...tries to include too many things in its delicate framework..."—
Hollywood Reporter.

UNDER FIRE (1957) B&W/Scope 76 min. Written by James Landis;
Produced by Plato Skouras; Directed by James B. Clark (debut).
Cast: Rex Reason, Harry Morgan, Steve Brodie, Peter Walker, and
Robert Levin.

Critics: "...a first-rate courtroom drama..."—*Hollywood Reporter*; "...does not measure up to the potential."—*Motion Picture Herald*; "...one of the best to emerge under the Regal banner."—*Variety*.

THE UNKNOWN TERROR (1957) B&W/Scope 76 min. Written by Kenneth Higgins; Produced by Robert W. Stabler; Directed by Charles Marquis Warren. Cast: John Howard, Mala Powers, Paul Richards, Gerald Milton, and May Wynn.
Tidbits: When Mala Powers read the script, then called *Beyond Terror*, she wondered why anyone would want to make it. Maybe she would have turned it down if she hadn't been pregnant, knowing she would be unable to work for a while. Her leading man, John Howard, didn't think much of the script, either. He couldn't make heads or tails of his character.

Charles Warren shot the movie very quickly at Producer's Studio. It features a lot of laundry detergent posing as dangerous fungus.
Critics: "...never really scrambles to its feet. The fungus looks like gargantuan quantities of good-quality detergent."—*Monthly Film Bulletin*; "...the type of audience that dotes on the mad doctor in far-off-surroundings...won't find much to start quibbling about."—*Motion Picture Herald*; "Lots of conversation..."—*Motion Picture Exhibitor*; "...script is distinguished only by its moldy gimmick."—*Variety*.
Exhibitors: "Doubled with *Back from the Dead* to fair business. Both pictures are just fair and the paper on each is not so hot."—Victor Weber, AR.

VALLEY OF THE REDWOODS (1960) B&W/Scope 62 min. Written by Leo Gordon and Daniel Madison; Produced by Gene Corman; Directed by William N. Witney. Cast: John Hudson, Lynn Bernay, Ed Nelson, Michael Forest, and Bruno VeSota.
Tidbits: "I made two pictures for Lippert," Gene Corman recalled. "One was *Secret of the Purple Reef* and the other was *Valley of the Redwoods*. Lippert was making pictures for 20th Century-Fox at that time and Buddy Adler, who was running the studio, liked *Valley of the Redwoods* so much he was talking about having me make bigger, more important pictures for the studio. As luck would

John Hudson, Ed Nelson and Lynn Bernay in Valley of the Redwoods *(1960).*

have it he died before that could happen. That's the way it goes sometimes."

Critics: "...a thin-edged melodrama..."—*Motion Picture Herald*; "...fast-paced direction..."—*Boxoffice*; "...simple, clean and straightforward..."—*Hollywood Reporter*; "...a brisk crime thriller..."—*Film Daily*; "...a ragged and unlikely plot..."—*Monthly Film Bulletin*; ...offers audiences brevity, a dash of suspense, and some pulsating jazz background music—little else."—*Variety*.

Exhibitors: "...this saved my day."—Arlon W. Peahl, OR.

VILLA!! (1958) Deluxe Color/Scope 72 min. Written by Louis Vittes; Produced by Plato A. Skouras; Directed by James B. Clark. Cast: Brian Keith, Cesar Romero, Margia Dean, Rodolfo Hoyos, Jr., and Carlos Múzquiz.

Tidbits: This picture was shot back to back with *Sierra Baron* on a location in Mexico outside of Cuernavaca. Most of the first day of production was spent waiting to film a train hold-up, which the fates seemed to be conspiring to keep from happening. Finally, when they were ready to roll they couldn't find Brian Keith's white horse, the only white horse in the bunch. It turned out that it was being used by the messenger sent across the valley to tell the locals to stay out of sight until they finished shooting.

"You had 200 horses to choose from," exasperated producer Plato Skouras said to the wrangler who had sent the messenger. "Why would you choose the star's horse?"

The wrangler replied: "He's the fastest, Señor."

Chatting with producer Benedict Bogeaus, who was making *From the Earth to the Moon* (1958) in Mexico at the time, Maury Dexter learned they had paid twice as much for the use of the train as Bogeaus had. Dexter assumed their production assistant had pocketed the difference. Furious, Dexter fired the P.A., but the P.A. told Dexter he didn't have the authority; only the syndicate could fire him.

"I was on a horse with the entire Mexican cavalry behind me," leading lady Margia Dean recalled. "I should never have agreed to it, but I rode that horse down that rock-filled hill! If it had slipped, I would have been crushed by all those horses behind me. A couple of them did slip and fall. I was later told, by a professional stunt-woman, that she would never do that—so I never should have agreed to do something a professional wouldn't do."

A deal was made with the commanding general of the Mexican army for the use of 200 Mexican cavalry soldiers and their horses for one week. The messenger sent to get their money was ambushed by a bunch of banditos. He managed to get away, and the soldiers were paid, but the fact that only a few people knew that the messenger would be carrying the money indicated an inside job.

The cameras were rolling on one of the stages at the Churubusco Studios when a loud commotion brought everything to a halt. The General and several of his aides exploded onto the set, yelling at the top of his lungs.

"When we finally got our interpreter to calm him down, we discovered that the thousands of dollars in pesos should have gone directly to him, not the soldiers!" Dexter recalled. "I knew the political system in Mexico was rotten, but I found out the military was, too. The General demanded full pay for himself. We suggested that he get the money back from his troops, but we were told he wasn't going to cause a small revolution over something that was rightfully his in the first place."

They came to an impasse—the soldiers had been paid, they had signed for the money, and that was that.

Not one to walk away empty-handed, the General said: "You will pay!" As he headed for the door he said again, "You will pay!" Of course, they did because, otherwise, the General would not let them ship their film out of the country.

Clark and his crew were invited to a wrap party at a very nice home in an upscale neighborhood of Mexico City. It was a first class affair with food and drink, and with musicians supplying live music. Most of the local people who had worked on the film were present. The whole affair was being paid for by someone, but they didn't know who. It turned out it was the P.A. they'd tried to fire. Before Maury Dexter could say something that would have caused some embarrassment, the auditor pulled him away from the crowd. "Please stay," the auditor said firmly. "It would be a great insult if you all left." "What about the insult of stealing our money?" Dexter asked. "In his heart," the auditor replied, "he didn't steal the money. He only took it so the Mexican cast and crew could throw a big party to thank all of you." So Dexter held his tongue, and everyone had a great time.

Critics: "A sound general audience pleaser."—*Film Daily*; "...appears a bigger presentation than the money that went into it."—*Variety*; "It is best classified as light entertainment."—*Hollywood Reporter*; "...ranges from the ludicrous to an almost epic sweep."—*Mirror News*; "...puts all its emphasis on action and makes of its characters both real and fictitious stereotypes."—*Motion Picture Herald*; "...magnificent scenic backgrounds...stirring battle sequences..."—*Boxoffice*.

Exhibitors: "It did very well and is recommended for your western fans."—A.P. Quesnel, Ontario; "Played this with a horror pair...to not-so-good results."—A.A. Richard. WV; "Was saved on this by the large Mexican population here."—L. R. Dubose, TX.

WALK TALL (1960) Color/Scope 60 min. Written by Joseph Fritz; Produced and Directed by Maury Dexter. Cast: Willard Parker, Joyce Meadows, Kent Taylor, Russ Bender, and Ron Sobie.
Critics: "...looks as if it were made up during the filming."—*Boxoffice*; "...there is little to distinguish this low-budget, trail-weary western..."—*Variety*; "...a good western for its class..."—*Hollywood*

Reporter; "Maury Dexter produced and directed, keeping events moving briskly."—*Film Daily*; "...routine U.S. Cavalry drama..."—*Los Angeles Times*.
Exhibitors: "I hate myself when I let myself get talked into product like this."—Jim Fraser, MN.

WILD ON THE BEACH (1965) B&W 77 min. Written by Harry Spalding; Produced and Directed by Maury Dexter. Cast: Frankie Randall, Sherry Jackson, Sonny and Cher, Cindy Malone, and Sandy Nelson.
Tidbits: A more appropriate title for this movie would have been *Mild in the House*. Except for the surfing sequence shown during the film's opening credits, most of the story takes place inside a beach house. There is no sun, no sand, no surf and, worst of all, no bikini girls! This was an attempt to make an even cheaper version of the Beach Party movies that were making so much money for American International.

In an interview conducted by Thomas Lisanti for his book *Hollywood Surf and Beach Movies*, singer-turned-actor Frankie Randall remembered that the picture was shot in two weeks: "I was a bit nervous and Maury [Dexter] was very helpful. He gave me some direction in terms of my performance and guided me with block and hitting my marks." It was Dexter's final film for Lippert.
Critics: "A raucous, swinging teenaged musical..."—*Boxoffice*; "...a spirited comedy with spirited music."—*Film Daily*.
Exhibitors: "It is a light story and the songs did not go over too well with our audience."—John Herbie, NY.

WITCHCRAFT (1964) B&W 80 min. Written by Harry Spalding; Produced by Robert L. Lippert; Directed by Don Sharp. Cast: Lon Chaney, Jack Hedley, Jill Dixon, Viola Keats, and Marie Ney.
Tidbits: Lippert liked making pictures in England because he could take advantage of the Eady money. He hooked up with a producer in England named Jack Parsons and together they made a dozen pictures. This one was inspired by the protests that took place in San Francisco when a graveyard was ravaged by a developer to make room for his new project.

Director Don Sharp was given 13 days to make the picture, and Lon Chaney was his star. Chaney was drinking heavily and was too sloshed to work past noon. "But by the next morning," Sharp recalled, "he would be so eager, so keen to do right."

For the film's climax, a real house (scheduled for destruction) was burned to the ground.

Witchcraft was packaged with *The Horror of It All*, a Pat Boone horror-comedy. Plastic "Witch Deflectors" were given away as an enticement to the ticket-buyers.

Critics: "...will produce more yawns than gooseflesh."—*Los Angeles Times*; "...a spine-tingler..."—*Los Angeles Herald Examiner*; "...a good example of its kind."—*Variety*.

WOLF DOG (1958) B&W 61 min. Written by Eric Norden; Produced and Directed by Sam Newfield. Cast: Jim Davis, Allison Hayes, Tony Brown, Don Garrard, and John Hart.

Tidbits: This movie, which was filmed in and around the quiet Ontario village of Markdale, was the second-to-last feature directed by Sam Newfield. Newfield, with over 200 feature films to his credit, is often celebrated as the most prolific feature film director of the American sound era. He had been in Canada the year before making the *Hawkeye* TV show which starred John Hart, one of the actors in *Wolf Dog*. There were four more veterans of Newfield's TV series in the cast: Don Garrard, Syd Brown, Daryl Masters, and Juan Root.

Critics: "...uneventful and often downright dull."—*Boxoffice*.

WOMANHUNT (1962) B&W/Scope 60 min. Written by Edward J. Lakso and Russ Bender; Produced and Directed by Maury Dexter. Cast: Steven Piccaro (Peck), Lisa Lu, Berry Kroeger, Bob Okazaki and, Ann Carroll.

Critics: "...it dawdles rather than dashes..."—*Boxoffice*; "...all of the violence has a rather pointless quality..."—*New York Herald Tribune*; "A taut crime drama that improves as it goes along."—*Monthly Film Bulletin*.

WOMEN OF PITCAIRN ISLAND (1956) B&W/Scope 72 min. Written by Aubrey Wisberg; Produced by Aubrey Wisberg and Jean Yarbrough; Directed by Jean Yarbrough. Cast: Lynn Bari, John Smith, Sue England, Arleen Whelan, and James Craig.

John Smith chats with Lynn Bari, one of the Women of Pitcairn Island *(1956).*

Critics: "...indifferently acted and directed...Lynn Bari and Arleen Whelan are unable to rise above the ridiculous plot situations and Miss Whelan suffers most from unflattering camera work."—*Boxoffice*; ...a fantastic follow-up to *Mutiny on the Bounty* if ever there was one..."—*Los Angeles Times*; ""...a dull programmer with little to recommend it."—*Variety*.
Exhibitors: "...stay away from this."—D. Ellickson, WI; "I get amused with all this talk of 20th-Fox helping the small theatres stay open. We are as small as any, and if we had to depend on 20th-Fox, we would have already been closed."—O.M. Shannon, TX; "This was a first class dog!"—D. Ellickson, WI.

THE YELLOW CANARY (1963) B&W/Scope 93 min. Written by Rod Serling, based on the novel *Evil Come, Evil Go* by Whit Masterson (Bill Miller); Produced by Maury Dexter; Directed by Buzz Kulik. Cast: Pat Boone, Barbara Eden, Steve Forrest, Jack Klugman, and Jesse White.
Tidbits: Peter Levathes had purchased the Whit Masterson's novel for $200,000 as a vehicle for Pat Boone. Rod Serling was paid $125,000 to script it, and contract player Boone would get $200,000 to be in it. All in all, the studio expected to spend a couple of million to make it until the out-of-control *Cleopatra*

threatened to close the studio. Spyros Skouras was forced to resign and Darryl Zanuck took over. He fired Levathes, put his son in his place, and cut the budget for Boone's picture. He gave Lippert $100,000 to finish it. For the first time in his career, Pat Boone found himself in a black and white quickie.

"This was presented to me and I suppose they thought I would turn it down," Boone recalled. "But, number one, I didn't want to lose the money by refusing the project; number two, I still thought it was a great script for me."[12]

Boone had always played clean-cut, wholesome types, and he welcomed the challenge of playing an egotistical jerk. He asked his acting coach, Jeff Corey, to help him prepare for the role. In the early 50s, shortly after his appearance in Lippert's *Superman and the Mole Men*, Corey's acting career was derailed because of his refusal to name names for HUAC. Boone persuaded the Fox executives to let Corey play a part in the picture.

Director Buzz Kulik was given 12 days to make the picture, most of which was shot on a soundstage. Even with this extra control, Kulik still ran out of time and was forced to cut one day of location shooting, eliminating some scenes that Boone felt were critical to the picture. Boone took $20,000 out of his own pocket to pay for another day's shooting.

The pictured was sneaked at the Theatre Owners Association convention in Dallas. Lippert gave a detailed synopsis of the movie to every exhibitor who was likely to play the picture, along with a personal request for some old-fashioned publicity stunts. "We've become too circumspect," he told them. "Let's throw some theatrical spit-balls a la Harry Reichenbach."

Critics: "...a nice little thriller."—*Newsweek*; "...weakly defined..."—*Variety*; "...doesn't sustain early promise of suspense or excitement."—*Los Angeles Times*; "...a fine chiller-thriller."—*Los Angeles Herald-Examiner*; "...so-so dialogue and weak direction..."—*Film Daily*; "[Boone] admirably succeeds in altering his popular, unspoiled-boy-next-door image."—*New York Times*.

Exhibitors: "If by some slim chance you haven't played this one yet, by all means grab it now!"—Herman Powell, Jr., TX.

YOUNG AND DANGEROUS (1957) B&W 78 min. Written by James Landis; Produced and Directed by William F. Claxton. Cast: Mark Damon, Lili Gentle, Eddie Binns, Frances Mercer, and Dabbs Greer. **Tidbits**: Favorable reactions at test screenings prompted Fox to order 400 prints of this film and its companion feature, *Rockabilly Baby*. The studio gave the package Class A treatment with plans to make sequels to them both.

Critics: "A realistic treatment of teenage maneuvers in its search for love and understanding..."—*Motion Picture Herald*; "...easily the most impressive and promising to date from Regal Films' active assembly line."—*Boxoffice*; "...well-made drama..."—*Variety*; "...one of the best small budget pictures of the year."—*Hollywood Reporter*; "...an intelligent effort..."—*Los Angeles Examiner*.

Exhibitors: "These teenage [double bills] have become my bread and butter here of late..."—Victor Webber, AR; "Bet the best audience for this type of show are the delinquents themselves..."—Dave S. Klein, Africa; "A good teenage picture which did slightly better than average business."—B. Berglund, ND.

Alana Ladd, James Mitchum and Jody McCrea from Young Guns of Texas *(1962).*

YOUNG GUNS OF TEXAS (1962) Color 78 min. Written by Harry Spalding; Produced and Directed by Maury Dexter. Cast: James Mitchum, Alana Ladd, Jody McCrea, Chill Wills, and Gary Conway. **Critics**: "…gets off to a solid start…then limps along lethargically the balance of the way."—*Variety*; "…downright entertaining…"—*Hollywood Reporter*; "…lacks suspense…"—*Los Angeles Times*. **Exhibitors**: "Just bought a new popcorn machine and it worked overtime with this western."—Carl W. Veseth, MT.

Ray Stricklyn and Merry Anders in Young Jesse James *(1960)*.

YOUNG JESSE JAMES (1960) B&W/Scope 73 min. Written by Orville H. Hampton and Jerry Sackheim; Produced by Jack Leewood; Directed by William Claxton. Cast: Ray Stricklyn, Willard Parker, Merry Anders, Robert Dix, and Emile Meyer. **Critics**: "…uneven pacing…"—*Variety*; "Students of western folklore may be surprised to learn that Jesse James was once spurned by Belle Starr, and spent the night sulking while Cole Younger enjoyed the lady's favors in the adjoining room…This brief but pregnant liaison between the legendary outlaws is less bizarre than *Frankenstein Meets the Wolf Man* or *I Married a Monster from Outer Space*, but it is clearly aimed to stimulate the same audience."—*New York Times*; "…well paced…"—*Limelight*.

Exhibitors: "Poorly produced, enacted and directed hunk of junk…"—Paul Fournier, NE.

THE YOUNG SWINGERS aka COME TO THE PARTY (1963)

B&W 71 min. Written by Harry Spalding; Produced and Directed by Maury Dexter. Cast: Rod Lauren, Molly Bee, Gene McDaniels, Jack Larson, and Jo Helton.

Critics: "…isn't much on plot…"—*Motion Picture Exhibitor*; "…at its best when the sound of music holds forth."—*Boxoffice*.

Exhibitors: "…this proved to be a dud. I asked my son (a teenager) why. He said, 'Nobody in it and the wrong kind of music.'"—M.W. Long, IA.

Notes:

1. Magers, Boyd and Michael G. Fitzgerald *Westerns Women*, McFarland and Company, Jefferson, N.C., 1999, page 21.
2. Weaver, Tom *Sci-Fi Swarm and Horror Horde: Interviews with 62 Filmmakers*, McFarland and Company, Jefferson, N.C. 2010, page 188.
3. Williams, Esther with Digby Diehl, *The Million Dollar Mermaid*, Simon and Schuster, New York, NY. 1999, page 327.
4. Weaver, Tom *Science Fiction Confidential*, McFarland and Co. Jefferson, N.C. 2002, page 226.
5. *Westerns Women*, page 98.
6. Harford, Margaret "Star of B Films Turns Producer of Westerns," *L.A. Mirror*, October 8, 1960.
7. *Boxoffice*, page 23, November 9, 1959.
8. Petkovich, Anthony "Stuart Whitman," *Shock Cinema*, No. 44, page 44.
9. Lewis, C. Jack *White Horse, Black Hat*, The Scarecrow Press, Inc., Lanham, MD. 2002, page 107.
10. Weaver, Tom *Science Fiction Stars and Horror Heroes*, McFarland & Co., Jefferson, N.C., 2006, page 76.
11. Ibid., page 75.
12. Kibbey, Richard D. *Pat Boone, The Hollywood Years*, Tate Publishing and Enterprises, Mustang, OK, 2011, page 299.

AMERICAN INTERNATIONAL PICTURES

THE LAST MAN ON EARTH aka **NAKED TERROR** (1964) B&W/
Scope 88 min. Written by Logan Swanson (Richard Matheson),
William P. Leicester, Furia M. Monetti, and Ubaldo Ragona, based
on the novel *I Am Legend* by Richard Matheson; Produced by
Robert L. Lippert; Directed by Sidney Salkow and Ubaldo Ragona.
Cast: Vincent Price, Franca Bettoja, Emma Danieli, Giacomo Rossi
Stuart, and Umberto Rau.

Tidbits: Knowing that his boss liked end-of-the-world movies
because they usually had small casts, Harry Spalding introduced
Lippert to Richard Matheson's novel *I Am Legend*. Lippert liked
the story about a man alone in a world of vampires and told
Spalding to buy it. Spalding got in touch with Matheson, who told
him the movie rights had been sold to Hammer Films back in 1957,
when Matheson adapted his novel for Tony Hinds. The picture,
which Hammer intended to call *Night Creatures*, was never made
because the British censors wouldn't pass it. Hinds happily sold the
property to Lippert, and Matheson was invited to Lippert's home
to talk about it.

"We're gonna get Fritz Lang to direct it," Lippert told
Matheson and Matheson was overjoyed. Of course, if Lang's better
days hadn't been behind him, he wouldn't have been available at
Lippert's price. Matheson's high hopes for the project were soon
dashed when he was later told that instead of Lang, Sidney Salkow,
a mediocre talent at best, would be the director. "Well," Matheson
replied, "there's a bit of a drop!"[1]

The movie was supposed to take place in Los Angeles, but
in spite of the fact that there are no locations in Italy that even
vaguely resembled Los Angeles, that's where Lippert wanted to
make the picture in order to cut costs.

"I was disappointed in the film," Matheson told William P.
Simmons, "even though they more or less followed my story. I think
Vincent Price, whom I love in every one of his pictures that I wrote,
was miscast. I also felt the direction was kind of poor. I just didn't
care for it."

Matheson was so "disappointed" that he used a pseudonym.

The Last Man on Earth was released by American International
in the U.S. 20th Century-Fox handled it overseas.

Critics: "Salkow allows the movie, which showed promise of being a superior horror film, to peter out during the final reels."— *Hollywood Citizen News*. "...weak ammunition for even the bottom half of a double bill..."—*Variety*; "...a one-man show and this versatile actor makes the most of it."—*Los Angeles Times*.

Notes:

1. Weaver, Tom *Science Fiction Stars and Horror Heroes*, McFarland & Co., Jefferson, NC. 1999, page 306.

PARAMOUNT

WALK A TIGHTROPE (1964) B&W U.S. 69 min. U.K. 78 min. Written by Mann Rubin; Produced by Neil McCallum; Directed by Frank Nesbitt. Cast: Dan Duryea, Patricia Owens, Terence Cooper, Richard Leech, and Neil McCallum.
Critics: "An adroitly made thriller..."—*Film Daily*; "...there are bothersome loopholes in the plot."—*Motion Picture World*.

WARNER BROS.

THE WOMAN WHO WOULDN'T DIE aka **CATACOMBS** (1965) Warner Bros. B&W 84 min. Written by Daniel Mainwaring, from the novel by Jay Bennett; Produced by Jack Parsons; Directed by Gordon Hessler (debut). Cast: Gary Merrill, Georgina Cookson, Jane Marrow, Neil McCallum, and Rachel Thomas.
Tidbits: This was a story that was turned down by Alfred Hitchcock Presents when Gordon Hessler was working on the show.
Critics: "...titillates and terrifies..."—*The Film Daily*; "...never believable or gripping."—*Hollywood Reporter*; "...taut, suspenseful and splendidly acted..."—*Boxoffice*; "...deserves, and undoubtedly will get, an enthusiastic reaction..."—*Motion Picture Herald*; "...last talky hour, embroided with spooky music, kills it."—*New York Times*; "...taut little thriller more than holds its own."—*Variety*.

APPENDIX TWO

MOVIES THAT DIDN'T HAPPEN

Robert Lippert and friends on the set of The Hat Box Mystery *(1947).*

The following is a list of projects that Lippert announced but were either never made or were given new titles: *The Abilene Kid* with Reed Hadley, Mary Beth Hughes and James Millican (probably became *Rimfire*); *Adventures of Archie*, a detective drama; *Aloha*; *Bandoleer*; *Before We Wake* directed by Seymour Friedman; *Berkeley* written by Frank Woods; *The Big Disc Jockey Platter Parade* produced by Jack Leewood; *The Blackmailers*; *Black Tulip*; *Caboose*; *Calibre .45* with Don Barry; *Cannibal Island*; *The Champaign Caper* with George Raft; *Come Out Fighting*; *Corny Rhythm*; *Crises Dirk Diamond*, a detective drama; *Cross-Currents*; *The Dalton's Last Raid*; *Daredevils of the Highway*; *Dark Bullets*; *Dead End Canyon*; *Dead Ringer* (most likely became *Gunfire*); *Desert Queen*; *Emergency Squad*; *Emergency Ward*; *End of the Santa Fe Trail, The Sister Blandina Segale Story* written by Guy Trosper; *Firebug Agent* (may have become *Arson Inc.*); *Fort Defiance*; *Fort Disaster*; *Fort Dishonor*;

Galveston written and directed by Charles Marquis Warren; *Ghost of Jesse James* (probably became *The Return of Jesse James*); *The Glass House*; *The Great Jewel* Robbery; *The Great Adventure* filmed in Africa; *Gringo*; *Headin' For Trouble* with Don Barry; *Isle of Zorda*; *Jailbreak* written by Jerome Fisk; *Kazan* produced by Walter Colmes; *King of the Safecrackers* aka *I Was King of the Safecrackers*; *The Lock and the Key* written and directed by Frank Gruber; *Madam Sheriff*; *Miss Galaxy 2000*; *Montana Badlands*; *Mustang Fury*; *Outlaw Hideout* with Don Barry; *Park Row* (later made by Sam Fuller for United Artists); Max Brand's *Pillar Mountain* with Greg McClure; *Police Force*; *Police Woman*; *Race Horse*; *Radio Patrol* (probably became *Motor Patrol* or *Radar Secret Service*); *Project X* "the amazing story of an undersea civilization"; *Redskin Renegades*; *Rolling Wheels* (probably became *Hi-Jacked*); *Shep Fights Back* with Harry S. Webb writing and directing; *Stranger in the House*; *Stratocrusier*; *Streamliner Limited*; *Sunset Rim*; *Tales of Captain Kidd*; *There is No Escape*; James Oliver Curwood's *Trail's End* in Sepiatone; *20,000 Leagues Under the Sea* starring Reed Hadley, produced by Carl K. Hittleman and directed by Sam Fuller (later Kurt Neumann); *Western Barn Dance* (may have become *Hollywood Barn Dance*); *Western Fury* with Don Barry; *The Wizard of Oz*; *Woman with a Gun* with Paulette Goddard; *Yosemite* in Cinecolor.

Appendix Three

LIPPERT THEATERS

Aladdin Theatre, Indo, CA
Alameda Theatre, Alameda, CA
Americana 5 Cinemas, Panorama City, CA
Arden Fair 4 Cinemas, Sacramento, CA
Auto See Drive-In, Yuba City, CA
Beverly Theatre, Beverly Hills, CA
Brentwood 4 Cinemas, Denver, CO
Broadway Theatre, Yreka, CA
Buena Park Theatre, Buena Park, CA
Centre I, II & II, Santa Rosa, CA
Ceres Drive-In, Ceres, CA
Cinema of North Hills, Granada Hills, CA
Cinerama, San Diego, CA
Coddingtown I, II & III, Santa Rosa, CA
Colorado 4 Cinemas, Denver, CO
Corbin Theatre, Reseda, CA
Corcoran Theatre, Corcoran, CA
Corcoran Theatre, Pixley, CA
Country Squire Theatre, Fresno, CA
Craterian Theatre, Medford, OR
Crest Theatre, Westwood Village, CA
Desert Theatre, Indo, CA
Dinuba Theatre, Dinuba, CA
Downtown Cinema, Phoenix, AZ
Eagle Rock 4 Cinemas, Los Angeles, CA
Edgebrook Plaza 5 Cinemas, Houston, TX
Embassy Theatre, Los Angeles, CA
Esquire Theatre, Fresno, CA
Festival 6 Cinemas, Tulsa, OK
Fig Garden Theatre, Fresno, CA
Fontana 4 Cinemas, Tulsa, OK
Foothill Theatre, Oakland, CA
Grand Theatre, Richmond, CA
Holly Theatre, Medford, OR
Indio Drive-In Theatre, Indio, CA

Irvington Theatre, Irvington, CA
Island Auto Movie, Alameda, CA
La Habra Cinemas I & II, La Habra, CA
Lake Theatre, Corcoran, CA
Liberty Theatre, Stockton, CA
Lincoln Theatre, Alameda, CA
Lincoln Theatre, Stockton, CA
Lucky Drive-In, Turlock, CA
Marina I, II & III, Redondo Beach, CA
McHenry Twin Drive-In, Modesto, CA
Medford Cinema Center, Medford, OR
Midway Drive-In, Dinuba, CA
Northridge 4 Cinema Center, Northridge, CA
Pablo Theatre, San Pablo, CA
Paducah Cinemas I & II, Paducah, KY
Park Cinema I & II, Santa Rosa, CA
Pepper Tree III Cinemas, Northridge, CA
Pix Theatre, Pixley, CA
Pleasant Hill Motor Movies, Pleasant Hill, CA
Prescott Drive-In Theatre, Modesto, CA
Rio Theatre, Alameda, CA
Rio Theatre, Richmond, CA
River Oaks Cinema, Houston TX
Round-Up Theatre, Hollywood, CA
Royal Theatre, Guadalupe, CA
Royal Theatre, Sanger, CA
Ryan Theatre, Fresno, CA
Shamrock 4 Cinemas, Houston, TX
Showcase Cinemas I & II, Alameda, CA
Showcase Cinemas I & II, Chattanooga, TN
Showcase Cinemas I & II, Downey, CA
Showcase Cinemas I & II, Fremont, CA
Showcase Cinemas I & II, Tucson, AZ
Showcase I & II, Oakland, CA
Showcase Theatre, Redding, CA
Sierra Drive-In, Marysville, CA
Sky-Vue Drive-In, Redding, CA
Starlight Drive-In, Keyes, CA

Starlite Drive-In, Medford, OR
Starlite Drive-In, Visalia, CA
Starlite North, Fresno, CA
Starlite South, Fresno, CA
Starlite Theatre, Salida, CA
Star-Vue Motor Movie, Santa Rosa, CA
Studio Theatre, Santa Maria, CA
Studio Theatre, Vallejo, CA
Studio Theatre, Richmond, CA
Sunnyside Drive-In, Fresno, CA
Sunset Drive-In, Fresno, CA
Times Theatre, Alameda, CA
Times Theatre, Richmond, Ca
Valley Drive-In, Medford, OR
Vanity Fair 4 Cinemas, Salt Lake City, UT
Victory Theatre, Hanford, CA
Village Cinema, Sacramento, CA
Village Drive-In, Santa Rosa, CA

INDEX

CPSIA information can be obtained at www.ICGtesting.com
Printed in the USA
BVOW08s0447170714

359353BV00012B/335/P